A RATTLING OF SABERS

PREPARING YOUR HEART FOR LIFE'S BATTLES

DR. GREG BOURGOND

iUniverse, Inc.
Bloomington

A Rattling of Sabers
Preparing Your Heart for Life's Battles

iUniverse Star
an iUniverse, Inc. imprint

iUniverse books may be ordered through booksellers or by contacting:

iUniverse
1663 Liberty Drive
Bloomington, IN 47403
www.iuniverse.com
1-800-Authors (1-800-288-4677)

ISBN: 978-1-938908-16-3 (pbk)
ISBN: 978-1-938908-17-0 (ebk)

Library of Congress Control Number: 2012916685

Printed in the United States of America

iUniverse rev. date: 9/6/12

CONTENTS

ACKNOWLEDGMENTS

I am indebted to so many people who have touched my life in profound ways during the years that this book was in incubation.

Darrel Johnson, missionary training director of College Avenue Baptist Church in San Diego, California, and my spiritual father and mentor, took the rough lump of coal that I was and poured his life into me. He deeply laid the foundation of my faith and built a house on solid rock. I would not be the person I am today if not for his love, patience, and watchful care over my soul. I am deeply grateful he saw something in me that I didn't see in myself.

Neil T. Anderson, of Freedom in Christ Ministries, provided the kindling wood that would eventually erupt into the Heart of a Warrior Ministries. His writings and personal counsel were very instrumental in my life, and he helped me grasp the fact that it's not what you do that determines who you are; it's who you are in Christ that determines what you do.

Erwin McManus, lead pastor of Mosaic in Los Angeles, California, and prolific author, has been a staunch supporter of my ministry to men and helped me understand the excitement of the journey. His sponsorship and counsel was immensely helpful along the way. He has been a great encourager, on whom I can count for clarity, insight, and honesty. His prophetic voice into my life is a great gift from God.

Gary Gonzales, former chief of staff of Promise Keepers and currently senior associate pastor of Overlake Christian Church in Redmond, Washington, and a close personal friend of over thirty years, was at many of the significant junctures of my life, offering friendship, wisdom, and perspective. His godliness and consistent integrity has been a model of leadership and spirituality for me.

J. Robert Clinton, professor of leadership in the School of Intercultural Studies, Fuller Theological Seminary, whose foundational research in leadership emergence theory, written works, and personal mentoring saved me from making many mistakes and provided a wonderful framework for personal growth. His blessing of me will always be one of the most significant events in my life.

Jerry Sheveland, president of Converge Worldwide, formerly the Baptist General Conference, provided many opportunities to serve. He opened the door so that I could soar. His trust allowed me to test out many of the things I learned along the way. He provided a platform for me to grow as a leader. His leadership example continues to inspire me.

John Cionca, professor of ministry leadership at Bethel Seminary in St. Paul, Minnesota, a member of my board, talked me off many a ledge. His humor and common sense gave life to me. His encouragement and support provided a good foundation from which I could launch many initiatives for kingdom purposes.

Jose, **Gunny**, **Dube**, **Kenny**, **Tony**, and other men in the Lino Lakes Correctional Facility took a two-year journey to wholeness, and I learned a great deal regarding commitment and focus from them. They are living proof that God is our Redeemer and life-giver. It has been a highlight of my life to invest in these men. They are well on their way to becoming men after God's heart.

I also owe a debt of gratitude to two men, **Ray Pruban** and **Mark Bierle**, who have taken the journey with me, are on my board, and were original members of a small group that eventually was the catalyst for the formal launching of this ministry. They have been alongside me all the way and have traveled with me around the world, wherever God opened doors, to share about heart transformation.

My life mate and wife, **Debby,** has been in my corner every step of the way. She is a great supporter of my ministry, providing a loving home of safety and refuge. She has been my greatest ally, my partner, friend, and supporter, who kept lovingly pushing me to complete this book. She gives me the platform I get to dance on.

There are many others I have failed to mention; for that, I am sorry. But know that God has used you to shape and mold me. To all the men I have had the privilege of serving, thank you. I have gained more from you than I gave to you. My life has been enriched because of you.

I am humbled by God's mercy and grace as I have stumbled along to serve Him amidst the trials and tribulations of this life. I am thankful He has not given up on me. All I did was show up at the train station; God gave me the ticket to ride, and I will ride this train until He decides it is time for me to get off. And when He calls me home, I hope to lay at His feet what little I have tried to accomplish in His name. I long to hear Him say, "Welcome home, Greg; you are a man after my heart."

Now to my daughter, **Monique**, and my precious **grandchildren**—Derrick (peace and justice), Braedan (strength and honor), Talisa (love and joy), Kieran (courage and valor), Gaelan (goodness and integrity), and Lochlan (truth and wisdom)—I dedicate this book. I hope its contents will continually minister to your soul. I hope it will serve as a reminder of what I have tried to become and how I have tried to live my life; what I hope will spur you on to do great things for God; what my deep longings are for you; and what sweet-smelling aroma I hope to leave in your lives, now and long after I am gone. I leave you with this one plea—above all else, guard your heart, for it is the wellspring of your life!

Strength and Honor,
Greg Bourgond
Heart of a Warrior Ministries

For the grace of God that brings salvation has appeared to all men. It teaches us to say "No" to ungodliness and worldly passions, and to live self-controlled, upright and godly lives in this present age, while we wait for the blessed hope—the glorious appearing of our great God and Savior, Jesus Christ, who gave himself for us to redeem us from all wickedness and to purify for himself a people that are his very own, eager to do what is good. Titus 2:11–14

PREFACE

In 1973 I was attending a U.S. Navy electronic maintenance school in Key West, Florida. I decided to follow Jesus Christ on August 23 of the same year. God gave me a passion for developing men spiritually almost simultaneously with my conversion. Being immature in my faith, I thought that Christians should be involved in ministry immediately. I decided to start a Bible study in my home and invited all my classmates to come. Initially, three showed up. Many more joined later, and many came to Christ in the process. My subject was the book of Revelation. I used as a text Hal Lindsey's *Late Great Planet Earth*—the subject matter of which covered difficult material to understand. Somehow, God used my passion, and I witnessed lives change dramatically.

As I continued to grow in the faith, I attempted to mentor men. It wasn't until I was mentored myself that my growth accelerated. God led me to a godly man named Darrel Johnson. He took me under his wing and mentored me for over a year in the foundations of the faith. Apparently, he saw something in me that I did not see myself and chose to invest in me. He became my spiritual father. I am deeply grateful for his love, patience, and wisdom. That experience convinced me that I, too, should mentor men in the same fashion. My wife and I both began a mentoring ministry, mine to men and hers to women.

Over the years I noticed that some men got it and others didn't. Some men grasped the journey, while others wallowed in mediocrity. I did the same things with everyone, but for some, something was missing. So I turned up the burner and tried desperately to adapt their behavior to that of a true follower of Christ. I increased the intensity of the process but had the same results—some got it and others didn't. I kept looking for the missing piece, the one thing that would make the difference. I added spiritual disciplines to the process. I required memorization of Scripture and followed up with each man regularly. I tried other methods and approaches but still got the same results.

I began to believe that only certain men were destined to become fully devoted followers of Christ, while others were not. I began to invest only in those who were very serious about the journey. But to my frustration, even then, some got it and some did not. I can remember many men over the years who grew, while some remained stagnant; some advanced while others retreated. I kept looking for the right formula, the right process, the right strategy, or the right method. I wasn't about to give up; the passion remained.

In 1992, I was the adult pastor and staff coordinator for a church in Southern California. Over time, I noticed how difficult it was for young men to break into the leadership ranks of the church. Most lay ministry positions were taken by mature leaders. If someone made it through the gauntlet of service, he or she was dumped into the caldron of leadership. Then, because that person was a proven commodity, he was recycled over and over again into different leadership positions. Constant use tired the most able of leaders. The only way out, it seemed, was to drop out or leave the church.

I went to the senior pastor and asked him if I could recruit young leaders who had raw leadership skills, put them under my wing, train them, and release them into ministry when I was finished. He granted my request. I interviewed thirty-three men and accepted thirteen for the initial group. We met in my home every other week. Over the course of four years, more than forty men came through the training—doctors, lawyers, navy pilots, roofing contractors, business leaders, and others.

Training leaders to do ministry is not that difficult; training them to be leaders is more challenging. I knew, even then, that competencies were the tools of effective leadership, but character was the power of leadership. So I began to work with them to develop biblically informed character—such a focus is far more subjective. Some men are natural, intuitive leaders, some are trained leaders, and still others are reluctant leaders, but all of us lead at some time.

Regardless of the type of leader, development of competencies is important. If people are serious about doing leadership well, if they learn the competencies with a degree of effectiveness and apply what they have learned, the outcome is usually predictable. It will be linear and additive. Take that same leader, however, and put his learned competencies against a backdrop of biblically formed character, and the results can be exponential in their effectiveness.

In addition, I knew that leadership development must be tailored to the wiring of a given leader. The training must also include helping a leader develop focus for his life in accordance with his unique God-given wiring. So, the training dealt with three primary areas: leadership character, leadership competence, and leadership congruence.

As I began to work with these men, my devotions took me to the book of Proverbs. One morning as I was reading in the book, I came across a passage that rocked my world. It was the key I was missing all along, and which was missing in my own life as well. After reading the passage, I realized I had been on the wrong battlefield. I was fighting on the battlefield of behavior. I was trying to help men grow in Christ from the outside in, instead of the inside out. The real battlefield was not behavior modification but heart transformation. The passage came to me like a neon light.

> ***Above all else, guard your heart, for it is the wellspring of life.* Proverbs 4:23**

It was then that I realized that true transformation comes from a recalibrated heart. Whatever is stored in our hearts will issue forth in behavior that will bring glory and honor to our Lord—or dishonor and shame. It is the corruption within that leads to corrupted behavior. I was on the wrong battlefield—the real battlefield is the heart. I did a study of the word *heart* and its derivatives. I pored over eight hundred verses.

Another passage blew me away in the course of my studies. In 1 Samuel 16:1–7, we learn that Samuel, God's judge and prophet, was sent to the house of Jesse to anoint the next king of Israel. As Jesse's son Eliab came before him, God stopped the review right there. Samuel felt that Eliab possessed all the appearances of a king. God said no. Then He made this startling statement:

> *"Do not consider his appearance or his height, for I have rejected him. The Lord does not look at the things man looks at. Man looks at the outward appearance, but the Lord looks at the <u>heart</u>."* **1 Samuel 16:7**

There it is again. God judges the motives of men's hearts. He is concerned about the condition of the heart. He implies that the state of the heart is a far better predictor of the quality of a man.

A clear picture began to emerge. God had a lot to say about the heart. I found that the verses coalesced around four biblical constructs—beliefs, values, attitudes, and motives. Not only that, there was an interactive relationship between these constructs. My study led to an understanding that beliefs establish values; values inform our perceptual attitudes; attitudes condition our motives; motives energize our behavior; and our behavior reflects the condition of our hearts.

I now saw the goal as helping men to identify the corruption within them, remove that corruption, replace it with God's truth, act on that truth through the power of the Holy Spirit, begin to live a godly life—the gift that keeps giving—and finish the race well, leaving a positive legacy in the lives of others for the glory of God.

I began to interject my findings in the process of developing young leaders. God showed up in dramatic ways. Lives were changed. Ministry advanced. Men developed clear focus for their lives. Families benefited; the Gospel was lived out in boldness. That was the informal beginning of Heart of a Warrior Ministries (see the material at the back of the book).

As I continued my studies and ministry, God brought others into my life, which underscored what I had learned and taught. Neil T. Anderson, Freedom in Christ Ministries, helped me. J. Robert Clinton, professor of leadership at Fuller Seminary, mentored me, and others touched my life along the way to help me mature, while at the same time enriching my findings.

I left the church in 1995 to begin work at Bethel Seminary in St. Paul. When I got to Minnesota I knew I could continue the ministry that God had given me. I decided, however, not to tell anyone what had happened in California. I could do it again, but I wouldn't know if it was me or God. I determined to wait on Him to let me know if He wanted me to begin again. I began teaching in the church I was attending. The subject was legacy, which was team-taught with a close friend of many years, Gary Gonzales. In one of my sessions, I talked about finishing well. I concluded my remarks by saying, "Some of you will finish poorly." It got their attention.

At the end of the class, a man came to me and asked if we could meet. He was a very successful channel director for AT&T. He told me that he and three other men were relatively new to the Lord and that they recognized a need to go deeper. Would I be interested in conducting a Bible study with them? I said no. After his initial shock, I said, "Mark, I am not interested in conducting another Bible study that will simply give you an intellectual grasp of God's word without a commensurate change in your soul. You go back to these men. If they are interested in digging the junk out of the closets of their lives and take initiative to make changes in the difficult areas of their existence, I will give them my life."

One year later, Mark came back to me and told me that he had six men who wanted to take the journey. That was my sign from God that He wanted me to continue what I had begun in California. We began a two-year process that added three more men. I shared with them what I had been learning about the heart.

At the end of the journey, Ray, one of the members of the group and now on my board for Heart of a Warrior Ministries, came to me and pressed me to write a manual with what they had learned so that he and others could do what had been done for them. That was the formal beginning of Heart of a Warrior Ministries, which is dedicated to helping men to live lives of authenticity, integrity, courage, and honor under the authority of God.

Since then, hundreds of men have taken the journey, and the ministry has expanded significantly in many states in the United States and many countries abroad. What began informally in California seventeen years ago has grown rapidly, leading to many *"advances"* here, around the country, and in other countries—we don't call them retreats because we believe God wants men to advance rather than retreat. Now, many groups are meeting to take the journey, led by men who have completed the journey. Many men's ministries have been launched or revitalized, with many opportunities to speak in churches around the world and recently, a launch of the ministry in prison.

A Necessary First Step

If you have not received Christ as your Lord and Savior, much of what follows may not make sense to you. Receiving Christ is a volitional decision, requiring acknowledgement that you need a Savior. You and I were born as fallen human beings with a sinful nature, inherited from Adam and Eve when they disobeyed God in the Garden of Eden. Sin is rebellion against God. Our relationship with God was broken at the Fall. Our predisposition to sin is demonstrated by our continued sinful behavior. Sin is choosing to live independent of our Creator and includes failure to do what we know to be right.

The Bible tells us that sin is an inclination toward evil. Disobedience of God is sin and requires punishment. Breaking God's laws has serious consequences, and the penalty must be paid. We are incapable of the payment, apart from God's initiative, which paid the price for us through the life, death, and Resurrection of His Son, Jesus Christ.[1] Only God, through Christ, can deliver us from the penalty of sin.[2]

Salvation in Christ is freely offered but costs a great price. We are saved by faith after hearing the good news of Jesus' sacrifice on our behalf—His death and Resurrection. We must believe (trust in, rely on, and cling to) the Lord Jesus Christ. This requires repentance; a conscious decision to turn away from independence from God and a turning to dependence on God.[3]

This act of contrition (remorse, regret, sorrow, or apology) is completed when we confess our disobedience and acknowledge Christ as our Savior and Lord. This is an act of submission to Him and represents a commitment to live in accordance with His pattern for a godly life. This

1   John 3:17; Romans 5:10; Ephesians 1:17; 2:5, 8
2   2 Timothy 1:9; Titus 3:5; Acts 4:12
3   Ephesians 1:13; Romans 1:16; Acts 3:19

is done through sincere prayer when we confess Him as Lord (Master, Mediator, and Messiah) and believe God raised Him from the dead.[4] Such confession and belief is a recognition that salvation is in Christ alone.[5]

If you have not received Him, I strongly recommend that you do so now. A simple prayer, acknowledging the facts I have just described to you, will make you a member of God's family and secure eternal life. You will become a citizen of His kingdom.[6]

- - - - - - - - - - - - - - - - - - - -

I wrote this book primarily for three reasons. First, many men and women have encouraged me to write it. Second, my wife, my greatest support, insisted that I write it. And third, I want my grandchildren to know what was most important in life and what was on and in the heart of their Papa.

What follows is what I have learned, what God has given me, and what I am obligated to pass on to others (2 Timothy 2:2). I encourage you to read it through. Yes, there is a lot here, but if you stay the course, I believe you will feel the time you spent was well worth the effort. You will notice numerous footnotes throughout the book. I chose to put almost all supporting scriptural references in the footnotes and not the text so that you would not be distracted by citations embedded in the narrative.

My hope and prayer is that God will speak to your soul and fan the embers in your heart into flame; that you will commit to bring glory and honor to God, renew your relationship with Christ, avail yourself of empowerment from the Holy Spirit, and revitalize your walk; that you will be encouraged to act and to live life in bold relief; that He will compel you to live a godly life; that you will focus on finishing well; and—when all is said and done, when God calls you home—that you will be carried on your shield before God, bearing in your person the scars you have accumulated because you chose to make a stand; and that you will hear these words: "Welcome, son, I have been waiting for you. You are a man after My heart."

---

4   Romans 10:9–10, 13; Ephesians 2:8–10; Titus 2:11–14
5   John 14:6, Acts 4:12; Philippians 2:5–11
6   Ephesians 2:19–22; Philippians 3:20–21

INTRODUCTION —
DÉJÀ VU ALL OVER AGAIN

There is a way that seems right to a man,
but in the end it leads to death.

Proverbs 14:12

Five Familiar Scenarios

Brad stared at the screensaver on his computer. The star field gave him an impression of hurtling through space. As he stared at the stars seemingly coming at him, he wondered about the twists and turns his life had made over the years. He remembered the day he gave his life to Christ and the hope it had given him for the future. But somewhere in the journey, he had lost his way. His life hadn't turned out as he'd expected. His new life in Christ started out pretty well, but somehow it went awry. Now, he was living a life of quiet desperation. Life was endured but not really enjoyed. Hopeful dreams gradually gave way to the tyranny of the urgent in his life. Where was the meaning?

He did what he thought would lead him to significance. He attended church regularly and was involved in the men's ministry. He was a good guy, for crying out loud. Why did he feel so empty? Why did he sense that life was passing him by? What would be left to mark his passage through life once it was over? What would be said of him by others? What aroma would he leave in the nostrils of those he encountered along the way? What would his children remember of him? How would his wife characterize him after he was gone? What legacy would he leave? He felt like his life was a waste, believing he would leave nothing of any lasting value. His life had been a random assortment of activities that meant little in the larger scheme of things.

Mark finished college and landed what he thought was a great job, but five years had passed, and already he realized that his work didn't deliver the satisfaction he expected. He saw more seasoned professionals scrambling for the next promotion, the next rung on the ladder to success. He recently had been promoted, but the joy lasted about twenty minutes before the demands of his new position hit him. He thought that if he worked really hard and put in the hours that were necessary to succeed, he would be able to give the time that his young family needed of him. Every new ascent to the top gave momentary satisfaction before the reality hit that another ascent was ahead of him.

His two small children and wife saw little of him because of the demands of his job—or so he believed. The argument he had with his wife the other night had become a familiar refrain: "Don't you know I'm doing this for you and the kids? Once this account is closed, I'll have more time to spend with you and the family." Deep down inside, he knew it wasn't true. If he was to get the next promotion, he had to show he was dedicated to the company. He had to work harder than his associates. His family didn't understand now, but they would later—or so he thought. The rationalization soothed his guilt.

Frank grew up in a pseudo-religious home. On a youth camping trip sponsored by his church, he gave his life to the Lord. He was baptized soon after. He did what he was told to do—went to church, read the Bible, prayed, and witnessed for Jesus. Several years had passed since his conversion, and the initial joy was replaced with boredom and mediocrity. In fact, he'd become quite cynical of those who were new to the faith. He reasoned that life hadn't caught up with them yet. Once the reality of life's difficulties hit them, they would come to realize what he had—that life was tough and it wouldn't get much better until we were home with the Lord. Sure, he believed once that the so-called abundant life was available this side of heaven. He had come to realize, however, that such a hope wasn't for our temporal existence on earth. Being faithful in reading Scripture, praying regularly, and so on hadn't delivered the kind of life he had been led to expect as a Christian. Something was missing. He had done all the right things he thought would guarantee a more fulfilled life. He followed the prescriptions for spiritual growth to the letter. Yet his private thoughts and outward behavior bore little congruity to what he said he believed. There was a growing incongruity between what he verbally affirmed as his beliefs and how he acted away from his church.

Brian was growing more afraid each day that he would be found out. Late nights spent in front of his computer, looking at images that stirred his lust, now invaded him in the daytime. If his boss saw what he was doing on his computer at work, he would certainly be fired. His daily visits to pornography sites had begun innocently enough— when he was a boy, he would watch his father do the same thing. He learned at an early age how to access the "forbidden" Web pages when his father wasn't home. The graphic depictions lured him deeper and deeper into a darkness that overwhelmed him. Repeated prayers of confession followed by an absolute commitment not to do it again lasted for a short time—and then he was at it once again.

He had gone to the pastor to ask for help "for a friend" who suffered from an addiction to pornography. The pastor's response was predictable: "Just pray about it, and give it over to the Lord." Brian wished it were that easy. His job took him out of town frequently. The pattern was the same. He would get to his motel room with an internal commitment not to visit the adult movies section of the TV menu, but as he looked at the general movie fare, he would ultimately wander to the adult section. Before he knew it, he was once again watching an adult movie. He rarely watched the whole thing, yet it was enough to feel dirty. Such episodes would conclude with a fervent prayer of confession and a declaration not to do it again. Deep inside, he knew better. He knew it was just a matter of time before the cycle would repeat itself. How long would it be before he acted on his fantasies? He was scared.

Jim had always wanted to be a pastor; he'd known what he wanted to be from an early age. There was a long line of pastors in his family tree. His calling was a sure thing. His first church was a struggle, but others that followed were easier. Each church was larger than the last. He was a "star" in his denomination and was being groomed for the presidency. His latest church was a mega-church of several thousand members. His growing staff permitted a focus on his gifts—preaching and teaching. The rest of the staff took care of the daily ministry activities. Once in a while he would visit the staff to see how things were going. He would teach on leadership occasionally and was invited to speak at many events outside the church.

He was under a lot of stress to perform. Few understood the pressures he endured. The relationship with one of his staff started out with casual conversations. She was always ready to listen to his dreams and aspirations for the ministry. Over time, the conversation moved to personal issues. She really understood him. The relationship quickly became physical, and the affair lasted for six months—until the relationship became public. His ministry began unraveling. Before he knew it, he was asked to resign, and his promising career now gave way to humiliation and despair. How could he have let himself get entangled to begin with? Where had he gone wrong? What were the telltale signs along the way? His future looked dismal. He had heard it happening to other pastors but not him. He was smarter than that. He could lose his family over his sexual immorality, not to mention squandering the spiritual authority he once had.

Common Response Strategies

What do these stories have in common? What threads of destruction are woven throughout these journeys? What factors contributed to these circumstances?

Our lives often reflect a lifestyle that is more reactive than proactive, more worldly than godly, more situational than transcendent. For many of us, our lifestyle repeatedly violates what and who we say we are—"a chosen people, a royal priesthood, a holy nation, a people belonging to God, that we may declare the praises of him who called us out of darkness into his wonderful light."[7]

Behavior like this is not uncommon in the world. And to our embarrassment, it is not uncommon in the church. Think honestly for a minute. If you knew that no one would know, no one would ever find out, no one would be the wiser, what would you be open to doing? In what kinds of behavior would you engage? In which activity would you be involved? What desires would you unleash? What hidden fantasies would you bring to life?

---

7   1 Peter 2:9

Response Strategy #1—Steel Band of Discipline

Well-meaning efforts to control our behavior last as long as the tenacity of our will or the strength of our discipline. As men, we have a tendency to wrap a steel band of discipline around our behavior. The band is kept in place by the tenacity of our will, the fellowship we keep, or the rules we obey. Sooner or later, life cascades in on us, and the steel band snaps. We revert to behaviors we thought were under control; behaviors we thought we had victory over; behaviors suppressed long ago.

These destructive behaviors, however, are just under the surface of our lives, ready to erupt at a moment's notice. These behaviors lie dormant until a circumstance, an event, or a personal interaction stirs them to life. Maybe it's a movie we are watching or a chance encounter with someone that brings the memory of our past—with all its attendant emotions—to the surface. Maybe it's a scent, or a familiar face, or a struggle we are in that causes the dormant behavior to spring to action. Once it's alive, it is very hard to control. We give vent to its alluring influence and play out its intent.

We feel bad after we succumb to the temptation, and we make hurried vows not to repeat such behavior again. Yet we might repeat the same scenario over and over again, with similar results, all the while expecting something different—perhaps victory. Repeated defeat seems to be a recurring theme in our lives.

Response Strategy #2—More Is Less

Generally, we employ a second common strategy at this point. We redouble our external efforts to control the beast within us. We read our Bibles more, pray more, worship more, witness more—only to find out that "more" is producing "less" in our lives. We become discouraged because our well-intentioned efforts meet with such little success. We increase the energy and frequency of such well-meaning disciplines, only to find out they are not producing the desired results we had hoped.

Such spiritual disciplines can be very helpful; they are most helpful when a vibrant relationship with Jesus Christ already exists. Such disciplines are meant to enhance what's already there in the life of the believer and follower of Christ. The embers of such a relationship are still hot but buried under the ashes of an impotent spiritual life. Adding the logs of spiritual disciplines to the smoldering embers can result in a welling up of vibrant flames, once the wind of the Holy Spirit is applied to the fire.

All too often, however, such well-meaning efforts do not produce the kind of revitalization we desire. We simply apply a discipline and hope the discipline—in and of itself—will spark renewal. When a spiritual discipline is the primary objective—which we expect will produce a byproduct of a restored relationship with Christ—then the result may be less than we hoped for. Spiritual disciplines are a means to a greater end, the continuance of a personal, healthy, ongoing, intimate relationship with Christ, not a panacea for corrupt and sinful behavior.

Response Strategy #3—The "Hail Mary" Pass

Frustrated and annoyed with the strategies we have used up to now, we look for a better solution to our dilemma. A third strategy is commonly exercised. We go to the Christian bookstore to find a more promising alternative to our futile efforts. We browse the contents of several books in the "how-to" section of the store. We purchase a few that promise some relief from our debilitating struggles. We read them carefully, noting any process, procedure, methodology, or strategy that can be applied to our situation. With fervent effort, we employ our favorite remedy found in the pages of a promising "how-to" book.

In this case, one size doesn't always fit all. Someone one else's experience may be instructive and could prove to be helpful sometimes—but not often. We may gather simple principles to consider or approaches to try. They may work for a season but may not produce a lasting remedy. In similar fashion, we have all heard sermons that give wonderful general application. To make such general application specific to our lives, however, we must meditate on its implications, pray for insight, and determine our personal application accordingly. Thoughtful and reflective meditation is the bridge we must cross from general application to specific personal application.[8]

Response Strategy #4—Surrender and Retreat

If nothing has worked up to this point, we embrace a final strategy of defeat. Our last option is to hunker down and hope that the storm will

---

8   Joshua 1:8; Psalm 1:2–3; 119:97–104

pass. Such rationale suggests that we are victims of a cruel Enemy who will not let us rise above our circumstances. After all, ultimate victory is ours once we leave this vale of tears called earth. In the meantime we are to bear the onslaught and tolerate a life of defeat, regardless of the promise of abundant living.[9] Life is simply too much for us.

So we dumb down our faith and live in the misty lowlands of mediocrity. We have forgotten what it's like to fly like an eagle. Instead, we must find what little comfort we can in living in a cage of our own making, as clipped-winged birds, until we are called home to glory. We must endure the in-between time. Those who appear to be living the abundant life are simply deluded. As soon as they face the difficulties we have faced, they will soon learn the truth—or so we tell ourselves. We live lives of quiet desperation, waiting for someone seven feet tall, wearing white, carrying a flaming sword, to come and usher us home. We live with our bags packed, suspicious of anyone who lives a more fruitful life than we are experiencing.

Same Old Story

We have a tendency to believe what is happening to us is unique. No one could possibly understand our situation. Wrong. Paul understood our dilemma exactly. He had personal experience with the spiritual dynamics I have discussed so far. In the book of Romans 7:15–24, we read:

> *I do not understand what I do. For what I want to do I do not do, but what I hate I do. And if I do what I do not want to do, I agree that the law is good. As it is, it is no longer I myself who do it, but it is sin living in me. I know that nothing good lives in me, that is, in my sinful nature. For I have the desire to do what is good, but I cannot carry it out. For what I do is not the good I want to do; no, the evil I do not want to do—this I keep on doing. Now if I do what I do not want to do, it is no longer I who do it, but it is sin living in me that does it.*
>
> *So I find this law at work: When I want to do good, evil is right there with me. For in my inner being I delight in God's law; but I see another law at work in the members of my body, waging war against the law of my mind and making*

---

9   John 10:10

> *me a prisoner of the law of sin at work within my members.*
> *What a wretched man I am! Who will rescue me from this*
> *body of death?*

Paul finally arrives at the answer in verse 25: *Thanks be to God—through Jesus Christ our Lord!* Thanks, Paul, that's helpful, but what does it mean? Jesus said that if we hold to His teaching, we are really His disciples. Then we will know the truth, and the truth will set us free.[10] But it's not just a matter of knowing the truth that will set us free. It's a matter of knowing the personification of truth, Jesus Christ, and submission to His Lordship over our lives that makes the difference.[11] An itinerant evangelist, Vance Havner, once said that when we come to Christ, we receive Him as Lord and Savior. We are under new management from that moment forward. He is Master, Mediator, Messiah, Lord of Lords, and King of Kings.

Unwrapping Paul's revelation, God's truth, in our lives requires more information and understanding if we are to live the abundant life now, in the in-between time. Victorious living is possible now. We don't have to wait until we are in heaven. The question is, how can we experience abundant living this side of glory? What concrete measures can we apply so that we live lives of glory and honor rather than shame and disgrace?

Why do we do what we do? Why do we do the very things we hate to do? Why is our behavior inconsistent with—even opposed to—what we say we believe? We are told to be self-controlled and alert. Our Enemy, the devil, prowls around like a roaring lion, looking for someone to devour. We are instructed to resist him and stand firm in the faith because we know that our brothers throughout the world are undergoing the same kind of sufferings.[12] There is a battle going on for our hearts. The heart is the battleground where the success of the daily Christian life is determined. Understanding and winning the battle for the heart is essential to Christian maturity and freedom.

The Journey Ahead

This book will help you become a man of honor and integrity by aligning your heart with God's heart. The objective of this book is to help you become men after God's heart. Your behavior, good or bad, is reflective of

---

10 John 8:31–32
11 John 14:6
12 1 Peter 5:8–9

what's in your hearts. Let the scalpel of God's Word perform surgery on your heart so that your life will bring glory instead of shame to the Father. I encourage all to engage in a life-transforming journey that will teach you how to live differently—to live victoriously, to live lives of integrity and honor under God's authority. The book is divided into three parts. Part one contains three chapters. Part two includes six chapters. Part three closes with two chapters. Although helpful suggestions and applications are provided throughout the book, the last two chapters focus entirely on application. They answer the question: "What do we do now that we know?"

Part 1: Preparing for Battle

Part 1 begins the journey by addressing what a man after God's heart looks like. In **Chapter 1**, twelve essential characteristics are described and explained. **Chapter 2** identifies situational lifestyles we adopt to navigate the pathways of our lives. These lifestyles promise victory but only result in dysfunctional approaches to life's problems. In opposition to these defective patterns, **Chapter 3** lays out God's preferred lifestyle, the one that indeed delivers what it promises—a victorious life—if we have the courage to train to reach it. This chapter sets the stage for all that follows in the next two parts; it sets the objective. The remaining chapters point to this objective and are designed to help us reach it.

Part 2: Surveying the Battlefield

Part 2 addresses the real battlefield for change and transformation that will help us reach our objective of God's preferred lifestyle. Counter to what we have come to believe, sanctified behavior modification is not the route to lasting transformational change, leading to the spiritual maturity and abundant living that is promised in the Bible. **Chapter 4** opens with a critique of five deadly lies that, if believed, will lead to insignificance and mediocrity. The chapter continues with an overview of the real battlefield, where the struggle for victory is fought.

Each subsequent chapter includes a ***Battle Plan*** at the end of the chapter. This gives us an opportunity to engage the material covered from a personal point of view. These sections help us grasp the impact of the material in our personal lives. Certainly, the book can be read and—I hope—enjoyed without interacting with the battle plans at the end of the chapters. I believe, however, that each of us will get much more out of the book by completing the battle plans along the way.

Chapter 5 briefly looks at the map of the battlefield that must be defended and guarded if we are to live godly and honorable lives as we wait for the blessed appearance of our great God and Savior Jesus Christ.[13] This part also describes the topography of the battlefield in detail. Four terrains are addressed. **Chapter 6** addresses central beliefs; **chapter 7**, core values; **chapter 8**, worldview; and **chapter 9**, motives. Each terrain builds on the one previous. Together, they comprise the complete landscape where the battle is fought and ultimately won or lost.

Part 2 illustrates the relationship between each of the battle terrains and their importance in determining victory or defeat. Each terrain affects the others but one terrain—central beliefs—can positively or adversely affect or infect the others. Just like a computer's operating software, this very important high ground on the battlefield determines how all application software functions.

Part 3: Winning the Battle

Our final section answers the question, "So what?" This part brings all that preceded it together into a functioning whole. **Chapter 10** puts it all in perspective and helps us to see the whole after having reviewed the parts. We can see how the individual parts interact with one another. An example will be provided to that end.

Chapter 11 provides guidance on how to correct corrupted behavior. This chapter gives specific, concrete steps we can take to remove and replace sinful behavior and the corruption in the heart that led to that behavior. Specific corrective measures will be described. **Chapter 12** offers guidance for proactively living godly lives. Once again, specific concrete steps will be presented, the completion of which help us to live a productive and godly life. Guidance in **Chapter 11** is corrective of destructive, sinful behavior that brings shame and dishonor on us and God. Guidance in **Chapter 12** is preventative in nature and presents help on how to live intentionally, as men after God's heart, before problems arise that require corrective measures.

---

13 Titus 2:11-14

The book is designed to help us become effective crime scene investigators. How do we become CSIs? What gives a CSI the edge to see things on a crime site that are there but overlooked by a casual observer? What gives a CSI the capability to put evidence together to determine what actually happened at the crime site? We may have some inherent qualities that lend themselves to becoming effective CSIs, but such intuitive knowledge is no replacement for solid training in disciplines that are needed to properly identify and interpret crime scenes. Each CSI must be trained in a variety of skills to be effective in the field, and then, to remain sharp, he must visit crime sites regularly.

This book will help is to become good crime scene investigators—of our own lives primarily, and of others secondarily. I hope to give each of you the best tools to determine what happened on your crime site and the accurate conclusions that can be drawn to prevent its happening again.

The end of the book is just the beginning. Once we understand the dynamics of spiritual formation and spiritual transformation and begin to apply what we have learned under the authority of God, in response to the finished work of the cross by Christ and empowered by the Holy Spirit, we will begin to live a legacy worth leaving in the lives of others. You will finish the race well.[14]

Let's begin the journey.

---

14 Acts 20:24; 1 Corinthians 9:24–27; 2 Timothy 4:7–8; Hebrews 12:1–3

PART I

PREPARING FOR BATTLE

CHAPTER 1
THE HEART OF A WARRIOR

Man looks at appearances, God looks at the heart.

1 Samuel 16:7

The term "a rattling of sabers" is a common phrase that indicates military aggressiveness. A military show of force to others is meant to put observers on notice that there are dire consequences brewing, should anyone press his interest too far. Any man committed to becoming a man after God's heart brings upon himself the focused attention of the Enemy. Such a man is perceived as a potential formidable foe. We have been warned.

> *Be self-controlled and alert. Your Enemy the devil prowls around like a roaring lion looking for someone to devour. Resist him, standing firm in the faith, because you know that your brothers throughout the world are undergoing the same kind of sufferings.*[15]

Negative circumstances, events, and people are brought to bear by the Enemy to dissuade a fully devoted follower of Christ from pressing his interests—God's interests—too far. That is why men run into such opposition from the world, the flesh, and the devil when they attempt to live upright and godly lives in this present age.

How many times have you encountered such opposition when you attempted to live in accordance with God's commands, precepts, principles, and values? How many times have you felt the hot breath of the Enemy on your neck when you chose to live differently from the world? How many times have you run into road blocks when you tried to forge an honorable life; a life that would bring glory and honor to your Creator? How many times have you encountered seemingly impossible barriers when you tried

---

15 1 Peter 5:8–9

to live a Bible-centered life? How many times have you been frustrated when you have attempted to stand for Christ?

In the opening scene of the movie *Gladiator*, the Romans faced a terrifying Enemy. Just before the battle began, the imposing horde shouted and beat their weapons against their shields. Roman soldiers, unaccustomed to such tactics, undoubtedly experienced fear and terror. Once the battle was engaged, the fear and terror soon gave way to a desperate fight for survival. In the 1800s the British army faced Zulu warriors, who often preceded the fight by beating their weapons against their shields. The frightening sound could be heard for miles as they approached the British.

Battles in the past were often preceded by "a rattling of sabers" in the form of disturbing drum beats, shrill war cries, the beating of weapons against shields, and other forms of disarming noises designed to instill fear in the opposing army. When heard, they created a visceral reaction—one felt in the pit of the stomach—that signaled impending doom. They were meant to scare and immobilize the opposition and often resulted in a hasty retreat to safer ground.

It has always been easier to go along and get along than to confront these fears with steely resolve. Victory is within our grasp when we temper our fear, submit ourselves to God, and resist the scare tactics of the devil.[16]

Life is full of battles to be fought and skirmishes in which to engage. Saints before us have had similar experiences and found the necessary strength to overcome their fears.[17]

> *And what more shall I say? I do not have time to tell about Gideon, Barak, Samson, Jephthah, David, Samuel and the prophets, who through faith conquered kingdoms, administered justice, and gained what was promised; who shut the mouths of lions, quenched the fury of the flames, and escaped the edge of the sword; whose weakness was turned to strength; and who became powerful in battle and routed foreign armies.*

---

16 James 4:7–8
17 Hebrews 11:32–35

We are told we can do all things in Christ who strengthens us.[18] So when you hear the "rattling of sabers" of the Enemy know that *"You, dear children, are from God and have overcome them, because the one who is in you is greater than the one who is in the world."*[19]

Also know that there is no battle you are in or skirmish you are fighting that escapes the knowledge of God. He goes before us, fights besides us, and protects behind us. Don't be frightened by the noise of the "rattling of sabers."

God told Joshua, Moses' successor, that no one would be able to stand against him because He would be with him; He would never leave Joshua or forsake him. Three times God said, "Be strong and courageous."[20] Whatever battle we face, skirmish we encounter, crisis we experience, struggle we go through, or trial we suffer, God is with us, and our weaknesses will be turned to strengths if we remain faithful to him.

The Bible is full of military metaphors, symbols, and stories designed to illustrate biblical principles and values—the **armor** of God,[21] enduring hardship like a good **soldier** of Christ,[22] the last **battle**,[23] the **sword** of the Spirit,[24] and the **rider on the white horse**.[25] These metaphors illustrate the fact that life is indeed a battle. We must approach the battle with discipline, diligence, dedication, and devotion if we are to have any chance of victory.

Preparing for Battle

The Bible predicts more perilous times ahead. We may witness in our lifetime the increased persecution of Christ's followers, described by Jesus:

> *"Watch out that no one deceives you. For many will come in my name, claiming, 'I am the Christ,' and will deceive many.*

---

18 Philippians 4:13
19 1 John 4:4–5
20 Joshua 1:1–18
21 Ephesians 6:10-18
22 2 Timothy 2:3-4
23 Revelation 9, 16, 20
24 Ephesians 6:17; Hebrews 4:12
25 Revelation 19:11–21

You will hear of wars and rumors of wars, but see to it that you are not alarmed. Such things must happen, but the end is still to come. Nation will rise against nation, and kingdom against kingdom. There will be famines and earthquakes in various places. All these are the beginning of birth pains. Then you will be handed over to be persecuted and put to death, and you will be hated by all nations because of me. At that time many will turn away from the faith and will betray and hate each other, and many false prophets will appear and deceive many people. Because of the increase of wickedness, the love of most will grow cold, but he who stands firm to the end will be saved. And this Gospel of the kingdom will be preached in the whole world as a testimony to all nations, and then the end will come."[26]

The Book of Revelation depicts cataclysmic battles that will take place between the forces of good and evil. Even though the war is already won, we will face continuous skirmishes and battles until the culmination of Christ's victory over Satan and his forces.[27] These skirmishes and battles are happening around us now. Unfortunately, many of us are oblivious to this spiritual warfare. Vance Havner, a widely respected itinerant evangelist and modern-day prophet, now with the Lord, said, "It is bad enough to be ignorant when it can't be helped; it is a thousand times worse to be ignorant on purpose."[28]

Paul the apostle wasn't oblivious. He warned us that if we want to live a godly life in Christ Jesus, we will be persecuted.[29] He knew life was a battle—that we had to be prepared for the fight and that it was a good fight.[30] Our primary offensive weapon is the sword of truth, God's Word, the Bible. By it we must be trained.[31] "For the Word of God is living and active. Sharper than any double-edged sword, it penetrates even to dividing soul and spirit, joints and marrow; it judges the thoughts and

---

26 Matthew 24:4–14
27 Revelation 19, 20
28 Vance Havner. *In Times Like These*, p. 21.
29 1 Timothy 3:12, 13
30 1 Timothy 1:18–20
31 1 Timothy 3:15–17

attitudes of the heart."[32] In fact we are to train to wear the full armor of God.[33]

We just don't get up one morning and decide that today is the day we will wear God's armor and go to the battle lines. A set of armor, uniquely fitted for each us, waits for us to don it. God superintended our formation in our mother's womb. He set the days for us.[34] He prepared the armor we are to wear before we ever came to be, but we must be trained to wear it. Roman soldiers trained in their armor, marched in their armor, and fought in their armor. Their armor became like a second skin, but each man's armor had to be broken in. It took time to learn how to wear one's armor and maneuver in it with dexterity and flexibility.

Paul further identifies followers of Christ as "soldiers."[35] He gives guidance to soldiers of Christ. We are to endure hardship like a good soldier of Christ. We are to be focused on the battle. To be a good soldier, we must be devoted to our Commander, Jesus Christ, as well as disciplined and diligent.[36] He reminds us of the discipline necessary to prepare us for the struggles ahead. He equates the journey as a race of endurance. The race is not a jog but a race to win, which requires strict training.[37] Near the end of his life, Paul writes to Timothy and declares that he has fought the good fight, finished the race, and kept the faith.[38]

Not preparing for battle is not an option. Scripture tells us that we are to "Be self-controlled and alert. Your Enemy the devil prowls around like a roaring lion looking for someone to devour. Resist him, standing firm in the faith, because you know that your brothers throughout the world are undergoing the same kind of sufferings."[39] Make no mistake; we all have a battle line to which we must go. When the Commander calls, will we be ready? We can go to the battle line wearing someone else's armor, which doesn't fit us; wearing no armor, leaving us defenseless; or wearing

---

32 Hebrews 4:12
33 Ephesians 6:10–18
34 Psalm 139:1–18
35 Philippians 2:25–26; Philemon 1–3
36 2 Timothy 2:1–7
37 1 Corinthians 9:26–27
38 2 Timothy 4:6–8
39 1 Peter 5:8–9

the armor that God forged for us before we ever came to be. The choice is ours. Which will it be?

Will you take your place on the battle line? Others on the line depend on you. Will there be a gap where you should be? Havner pointedly stressed that "Those who fail to take their place in battle, by their very absence, have taken sides with the Enemy.[40] They may seek to justify themselves, but they have no reasons, only excuses, and one excuse is the skin of a reason stuffed with a lie. This is no time for professed Christians who attend flag-wavings and the bugle-blowings but never show up for the battle. Too many are trying to be neither/nor in a world that is either/or. We cannot escape involvement today; if we gather not with the Lord, we scatter abroad. Too many of the soldiers of the cross today will never be decorated for extreme courage under fire. They will be known only for extreme caution under cover."

The War Rages

The war rages, even though the outcome has been determined.[41] We serve a great Commander and Chief, the Lord Jesus Christ. Let me introduce you to the General of Generals, the King of Kings, and the Lord of Lords!

> *I saw heaven standing open and there before me was a white horse, whose rider is called Faithful and True. With justice he judges and makes war. His eyes are like blazing fire, and on his head are many crowns. He has a name written on him that no one knows but he himself. He is dressed in a robe dipped in blood, and his name is the Word of God. The armies of heaven were following him, riding on white horses and dressed in fine linen, white and clean. Out of his mouth comes a sharp sword with which to strike down the nations. "He will rule them with an iron scepter." He treads the winepress of the fury of the wrath of God Almighty. On his robe and on his thigh he has this name written: KING OF KINGS AND LORD OF LORDS.[42]*
>
> *The LORD is a warrior; the LORD is his name.[43]*

---

40   Matthew 12:30
41   Revelation 20:1–15
42   Revelation 19:11–16
43   Exodus 15:3

*The LORD will march out like a mighty man, like a warrior
he will stir up his zeal; with a shout he will raise the battle
cry and will triumph over his enemies.*[44]

There will come a time when the whole earth will tremble at the hands
of the Lord of Lords; no "meek and mild Clark Kent," no frail caricature
depicted in so many paintings. His mercy is unmerited, but it's not
unlimited. The climactic battle just mentioned is coming—but not yet.
No, not yet. There is still time; time to change our ways, time to prepare
for the battle, time to get ready for the orders we will receive—but not a
lot of time.

Whose side will you be on when the time comes? Where will your allegiance
lie? Will you be ready? We live in the "in-between" time. You sense that it's
coming. Something is stirring within your soul. It is strangely exhilarating
and fearful at the same time.

You can hear it, can't you? The rattling of sabers on a distant battlefield?
It's getting louder. Are you ready?

Let's make one point clear: He is building an army for the battles that
are raging now, for the battles that will rage in the future, for the battles
leading up to the final decisive battle. We will need the heart of a warrior
if we are to prevail against the gates of hell.[45]

A Man after God's Heart

What does it mean to have the heart of a warrior? Simply stated, to have
the heart of a warrior we must be men after God's heart. God declared
David as king of Israel, son of Jesse, a man after His own heart. Why?
Because he would do everything God wanted him to do.[46] David's life was
a series of ups and downs, highs and lows, victories and defeats, integrity
and treachery, honor and dishonor, consistency and inconsistency,
godliness and compromise, happiness and sadness, triumphs and failures,
high roads and low roads, mountain tops and valleys, and excellence and
mediocrity. Yet God declares David a man after His heart. Aren't you glad
that God uses marred individuals to carry out His purposes? Aren't you
glad that we don't have to be perfect before God can use us? Aren't you

---

44 Isaiah 42:13
45 Matthew 16:18
46 Acts 13:22

glad that God does not give up on us? In fact, He has plans to prosper us and not to harm us; plans to give us hope and a future.[47]

What does a warrior after God's heart look like? Let me suggest twelve characteristics of a man after God's heart. Certainly, others could be added but these seem to me to be particularly relevant.

As you read these characteristics, please remember that we are all in the process of becoming yet not having arrived. What is important is for us to acknowledge the characteristics and to strive to comply with them. Try to determine where you fall along the following continuum for each characteristic.

Not true of me   Completely true of me

1. A warrior after God's heart is loyal to his Commander.

He recognizes that he is under new management; he is under Christ's authority. His allegiance is to Him above all others. Christ sets the parameters for allegiance. We who would submit to His authority recognize that we must follow new rules and embrace new values if we are to be loyal to our Commander. "We are to say no to ungodliness and worldly passions and to live self-controlled, upright, and godly lives in this present age, while we wait for the blessed hope—the glorious appearing of our great God and Savior, Jesus Christ, who gave Himself for us to redeem us from all wickedness and to purify for Himself a people that are His very own, eager to do what is good."[48]

Dr. Havner once said that if Jesus is not Lord of all, then He is not Lord at all. He also suggested that if we were 95 percent faithful to Christ, we were not faithful at all. Christ is not looking for divided allegiance. He is looking for warriors who are completely loyal to Him. Such loyalty also recognizes that allegiance to Him will embrace a new identity—His identity. In other words, we are to live in accordance with who we are in Christ:

---

47 Jeremiah 29:11
48 Titus 2:11–14

- Salt and light of the earth[49]
- A branch of the true vine, a channel of His life[50]
- Chosen and appointed to bear fruit[51]
- God's temple[52]
- A minister of reconciliation for God[53]
- God's co-worker[54]
- God's workmanship[55]
- Established, anointed, and sealed by God[56]
- A child of God[57]
- Christ's friend[58]
- A member of Christ's body[59]
- A saint adopted by God[60]
- Complete in Christ[61]

2. A warrior after God's heart is a citizen of God's kingdom.

A man after God's heart abandons his worldly citizenship for a new citizenship under a new flag. According to the Scriptures, our new citizenship is in heaven.[62] We are now aliens and strangers in the world. We are to abstain from its sinful practices, which war against our souls. But we are required to live in the world in such a way that we model our new citizenship with its values to the world around us, in hope of rescuing others trapped by worldliness. We are to live such good lives in the face of ridicule so that the world may see our good deeds and glorify God accordingly.[63]

---

49 Matthew 5:13, 14
50 John 15:1, 5
51 John 15:16
52 1 Corinthians 3:16
53 2 Corinthians 5:17
54 1 Corinthians 3:9
55 Ephesians 2:10
56 2 Corinthians 1:21, 22
57 John 1:12
58 John 15:15
59 1 Corinthians 12:27
60 Ephesians 1:1, 5
61 Colossians 2:10
62 Philippians 3:20, 21
63 1 Peter 2:11–12

Such allegiance requires us "not to conform to the pattern of this world, but be transformed by the renewing of (our) minds. That (we) will be able to test and approve what God's will is—His good, pleasing, and perfect will."[64] We are not to love the world or the things in the world. In fact, we are told that if we love the world, the love of the Father is not in us. Everything in the world—the cravings of sinful man, the lust of his eyes, and the boasting of what he has and does—comes not from the Father but from the world. The world and its desires pass away, but the man who does the will of God lives forever.[65] The Bible also informs us that friendship with the world is hatred toward God. Anyone who chooses to be a friend of the world becomes an Enemy of God.[66] Pretty strong language, wouldn't you agree? Nevertheless, our new citizenship demands a separation from the world and alignment with the kingdom of God. There is no middle ground.

Alister McGrath, Christian historian and theologian, stresses that we should think of ourselves, our churches, and our families as "colonies of heaven, as outposts of the real eternal city, who seek to keep its laws in the midst of alien territory." C. S. Lewis, famed author of *Mere Christianity* and *The Chronicles of Narnia*, in thinking about the Christian life, sees the world "as Enemy territory, territory occupied by invading forces."

Building on this theme, McGrath adds: "In the midst of this territory, as resistance groups are the communities of faith." He goes on to say that "we must never be afraid to be different from the world around us. It is very easy for Christians to be depressed by the fact that the world scorns our values and standards."

"But the image," he says, "of the colony sets this in its proper perspective. At Philippi the civilizing laws of Rome contrasted with the anarchy (a state of lawlessness or political disorder) of its hinterland (regions outside of Rome). And so," he continues, "our moral vision—grounded in Scripture, sustained by faith, given intellectual spine by Christian doctrine—stands as a civilizing influence in the midst of a world that seems to have lost its moral way."[67]

---

64 Romans 12:2

65 1 John 2:15–17

66 James 4:6

67 Alister E. McGrath, "Doctrine and Ethics," *Journal of the Evangelical Theological Society* 34, 2 (June 1991): 145–56.

In summary, allegiance to a new Commander and to a new kingdom requires its citizens to live under new authority and a new value system. A man after God's heart is loyal to his king first. He does not have dual citizenship—in the world and in the kingdom of God. His citizenship is squarely in the kingdom of God. Such loyalty, such allegiance is not for the faint of heart. Such commitment, however, is not exercised devoid of fear. God is asking us to lean into our fear. He can do this because He has given us everything we need to live a life of godliness.[68]

3. A warrior after God's heart follows orders.

After removing Saul, God made David king. He testified concerning him: "I have found David, son of Jesse, a man after my own heart; he will do everything I want him to do."[69] How do we show our love for God? We show our love by obeying His commands. This concept should not be foreign to us. How many parents have uttered the following words? "Will you just do what I ask you to do?" How do we gauge the love of our children? By their obedience.

As a devoted follower of Christ, we also show our love by our obedience. Those who have come to know God will obey His commands. Scripture is very clear on this matter—"The man who says, 'I know Him' but does not do what He commands is a liar, and the truth is not in him. But if anyone obeys His word, God's love is truly made complete in him. This is how we know we are in Him: Whoever claims to live in Him must walk as Jesus did."[70] The Spirit who lives in every believer testifies internally to the validity of our commitment—those who obey His commands live in Him, and He in them. "And this is how we know that He lives in us: We know it by the Spirit he gave us."[71] Obedience is the single indicator of our love for God. Our service for Him should be marked by uncompromising obedience to Him.[72]

We are to endure hardship like a good soldier of Christ Jesus. No one serving as a soldier gets involved in civilian affairs—he wants to please

---

68 2 Peter 1:3, 4
69 Acts 13:22
70 1 John 2:3–6
71 1 John 3:21–24
72 1 John 5:1–5; 2 John 5, 6

his commanding officer.[73] Our focus should be intentionally singular. In other words, we are to live our lives for an audience of one.

What are His orders? Say no to ungodliness and worldly passions and live self-controlled, upright and godly lives in this present age, eager to do what is good.[74]

4. A warrior after God's heart prepares for the battle.

As stated earlier, there are only three ways we can show up on the battle line: no armor at all, leaving us defenseless; wearing someone else's armor, which doesn't fit us; or wearing the armor God forged for us before we ever came to be.

The pieces of armor are the same, but one size does not fit all—it fits each man differently. "Stand firm then, with the belt of truth buckled around your waist, with the breastplate of righteousness in place, and with your feet fitted with the readiness that comes from the Gospel of peace. In addition to all this, take up the shield of faith, with which you can extinguish all the flaming arrows of the evil one. Take the helmet of salvation and the sword of the Spirit, which is the word of God."[75]

What should be the frame of mind of a warrior after God's heart? "Be on your guard; stand firm in the faith; be men of courage; be strong. Do everything in love."[76]

A friend of mine once asked me to define courage and valor. At the time, the movie *The Last Samurai* was playing in the local theaters. Knowing that men are often stimulated by images and symbols before words, I suggested that he and I go to the movie. Men must feel the power of words viscerally before the definitions are truly understood. I instructed him to pay close attention to the warlord of the Samurai—he epitomized courage and valor. After viewing the movie, the friend indicated that he certainly felt the implications of courage and valor. I then defined these qualities for him. Erwin McManus, lead pastor of Mosaic in Los Angeles, has given a helpful and clarifying definition of courage: "Courage is not the absence

---

73 2 Timothy 2:2–5
74 Titus 2:11–14
75 Ephesians 6:14–17
76 1 Corinthians 16:13–14

of fear; it is the absence of self." When we exercise courage, we lean into our fear. Valor is facing overwhelming odds without ever turning your back on the Enemy. Regardless of the forces arrayed in front of you, valor dictates that you face the Enemy head on, even if it means great loss.

Engagement in the battle requires courage and valor. Such an attitude recognizes the importance of self-preservation but sets it aside for the higher cause of one's comrades, and it does what is uncommonly expected in the face of danger. Every warrior prepares himself for battle. He learns how to wear his armor and how to fight in his armor. He digs deep down inside and musters the courage necessary to face overwhelming odds. He leans into his fear and faces the Enemy head on. He is not alone; he has a brave Commander in the lead and other warriors by his side. If he falls in battle, others will lift him up. As iron sharpens iron, each man sharpens another.[77]

5. A warrior after God's heart guards his heart.

One of the most vulnerable organs in a human body is the heart. A well-placed shot to the heart will quickly incapacitate or kill the strongest warrior. The heart of a warrior must be guarded at all times. Foreign substances must be kept away from the heart. The Bible tells us that "Above all else, guard your heart, for it is the wellspring of life."[78] We are to be ever vigilant, alert, and on guard at all times. If we drop our guard, we become vulnerable to the tactics of the Enemy. Others who depend on us may be in jeopardy if we fail to protect ourselves.

Every warrior needs a strong heart. If we flag in zeal, if we do not embrace healthy lifestyle patterns, or if we permit toxins or other contaminants to invade the heart, we will not have the strength to prevail in times of battle. Bad habits, lack of exercise, and poor dietary discipline can result in debilitating weakness. The Bible recognizes that physical training is of some value, but godliness has value for all things.[79]

The heart is the central repository of our strength. An unhealthy heart robs us of our strength. Cyclist Lance Armstrong accomplished what no other cyclist has ever attained—an unprecedented seventh Tour de France

---

77 Proverbs 27:17
78 Proverbs 4:23
79 2 Timothy 4:8

victory. Because of his meticulous attention to detail and arduous training regimen, he performed at a level superior to all others. His training, however, placed huge demands on his physical capacity. Because he continually pressed the limits of his physical capacity, he made his body into a machine capable of great feats of strength and stamina. His physical heart is said to be 30 percent larger than those of other humans.

Not only must a warrior after God's heart develop healthy practices, he must nurture a healthy heart if he is to weather the demands of the battle. His strength and stamina depends on it.

6. A warrior after God's heart is a man of integrity.

What is a man of integrity? John Maxwell, author of numerous books on leadership, gave a great definition of integrity:

> *Integrity binds our person together and fosters a spirit of contentment within us. It will not allow our lips to violate our hearts. When integrity is the referee, we will be consistent; our beliefs will be mirrored by our conduct. There will be no discrepancy between what we appear to be and what our family knows we are, whether in times of prosperity or adversity. Integrity allows us to predetermine what we will be regardless of circumstances, persons involved, or the places of our testing.*

Are we the same in the dark as we are in the light? Are we the same at home as we are at work? Are we the same at work as we are at church? Is there incongruity between what we say we believe and how we act? Integrity requires unanimity.

In the opening scenes of the movie *Gladiator*, Roman legions are poised for battle against the last barbarian stronghold in Germania. Marcus Aurelius, the last philosopher-emperor of Rome, is hoping to bring a twelve-year war to a close and usher in an era of peace across the empire. The general of the armies, Maximus, is a principled man who lives his life in accordance with three values: allegiance to Rome, love for his family, a passionate commitment to strength and honor. Before the climactic battle is about to begin, he addresses his cavalry and makes a profound statement: "What we do in life echoes in eternity." Although a pagan, he mouths a biblical principle forgotten by most of us today.

The story proceeds. After the battle is won, Commodus, the devious son of Marcus Aurelius, kills his father upon the news that he will not be emperor. Marcus, he learns, intends to make Maximus the protector of Rome until a republican form of government is once again in place. Maximus is almost assassinated because he refuses to give his allegiance to Commodus. He escapes, is made a slave who becomes a gladiator, and ultimately defies the emperor. The two meet in a fight to the death in the Coliseum.

What takes place in the arena is not important. The power of the story is about the honor and courage of a man under extreme circumstances, living his life in absolute commitment to his values—a man of integrity. Think about it for a minute—if we, as men, lived our lives committed to God, our families, and biblical beliefs and values with intentionality, intensity, passion, and focus, what kind of men would we become? What could we accomplish for our Lord? What kind of legacy would we leave our loved ones and those God has called us to influence for His redemptive purposes and plans? From a biblical point of view, what does a man of integrity look like?

> *LORD, who may dwell in your sanctuary? Who may live on your holy hill? He whose walk is blameless and who does what is righteous, who speaks the truth from his heart and has no slander on his tongue, who does his neighbor no wrong and casts no slur on his fellowman, who despises a vile man but honors those who fear the LORD, who keeps his oath even when it hurts, who lends his money without usury and does not accept a bribe against the innocent. He who does these things will never be shaken.*[80]

7. A warrior after God's heart is a man of authenticity.

In many cases, our impact on others is minimal at best because we haven't modeled authenticity. We are too much like those to whom we hope to bring to Christ. What we verbally proclaim—sometimes sincerely, intently, and occasionally loudly—is not always consistent with how we

---

80 Psalm 15:1–5

behave. Our behavior does not always coincide with what and who we say we are.

What does it mean to be authentic? Webster's Dictionary defines the term to mean trustworthy; not imaginary, false, or imitation; conforming to an original so as to reproduce its essential features. In other words it's being exactly what one claims to be.

Dr. Robert Lewis, founder and president of Men's Fraternity, defines an authentic man as one who rejects passivity, accepts responsibility, leads courageously, and expects God's reward. That's a great definition for authentic manhood.

What does an authentic Christian look like? An authentic Christian is one who conforms to the original, Jesus Christ, and reproduces those features that reflect His character. Such a person leaves little doubt to whom he belongs because he bears the imprint of the Master. He carries in his person God's certificate of authenticity. The question that needs to be asked is: Do we bear the imprint of the Master? Do our lives, our behavior, reflect His character? Would He authorize a certificate of authenticity for us?

To travel by plane today, we first must pass through the airport's metal detector. An alarm rings when certain objects are detected. An attendant passes a special wand over our bodies to locate these objects. Our baggage passes through a machine that gives another attendant a view of its contents. What if a detector could be designed to detect an authentic Christian, and we were asked to pass through the detector. Would it go off?

For many of us, our lifestyle repeatedly violates what we say we are—a chosen people, a royal priesthood, a holy nation, a people belonging to God—that we may declare the praises of Him who called us out of darkness into His wonderful light.[81]

8. A warrior after God's heart lays his life on the line.

A warrior after God's heart realizes that God has preordained unique purposes for his life in close alignment to how He has wired him. He is not here to aimlessly meander through the years without purpose or reason for being. He is to calibrate his life in accordance with God's purposes and give himself fully to accomplishing those purposes. "For we

81   1 Peter 2:9

are God's workmanship, created in Christ Jesus to do good works, which God prepared in advance for us to do."[82] In so doing, the warrior will find significance, satisfaction, and convergence—that place along life's continuum where 80 percent of who we are overlaps 80percent of what we do. And these purposes, for which he is willing to lay his life on the line, are not self-centered but Christ-centered. Neil Anderson, president and founder of Freedom in Christ Ministries, said, "It's not what we do that determines who we are. It is who we are in Christ that should determine what we do."

To what must each man align himself? In my humble opinion, John Eldredge, in his book *Wild at Heart*, provides the answer. He correctly identifies the soul of man. Men find their identity in three primary areas: a cause to die for, a challenge to embrace, and loved ones to protect. Every man longs to be a part of something larger than himself—a cause that is worth living for and worth dying for. Every man longs for a challenge that compels him to reach for what is just out of reach, to stretch the limits of his capacity. And every man is driven to protect the defenseless, the underdog, the underrepresented, his loved ones—those who cannot adequately protect themselves.

Not too long ago, I was asked to record a radio spot and briefly respond to the question of what makes a man a man. I made the following comments:

> *During the impeachment hearings some years ago, a politician was asked to explain why the president did what he did. She responded, "Men will be men." The implication is that men have a base nature from which they can't escape—a lecherous, self-indulgent need for gratification. Is that really true? What makes a man a man? The Bible is clear—we are created in the image of God. Sin has marred that image. Christ has repaired the image. When men receive Jesus as their Savior and Lord, He gives them back their true selves. He, in essence, resurrects our true identity as men. What makes a man a man? Christ is our model for manhood. He had a "cause" to die for (atonement for the sins of the world), a challenge to embrace (the suffering of the cross), and loved ones to protect (the redemption of mankind). As men, we too*

---

82 Ephesians 2:10

have a cause to die for, a challenge to embrace, and loved ones to protect. Take any one of these away, and you rob a man of his true identity. What cause, larger than yourself, are you prepared to die for? What challenge does God want you to embrace? Who has God called you to protect? You may not need to look any further than your home.

So our challenge is clear. We are to always give ourselves fully to the work of the Lord because we know that our labor in the Lord is not in vain.[83] We were not meant for the sidelines. Life is to be lived, not endured. Just as ships were not meant to spend their existence tied up to a pier, men are not meant to passively stand back from the battle lines. We can spend our whole lives polishing the brass, making sure our engines are finely tuned, and ensuring that our hulls are seaworthy. We were meant to be at sea. Get your ship away from the pier. What are you waiting for? Engage!

9. A warrior after God's heart rises to the challenge.

I have spent a great deal of time observing the world around me. I have observed that the world is getting darker.

In *After Virtue*, Alasdair MacIntyre, senior research professor at Notre Dame, commented on our culture today by comparing it to the Dark Ages. He makes the following comment:

A crucial turning point in that earlier history occurred when men and women of good will turned aside from the task of shoring up the Roman imperium and ceased to identify the continuation of civility and moral community with the maintenance of the imperium. What they set themselves to achieve instead—often not recognizing fully what they were doing—was the construction of new forms of community, within which the moral life could be sustained so that both morality and civility might survive the coming ages of barbarism and darkness. If my account of our moral condition is correct, we ought also to conclude that for some time now we too have reached that turning point. What matters at this stage is the construction of local forms of community within which civility and the intellectual and moral life can be sustained

---
83 1 Corinthians 15:58

> *through the new dark ages which are already upon us. And if the tradition of the virtues was able to survive the horrors of the last dark ages, we are not entirely without ground for hope. This time, however, the barbarians are not waiting beyond the frontiers; they have already been governing us for quite some time. And it is our lack of consciousness of this that constitutes part of our predicament.*[84]

The old Dark Ages was marked by fear of the unknown and reliance upon the learned for interpreting the world around them. Knowledge and wisdom resided with the aristocracy and the church. Individual study of God's word was left to the so-called scholars with agendas, and interpretation was under the sole purview of these authorities. The common man and woman relied upon others for truth. But the Reformation broke that bondage. Luther's rebellion essentially gave the Scriptures back to the people.

MacIntyre suggests that we are in a new dark age. Living in the fast lane and being susceptible to the tyranny of the urgent has compelled many of us to rely on new authorities for knowledge and wisdom. These subject matter experts can be found on newscasts, talk shows, newsstands, and some pulpits. Because of our hectic lifestyles, we turn to "sound bites" from popular celebrities, inside and outside the church, for "truth." I agree with MacIntyre—we are living in the new dark ages. When the organizing center of our beliefs, values, worldview, and motives shifts from the Bible to a pluralistic syncretism and amalgamation of philosophies and ideologies, it isn't long before we lose our way and fall into factions and special-interest groups that fit our preconceived notions and whims.

The Bible tells us that we are to "watch our lives and doctrine closely."[85] We are to "Preach the word; be prepared in season and out of season; correct, rebuke, and encourage—with great patience and careful instruction. For the time will come [and I believe is upon us now] when men will not put up with sound doctrine. Instead, to suit their own desires, they will gather around them a great number of teachers to say what their itching ears want to hear. They will turn their ears away from the truth and turn aside to myths. But you, keep your head in all situations, endure hardship, do the work of an evangelist, (and) discharge all the duties of your ministry."[86]

---

84 Alasdair MacIntyre. *After Virtue.* 1984, 263.

85 1 Timothy 4:16

86 2 Timothy 4:2–5

In many discussions with men, I have come to conclude that the Spirit of God is moving in two powerful ways. Each movement compels men to rise to the challenge. Each movement is felt in the souls of men before they can articulate it.

1. *The middle ground has disappeared …*

It used to be quite comfortable to have one foot in the purposes of the world and one foot in the purposes of God. No more. The gap between them is too large and has always been that way. Committed followers of Jesus Christ are being asked to stand in bold relief against the backdrop of their culture and give a defense for the hope that is in them.[87] The only other option is to give in, fold back into our culture, becoming transparent with it, and not be distinguishable apart from it. There is, at this point, nothing of our lives that draws anyone to the foot of God's Son's cross. The choice is ours. Where will we plant our feet?

2. *The rattling of sabers is getting louder …*

Metaphorically speaking, the rattling of sabers on distant battlefields is getting louder. Can you hear them? They indicate the coming of the Lord, preceded by the world's getting darker, sin becoming more widespread, godlessness becoming more rampant, hatred for God becoming more verbal, and followers of Christ becoming more marginalized. We were told it was going to happen.[88] God is calling men after His own heart who are stirred by the sounds and anticipation of holy battle. We don't know exactly where the battles will rage, but we sense the need to prepare for orders from the Holy One. We sense the need to be conformed to the image of Jesus Christ in anticipation of the battlefield to which we will be called. One day, we will receive our orders. Will we be ready? Now is the time to become a man after God's heart.

10. A warrior after God's heart takes a stand.

Scripture admonishes us to stand our ground.

> *Now it is God who makes both us and you stand firm in Christ. He anointed us, set his seal of ownership on us, and*

---

87 1 Peter 3:15
88 2 Timothy 3:1–9; Matthew 24:1–51

put his Spirit in our hearts as a deposit, guaranteeing what is to come.[89]

So then, brothers, stand firm and hold to the teachings we passed on to you, whether by word of mouth or by letter.[90]

"Be strong in the Lord and in His mighty power. Put on the full armor of God so that you can take your stand against the devil's schemes. For our struggle is not against flesh and blood, but against the rulers, against the authorities, against the powers of this dark world and against the spiritual forces of evil in the heavenly realms. Therefore put on the full armor of God, so that when the day of evil comes, you may be able to stand your ground, and after you have done everything, to stand."[91]

Roman armor was made to protect the front of the body. In battle, Roman soldiers were not permitted to turn their backs to the Enemy. If they should lose heart and run, dire consequences would result—Roman history tells us that the practice of decimation was exercised when soldiers retreated from battle. The cohort would be lined up and counted off. Every tenth man was condemned to die by the hands of his fellow soldiers. The command was odious and gut-wrenching, but it drove the point home—don't ever leave the battle lines and run to safety.

A beloved professor of Bethel Seminary, Dr. Ralph Hammond, died unexpectedly while exercising at his health club. Before his death, he penned this powerful call to stand:

When you get weary, stand.
When you're tired, stand.
When you feel alone, stand.
When your strength is almost gone, stand.
When you feel overpowered, stand.
When you feel you are out of everything, stand.
When you don't feel up to it, stand.
When you're not in your spiritual rhythm, stand.
When the path is not clear, stand.
When you've done everything, stand.

---

89 2 Corinthians 1:21–22
90 2 Thessalonians 2:15
91 Ephesians 6:10–13

When you don't know anything else to do, stand.

Stand! Stand!

Stand because God has commanded us to stand.
Stand because God has instructed us to stand.
Stand because it's God's will for us to stand.
Stand because Jesus said He would never leave us or forsake us.
Stand because greater is He that is in us, than he that is in the world.
Stand because the Holy Spirit is the source of our strength.
Stand because we can do all things through Christ who strengthens us.
Stand because God is able.
Stand because God is faithful.

Stand! Stand!

Stand as a witness to God's mercy.
Stand as an object of God's love.
Stand as the recipient of God's grace.
Stand to follow Him.
Stand to share Christ with others.
Stand to be a testimony for Christ in word and deed.
Stand as an ambassador for Jesus Christ.

Stand! Stand!

Stand for justice.
Stand for righteousness.
Stand for goodness.
Stand for godliness.
Stand for peace.
Stand as God's instrument of holiness.
Stand for the glory of God.
Stand for you labor not in vain.
Stand because we have victory in Christ.
Stand because Christ first stood for us.

Stand! Stand! Stand!

11. A warrior after God's heart provides for his loved ones.

Scripture once again sets the appropriate standard. "If anyone does not provide for his relatives, and especially for his immediate family, he has denied the faith and is worse than an unbeliever."[92]

Men need affirmation, respect, and love from their families, from the people who mean most to them. To receive, you must first give. Do you love others as God loves you? If you are married, do you love your wife as God loves you? Are you modeling the character of Christ for your children?

Dr. Robert Lewis identifies three types of fathers: the absent father, the involved father, and the strategic father. The absent father exists, but little else. He gets up in the morning, eats, goes to work, comes home, eats, watches TV, and goes to bed. The routine seldom varies, no matter what happens around him. He is generally detached from his family, except to provide the basics for them. The involved father is at his child's school plays and athletic events. He cheers on the sidelines, but rarely, if at all, gives any constructive life guidance to his children. The strategic father recognizes that his children don't need a buddy as a father; they need a father who will teach them how to live life.

Be careful what you model.

I have six grandchildren. The second youngest is my clone; he mimics everything I do. He follows me around the yard with his toy lawnmower when I cut the lawn. He helps me rake the leaves in the fall. He even pretends to lift weights when I work out in my home gym. He watches me closely.

If you are not married, then the loved ones you are to protect are the unloved, the uncared for, the under-represented, the unwanted, the underprivileged, and those on the margins.

Be careful what you model.

Are you fulfilling your responsibilities and obligations to your loved ones? Are you investing in the lives of your loved ones? Are you providing for their basic needs? Are you living in such a way that they will call you

---

92 1 Timothy 5:8

blessed? Are you serving or expecting to be served? Are you expressing unconditional love to them? Action speaks louder than words!

12. A warrior after God's heart finishes well.

To Timothy, Paul writes: *"In the presence of God and of Christ Jesus, who will judge the living and the dead, and in view of his appearing and his kingdom, I give you this charge: Preach the word; be prepared in season and out of season; correct, rebuke, and encourage—with great patience and careful instruction. For the time will come when men will not put up with sound doctrine. Instead, to suit their own desires, they will gather around them a great number of teachers to say what their itching ears want to hear. They will turn their ears away from the truth and turn aside to myths. But you, keep your head in all situations, endure hardship, do the work of an evangelist, discharge all the duties of your ministry."*

"For I am already being poured out like a drink offering, and the time has come for my departure. I have fought the good fight, I have finished the race, I have kept the faith. Now there is in store for me the crown of righteousness, which the Lord, the righteous Judge, will award to me on that day—and not only to me, but also to all who have longed for his appearing."[93]

The greatest gift you can give to your family, your friends, your work mates, your community, or to the world at large is a godly life. What kind of legacy would you leave if God called you home tonight? Legacy is the aroma left in the nostrils of those God calls you to influence for His sake, long after you are gone. There are only four legacies you can leave: no legacy, a perishable legacy, a bad legacy, or the only legacy worth leaving in the lives of others—a godly legacy.

It's never too late or too early to live a legacy worth leaving in the lives of others. Dr. J. Robert Clinton, professor of leadership at Fuller Seminary in Pasadena, California, has given his life to the noble task of determining how to finish the race well. Using qualitative research methodologies, he and his team have completed over 3,500 cases studies of the lives of biblical, historical, and contemporary Christian leaders. After a study of one hundred of the prominent leaders in the Bible, Dr. Clinton concluded that there was enough information provided about forty-nine of them to assess whether they had finished well. To finish well meant "they were walking

---

93 2 Timothy 4:1–8

with God personally at the end of their lives and probably contributed to God's purposes at some high-realized level of potential." Clinton discovered that less than 30 percent of these leaders finished well.[94]

Those who finished well possessed the following characteristics:

1. They had a personal, vital relationship with God, right up to the end.
2. They maintained a lifelong learning posture.
3. Christ-likeness in character was evidenced by the fruit of the Spirit in their lives.
4. They lived out God's truth in their daily lives.
5. They left a godly legacy behind in the lives of others.
6. They walked with a growing awareness of God's destiny for them.

Clinton also identified seven characteristics of those who didn't finish the race well:

1. Their finances were out of control.
2. They abused power.
3. They had self-centered pride.
4. They were involved in immoral behavior.
5. Their family life was out of control.
6. They had reached a plateau in their spiritual journey.
7. They made many compromises along the way.

When God calls us home, will we have left it all on the floor of the arena? As Maximus in *Gladiator* lay dead on the floor of the Coliseum, Lucilla says, "Is Rome worth one good man's life? We believed it once. Help us believe it again. He was a soldier of Rome; honor him." Will there be someone who says of you and me, "He was a soldier of God; honor him"?

The journey begins with a commitment to the ideal of a warrior after God's heart. Do you have the courage to lean into your fear for the journey ahead? I hope so. We need you on the battle line.

The Chinese philosophers were right: The journey of a thousand miles begins with the first step.

---

94 J. Robert Clinton. *The Mantle of the Mentor.* 1993, 5.

CHAPTER 2
SITUATIONAL LIFESTYLE STRATEGIES

Make level paths for your feet and take only
ways that are firm. Do not swerve to the
right or the left; keep your foot from evil.

Proverbs 4:26–27

Most men hate to stop and ask for directions. There are lots of resources available to help us find our way. Internet navigators use MapQuest or some other computer tool. Others like to use old-fashioned folded maps. The automobile industry has made getting directions easier—navigation systems are becoming common features in cars. You punch in an address or verbally tell it where you want to go, and directions are presented. Hiking in unfamiliar surroundings is no longer a challenge. Global positioning systems (GPS) can pinpoint your location in a matter of seconds.

But it is easy to lose our way. We stumble along, getting directions from others who seem to know the way. Too many times we are led to destinations where we don't want to go. Unless we have a good map and a calibrated compass or a GPS device—and know how to use them—we can get lost. Such devices, however, help us to find our way and stay on course. They provide the means to determine the direction we need to go so that we will reach our destination and not get lost along the way.

Navigating through life is another matter. How can we tell the right direction from the wrong direction? How do we avoid getting lost along the way? We think we're climbing the right ladder but find out it's leaning against the wrong wall. For many of us, navigating through life is a guessing game.

Wouldn't it be nice to have a voice-activated navigation system for life? You simply verbalize a concern, and it would give us the answer we seek:

- "Show me the quickest way to a godly life."
- "Where should I look in the Bible to get the nourishment I need right now?"
- "Should I take this job or that one?"
- "Whom should I marry?"
- "What school should I attend?"
- "What will happen if I take this direction?"
- "What will happen if I make this decision?"

We often resort to our own methods to find our way.

Why do people do what they do? Are there recognizable patterns of behavior? Do people behave in predictable ways? How do people respond to situations, circumstances, and crises? Many of us adopt situational lifestyles that offer perceived solutions to life's problems. These patterns help us navigate through life. We tend to adopt a variety of situational lifestyles as our compass to find our way. These strategies are consciously selected. They seem to help us navigate life's decisions, difficulties, and crises.

These patterns of behavior are developed early in life to cope with any difficulties and accommodate our predispositions and biases when we choose to live our lives apart from God. They may be the by-product of tragic circumstances, events, or people who have hurt us at times in our lives when we were defenseless, unaware, or immature.

They become a part of the natural rhythm of our lives over time. When faced with a dilemma, we may opt for a particular course that proves to be a good temporary solution. So when faced with certain issues, we use a particular response pattern again, again, and again.

For instance, because of our personality temperament, we may choose to fight, appease (pacify), or flee from perceived or real dangers. Do it often enough, and it becomes a predictable pattern for us whenever conflict arises.

This behavior is generally brought into play by some catalyst—a difficult situation we are facing, an event that spins us into a reactive mode of response, or an interaction with a particular person. Those circumstances, events, or persons that originally compelled us to adopt a mode of response

29

to life's situations often recede back into our subconscious. What remains is the pattern brought into play by the problems or issues we face. The repeated use of these patterns becomes habitual over time, and we employ them without thinking.

The point to remember is that they are relative and situational. These patterns of behavior are defense mechanisms to help us get through life. They accommodate our humanistic bent to solve life's problems on our own. They are unhealthy patterns that provide temporary solutions. Ultimately, they create more problems than they solve. They are not God's preferred lifestyle pattern for our lives. *"There is a way that seems right to a man, but in the end it leads to death."*[95]

Five Situational Lifestyle Patterns

Countless interactions with others have led me to conclude there are essentially five possible strategies that people use to get through life. In many cases, people adopt a combination of patterns or easily move from one pattern to the next, depending on the circumstances, events, or persons encountered. I am certain there are probably many more patterns, but the following seem to be the most common:

Pinball Wizard—Reactionary Pattern

Like a pinball machine, these people react to circumstances—they live life ricocheting from one emergency to the next. If there isn't a crisis to embrace, they tend to create one to fill the void. They are often people who need to be needed and tend to see more in a given situation than is actually there. They live on the edge.

Perhaps you have met someone like this. Upon meeting you, he will immediately ask how you are doing. You respond, "Fine." He isn't satisfied. He leans in closer and asks more intensely, "How are you *really* doing?" You wonder if he knows more about you than you are willing to communicate. Such a reactionary lifestyle pattern may evidence itself in a mother who gives her undivided attention to the child who is perpetually in trouble, to the neglect of her other children. These folks bounce from one problem to the next in hope of soothing their unhealthy need to be needed.

---

95 Proverbs 16:25

Saul, the first king of Israel, was such a person. In one instance, Saul became impatient while waiting for Samuel the prophet to come and offer a sacrifice. His men were scatted, and he once again panicked and reacted without thinking. He offered a burnt offering, although he was not authorized to do so. His action was condemned by Samuel, and he suffered a terrible consequence—his replacement as king.[96]

In another instance, Saul disobeyed God, who had commanded him to utterly destroy the Amalekites. Instead, he spared the king and kept the best of the captured livestock for the army and himself.[97]

In yet another instance, Saul's jealousy of David and angry reaction to the accolades given to David led to his trying to kill David.[98] Finally, in a panicked reaction to the Philistines closing in on him, he sought the counsel of the witch in Endor. His fear paralyzed him and propelled him to take immediate, reactive action, in opposition to God's expressed condemnation against such activity.[99]

Do you know anyone who fits this **reactionary** lifestyle? It may be a fireman who starts a fire so that he can be a hero by putting it out. It may be a lab technician who manipulates the data of an experiment to construct a solution that will garner him the respect of his colleagues. It may be a daughter who never finishes what she starts. She moves from one crisis to another, leaving chaos behind. If God does not intervene, this person will continue to respond in a similar fashion to every perceived crisis—or simply make up a crisis to address. They may neglect their responsibilities to others by continually focusing on people who never seem to rise above their circumstances but find themselves in one mess after another.

Electric Current—Avoidance Pattern

Like electric current, these people avoid problems in life by choosing the path of least resistance. They embrace choices that cause the least amount of pain and discomfort. Because character is formed over the anvil of difficulty, these folks' lives are usually shallow and undefined. They lack depth and often prefer superficial conversation. In a particularly intense interchange, you may hear them say, "Can't we talk about something more

---

96 1 Samuel 13
97 1 Samuel 15
98 1 Samuel 18
99 1 Samuel 28

positive? Isn't there something more cheery to discuss?" They play the "glad game" regularly. Their ship may be sinking, but they are still dancing.

Lot in the Old Testament was such a person. Lot offered his daughters to a riotous crowd to appease their lust in hope of abating their evil intentions.[100] Weighing his options carefully to avoid discomfort and difficulty, he chose the refuge of a town to the disaster he believed would happen to him in the hills.[101] Lot, forced out of his city sanctuary by fear, settled in the mountains. In a drunken stupor, he succumbed to his daughters and slept with them.[102]

Do you know anyone who fits this **avoidance** lifestyle? Maybe it's a father who wants to be "friends" with his children and gives in to their every whim. Maybe it's a church board member who knows he's right but gives in to the pressures of other board members so that he can avoid conflict. Maybe it's a relative whose home has deteriorated beyond repair because he didn't address the deterioration when it first occurred. Maybe it's the parents of a child who has academic problems and has changed schools each time the problems were brought to the parents' attention because they refused to believe their child was deficient in any way. Maybe it's a brother who refuses to deal with the problems between him and his wife or to seek counsel. He thinks the problem will go away. If God does not intervene, this person will continue to respond in a similar fashion to every potential and perceived source of pain—they will avoid it.

Super Glue—Transference Pattern

These people live vicariously through others that represent who they want to be. They are not satisfied with who they perceive they are. Like Super Glue, they attach themselves to others, losing their own identity in the process. Because all humans let us down over time, extraction is painful, and latching on to someone else is predictable. Have you ever tried to separate two fingers held together by Super Glue? It's a painful exercise. Similarly, when the object of these people's identity lets them down, removing themselves from their identity often creates psychological damage, leaving emotional "scar tissue." Their identity is wrapped up in others they admire, so separation simply moves them to quickly embrace

---

100 Genesis 19:6–9
101 Genesis 19:18–20
102 Genesis 19:30–36

someone *else's* persona. Not knowing who they really are, they desperately try to identify with someone whom they think has it together.

Jacob, the son of Isaac and the brother of Esau, used this pattern for his life. In complicity with his mother, he tricked Isaac into believing he was Esau to receive a coveted blessing that was reserved for the eldest son. Knowing Isaac's eyesight had failed him, Jacob wore the skin of an animal to fool his father and steal Esau's birthright.[103] He changed his identity to that of his brother. Much later, he finally came to his senses, with God's help, and became who he was meant to be all along. The consequences of his deception were many and required attention before he got on with his life.

Rehoboam, successor to his father, Solomon, in Israel, refused the counsel of wise men and sought the counsel of friends from his youth. Instead of following the wisdom of his father's counselors, he chose to listen to unwise counselors because he lacked discernment. He appealed to others who lacked wisdom because of his identity with them.[104]

Maybe you can think of someone who fits this transference lifestyle. Maybe it's your son or daughter, who has lost his or her identity to a cult or to a group of young people who wear all black and dark makeup. Maybe a friend of yours has begun speaking in language normally heard from rappers or streetwise young men. Maybe it's a relative who has joined a gang and acts and dresses much differently as a result. Maybe a work associate has changed his entertainment habits in hope of getting close to the "in crowd" or has joined a country club and drives a particular model of car similar to those driven by those she hopes to emulate. Maybe a coach embellished his résumé to leave the impression he is a graduate of a prestigious school and played in competitive professional sports. If God does not intervene, these people will continue to respond in a similar fashion every time they become discouraged with whom they are and continue to long to be someone they are not.

Log Jam—Indecision Pattern

These people hate to make decisions because they are fearful of the outcome. They decide not to decide, which, in fact, is a decision. When crisis or important issues demand a response, they tend to procrastinate.

103 Genesis 27:5–29
104 1 Kings 12:1–16

A log of indecision gets wedged in the stream of life, causing a log jam over time. The log jam is abandoned but is repeatedly begun again in some other place. These people are paranoid about making a mistake. They tend to compartmentalize life's problems, hoping instead that their problems will just go away. When a critical decision is left unmade, however, many secondary issues arise that demand decisions. Life can quickly become a real mess. They leave a marriage, a job, a location, or a responsibility, only to create a similar chaotic situation again with similar results.

Peter the apostle is a good example of this lifestyle for a certain portion of his life. When asked a potentially self-incriminating question about his relationship with Jesus Christ on the night of Jesus' inquisition by the high priest, he denied the relationship three times. He was indecisive because of fear. Each denial compounded the problem.[105] Much later, Peter was confronted by Paul for his hypocritical action, when he separated himself from Gentile converts for fear of the Jewish circumcision group.[106]

Maybe you can think of someone who fits this indecision lifestyle. Maybe a friend from your youth has left three marriages because of his unwillingness to resolve the problems that ultimately led to the demise of the marriages. Maybe a business associate leaves yet another job when the heat begins to build due to his less-than-satisfactory performance of his responsibilities. The pattern seems to be repeated frequently. Maybe it's your pastor, who stays in each church for a short period before moving on to another city to start all over again. If God does not intervene, these people will continue to respond in similar fashion every time they are required to make critical decisions or address difficult situations.

Loose Canon—Driven Pattern

This lifestyle pattern is my personal favorite. "Hi, I'm Greg Bourgond, reformed loose cannon. Before Christ intervened, I was headed toward a lonely end. If Christ had not touched my life and saved me from such an end through salvation in Him, I was destined to live life in the fast lane. I got my sense of identity by my achievements."

These people have one purpose in life—to achieve or succeed at all costs. They blow through every obstacle, with a focus always on the goal, regardless of the strain it places on their relationships. They generally

105 John 18:15–18, 25–27
106 Galatians 2:11–14

will do whatever it takes to obtain their objectives. They often justify and rationalize their frenzied activity by forcefully declaring, "Don't you understand? It's all for you and the kids. As soon as I finish this project (secure this account, receive a promotion, get the business established), I'll have time to spend with you." At the end of their lives they have little else but their accomplishments to keep them company. There is no one with whom to share them and nothing but memories of unfulfilled commitments, broken promises, and missed relationship opportunities left in the wake of their life. Sound familiar?

During my daughter's senior year in high school, she repeatedly asked if I could attend one of her school's basketball games—she was a varsity cheerleader. At the time, I was a general manager of a business. I remember giving perfectly legitimate and rational reasons why it was impossible to be there. To this day, I cannot remember any of those reasons. What I remember is that I wasn't there for my daughter. My primary focus was on the business sphere of influence. A devotion to one's chosen profession or dedication to becoming successful is commendable. When such devotion and dedication, however, become an excuse for neglecting our obligation to be light to a lost world, we sacrifice our God-given purposes, talents, and potential on the altar of expediency.

Maybe you can think of someone who fits this driven lifestyle. Do you know anyone who has been involved in an argument with their spouse to justify their being a workaholic? Do you know anyone who justifies his predisposition for the tyranny of the urgent at the loss of the important? Do you know anyone who derives his identity from his accomplishments? Do you know anyone who defines his worth by what he does instead of who he is? If God does not intervene, these people will continue to respond in similar fashion every time they give in to the need to achieve, excel at all costs, and make it to the next mountain peak, only to find still other mountains yet to climb.

In summary, these patterns are characteristic of those who would choose to live their lives on a horizontal plane, devoid of a vertical relationship with their Creator. These situational lifestyle patterns promise success but only result in more problems over time. Maybe you can identify with one or more of these patterns. Maybe your life is characterized by a combination of these approaches used to resolve life's difficulties. Maybe one or more of these patterns has been modeled to you by people you trusted. Maybe these timeworn patterns are comfortable to you, even though they don't deliver the solutions for which you had hoped.

Before I present God's preferred lifestyle pattern in the next chapter, let's look at the rich soil out of which His preferred pattern is cultivated.

Good Soil for a Healthy Lifestyle

With our penchant to want to live life on our terms, it may be helpful to hear what God has to say about His design for us. When men live their lives on a horizontal plane, without a vertical relationship with the Creator, their lives become meaningless. Without an understanding of God's intentional design for us, we are left to draw our own erroneous conclusions about the nature of true humanity.

Created by God's Hand[107]

First of all, we are not an accident, a happenstance, a coincidence, or a mistake. You and I were planned before we ever came to be. You see, God was intentional about our existence. Our birth, nationality, ethnic group, natural abilities and talents, personality temperament, and DNA were predetermined by God Himself. Our existence was planned and supervised by God. The Scriptures are clear: God knew us before our parents. He was and is familiar with all our ways. We cannot escape His overarching presence.

We are not the product of an accidental combination of molecules, but of divine intelligence; of a personally involved Creator. Our total existence on earth was determined before we were born. In fact, the exact number of days we will live has been predetermined by God. We are "fearfully and wonderfully made." He also has unique purposes for each of us. Alignment with those purposes will bring us to completeness and produce deep satisfaction.[108]

Created in the Image of God[109]

---

107 Psalm 139:1–18
108 Ephesians 2:10
109 Genesis 1:26, 27

Second, we bear in our person the DNA of God. God's transferable attributes were instilled in every human being who has lived, is living, and will live in the future. One of those attributes is an internal sense of an eternal reality.[110] God has placed eternity into our hearts. Yet this general revelation does not give us the ability to understand what God has done from the beginning to the end. That requires the special revelation of Jesus Christ, the counsel of the Holy Spirit, and the written inspired word of God, the Bible.

So what does it mean to be created in the image of God? J. I. Packer, the world-renowned theologian and author of the best-selling *Knowing God*, offers helpful counsel at this point:[111]

> *When God made man, he communicated to him qualities corresponding to His moral attributes. This is what the Bible means when it tells us that God made man (meaning both men and women) in His own image—namely, that God made man (and woman) a free spiritual being, a responsible moral agent with powers of choice and action, able to commune with Him and respond to Him, and by nature good, truthful, holy, upright: in a word, godly.*
>
> *The moral qualities which belonged to the divine image were lost at the fall; God's image in man has been universally defaced, for all mankind has in one way or another lapsed into ungodliness. But the Bible tells us that now, in fulfillment of His plan of redemption, God is at work in Christian believers to repair His ruined image by communicating these qualities to them afresh. This is what Scripture means when it says that Christians are being renewed in the image of Christ[112] and of God.[113]*

Created to Live in Accordance with God's Design

We are designed to live in accordance with God's design and if we don't, there are consequences. What would eventually happen if you filled your automobile tank with sugar water? Your engine would ultimately seize up

---

110 Ecclesiastes 3:10, 11
111 J. I. Packer. *Knowing God*, 1973, 89-90.
112 2 Corinthians 3:18
113 Colossians 3:10

and not run. What would eventually happen if you filled your automobile tank with diesel fuel? It would run for a while but would ultimately quit running. The plugs would be gummed up and refuse to fire.

I was mentoring several men from a church in which I was an associate pastor. We spent a week in Montana, fishing for trout. I decided to wash the dishes after a meal one evening. The cabin had a dishwasher, but I couldn't find any soap except a box of Tide laundry detergent. I figured that soap was soap, so I poured some Tide in the receptacle in the dishwasher, set the wash cycle, and went outside. To my utter surprise, I came in to find soap suds knee-deep throughout the kitchen and slowly making its way into the other rooms in the cabin. I learned the hard way that laundry detergent is not made for dishwashers.

J. I. Packer is again instructive about God's design:[114]

> *We are familiar with the thought that our bodies are like machines, needing the right routine of food, rest, and exercise if they are to run efficiently, and liable, if filled up with the wrong fuel—alcohol, drugs, poison—to lose their power of healthy functioning and ultimately to "seize up" entirely in physical death. What we are perhaps slower to grasp is that God wishes us to think of our souls in a similar way.*
>
> *As rational persons, we were made to bear God's moral image—that is, our souls were made to "run" on the practice of worship, law-keeping, truthfulness, honesty, discipline, self-control, and service to God and others. If we abandon these practices, not only do we incur guilt before God; we also progressively destroy our souls. Conscience atrophies, the sense of shame dries up, one's capacity for truthfulness, loyalty, and honesty is eaten away, one's character disintegrates. One not only becomes desperately miserable; one is steadily being de-humanized.*

When we violate God's designed purposes, we can expect less than favorable results.

---

114 J.I. Packer, 102, 103

Created to Be Like Christ[115]

Even though we each have a unique identity, we are all to be like Christ. "And we know that in all things, God works for the good of those who love Him, who have been called according to His purpose. For those God foreknew, He also predestined to be conformed to the likeness of His Son, that He might be the firstborn among many brothers."[116]

Many of us have heard sermons about the purpose of the church. We are familiar with the often-quoted verse that suggests that the purpose of the church is "to prepare God's people for works of service, so that the body of Christ may be built up."[117] I disagree. Before you label me a heretic, let me suggest that this verse is, instead, a means to a greater end. Looking a little further in the passage, we can conclude that Paul points to the clear objective of Christ-likeness. We read the following remarkable statement that the objective in preparing God's people for works of service has as its goal the "Unity in the faith and in the knowledge of the Son of God [to become] mature, attaining to the whole measure of the fullness of Christ."[118]

In case we miss the point, Paul reiterates the proposition. He repeats the purpose of building up the body of Christ by restating his original premise. "Instead, speaking the truth in love, we will in all things grow up into Him who is the Head; that is, Christ. From Him the whole body, joined and held together by every supporting ligament, grows and builds itself up in love, as each part does its work."[119]

He further draws an amazing conclusion. Becoming like Christ brings godly discernment. If we pursue becoming Christ-like, "we will no longer be infants, tossed back and forth by the waves, and blown here and there by every wind of teaching and by the cunning and craftiness of men in their deceitful scheming."[120] We will no longer be led astray. We will know the truth and the truth will set us free.[121] But there is a catch—we must hold to Christ's teaching. We must obey His teaching and act on it in the

115 Ephesians 4:11–16
116 Romans 8:28, 29
117 Ephesians 4:12
118 Ephesians 4:13
119 Ephesians 4:15, 16
120 Ephesians 4:14
121 John 8:31, 32

same direction over time, until it becomes a part of us. In so doing, we will be His disciples—learners after Him, men after His heart.

In summary, we are created by God's hand, in His image, in accordance with His design, and to grow in Him is to become Christ-like. This is God's ordained cultivation of the soil, which is necessary to plant the seed of salvation that will lead to spiritual transformation, in accordance with God's preferred lifestyle for His children.

The final element needed is salvation through Christ. It is only after you receive Jesus Christ as your Lord and Savior and experience conversion that you are forgiven, justified, and adopted into the family of God, into His kingdom. A fundamental step of faith must be exercised to receive God's gift of eternal life.

> *For there is one God and one mediator between God and men, the man Christ Jesus, who gave Himself as a ransom for all men—the testimony given in its proper time.*[122]

> *"I am the way and the truth and the life. No one comes to the Father except through Me."*[123]

> *That if you confess with your mouth, "Jesus is Lord," and believe in your heart that God raised Him from the dead, you will be saved. For it is with your heart that you believe and are justified, and it is with your mouth that you confess and are saved. As the Scripture says, "Anyone who trusts in him will never be put to shame." For there is no difference between Jew and Gentile—the same Lord is Lord of all and richly blesses all who call on him, for, "Everyone who calls on the name of the Lord will be saved."*[124]

It is important to note that the Bible does not say we must "accept" Christ, but it does say we must "receive" Christ. Who is accepting whom in this case?

---

122 1 Timothy 2:5–6
123 John 14:6
124 Romans 10:9–13

Once you become a member of His family, then you are given the capacity and empowerment to live life abundantly.[125] The pattern for a victorious life will be described in the next chapter.

It seems appropriate at this juncture to share my story with you. My hope is that it will give you hope. The amazing journey toward spiritual transformation begins with conversion. My story is fundamentally like many others who have come to a saving knowledge of Christ. It contains the essential elements, such as an acknowledgement of God's sovereignty and authorship of life, an independent intention to live life our way in opposition to God's divine plan, a provision for resolving the broken relationship between the Creator and creature through the finished work of Christ's cross, and a reception of God's gift of salvation that brings with it "everything we need to live a life of godliness."[126] The specifics, however, are unique, as they are for anyone who comes to Christ. God personally seeks us out in unique and special ways. You see, none of us comes to Jesus unless the Father who sent Him draws us to Him.[127]

My Personal Story

As I review my journey, I have come to believe that the perceived random incidents of our lives fall into a perceptible mosaic. The clarity of the relationships between events is best understood in retrospect. As I look over the topography of my life, an unmistakable pattern of God's activity emerges—a pattern that comes into focus as I connect the dots. The richness and tender care and processing of God is obvious to me.

Early Years

I grew up in a traditional Catholic home, attended parochial grade school, was an altar boy, and sensed God's hand on me at an early age. Although immature, I thought at the time that there was no higher calling than to serve God. I developed a deep and awesome respect for the majesty of God, even though I had no personal relationship with Christ from an evangelical point of view. In those days, young boys were identified early for the priesthood. That dream for me quickly ended when my parents divorced. At age twelve, I had to assume responsibilities usually embraced much later in life.

---

125 John 10:10
126 2 Peter 1:3, 4
127 John 6:44

This new responsibility was precipitated by appearing before the judge who presided over my parents' divorce. I remember his piercing eyes as he asked me which parent I wanted to live with; society was less sensitive then. I loved both my parents equally, and I couldn't choose. The judge grew impatient with me and blurted out, "Make up your mind, son. We haven't got all day." I blurted out a response and ran from the chambers. Outside the courthouse, two cement lions flanked the steps. I remember throwing my arms around one of them. Through my profuse tears, I determined I would never be put into such a position again. I would never let anyone have that kind of control over me again. My childhood was over that day.

When my mother later married a man in the U.S. Air Force, our family began to move around the country. My stepfather provided for us, and I will always be grateful for his watchful care over me. He became my surrogate father. I rambled through high school and stumbled through two years of college. During that period, I met my wife-to-be, just prior to my joining the navy. She came from a Christian home. Her father was in charge of Project Head Start for a tribe of Indians living in the Everglades. I noticed right away he was different. I remember coming over to the house one evening when Doc was at the dinner table by himself with his head in his hands. I asked, "Are you all right, Doc?" He replied, "I'm praying." I responded, "It's not dinner time." I didn't know any better.

Debby and I were married in 1969. She had made a commitment to Christ at age ten at a Billy Graham Crusade. She thought I was a Christian because I talked like one. For us, tragedy came early. We experienced three miscarriages over the next few years. Carrying on the family name was the highest priority for me; this was a very difficult period in our lives. She persuaded me to attend a few Baptist services, where I heard the Gospel clearly articulated, but I felt no need at the time to respond, believing my religious upbringing was enough.

God's Pursuit

I began to focus all my energy on advancing in the navy. I was selected for a prestigious officer development program that consisted of ten weeks of prep school, followed by a college education at one of twenty-two universities in the country. If I graduated, I would become an officer and serve aboard ships. In the sixth week of the prep school, I was called into the dean's office, where I was told that I had been dropped from the program. I had applied for a waiver for uncorrectable vision in my left eye, but it was denied, which meant I could not continue in the program. This was especially disappointing because I was in the top 10 percent of my class. I had just received orders to North Carolina State University and had just picked up my officer uniforms. I was devastated. The next several weeks I directed road traffic as I waited for orders to a ship going to Vietnam.

During my stay at prep school and subsequent traffic duty, my wife worked with her uncle in Albany at a medical research and teaching institute. A doctor who had taken an interest in her case diagnosed her problem with keeping a baby beyond the first or second trimester. After successful treatment she became pregnant just before I left for Vietnam. I went to Vietnam shaking my puny little fist in the face of God, thinking He would take the life of this baby, too. Seven and half months later, my ship returned from Vietnam. We were just off the coast of Recife, Brazil, heading up the eastern seaboard to our homeport in Newport, Rhode Island, when I received a radio message that my wife had given birth to our daughter. I was elated. I received permission to leave the ship in Puerto Rico and flew to Miami—Debby had no idea that I was coming. I walked into her hospital room just as the nurse was carrying out our daughter after her feeding. I asked if I could hold my daughter.

My Conversion

Six months later we were in Key West, Florida, for training. Now, I didn't attend church often but considered myself religious all the same. One evening, I walked into our daughter's room, where she was sleeping peacefully. I admired her beauty and acknowledged that she was indeed a gift from God, all the more meaningful in light of the fact we could not have any more children. As I was staring at her, one thought kept going through my mind: "God's gifts are meant to lead you to repentance." Somehow, at that moment, I realized that Jesus was God's gift to me. The Gospel became crystal clear. I dropped to my knees before my daughter's crib and gave my heart, body, and soul to Jesus Christ. I knew I was alienated from God through sin and that Christ paid the price for my independent disobedience.

From that day forward, my life changed dramatically. I began to attend the little Baptist church in the Keys regularly. Feeling the need to serve God immediately, I began a Bible study in my home with a few of my fellow students. Over time, seventeen students were in study with me, many of them coming to Christ in the process. I couldn't get enough of God's word. I studied the Bible for hours, the very Bible given to my wife and me when we were married, but which had remained in its box until I was saved on August 11, 1973. This was my "road to Damascus" experience. It was like a light switch had been turned on. My daughter was God's way of bringing me to His Son.

In the following years, I continued to serve the Lord with passion and commitment. I either led a small group, worked as a volunteer in the church, or a combination of both. A godly soldier of the cross mentored me, a pastor who taught me what the Lordship of Jesus Christ was all about. He taught what is meant by dying at the foot of the cross and living uncompromisingly for God. I grew rapidly under his leadership and the empowerment of the Spirit. I was introduced to lifetime mentoring through the works of D. Martyn Lloyd Jones, G. Campbell Morgan, A. W. Tozer, and Vance Havner. One particular sermon by Vance Havner, which I listened to on tape, had a significant impact on my life: "The Lordship of Christ." In that tape, he stressed the importance of making Christ the Lord of our lives. He explained the ramifications of such a life and how we are to live like eagles, not birds in a cage.

My Development

In 1976 I received orders to San Diego to teach anti-submarine warfare in a sonar school. A man of God began to mentor me in the basics of the faith. During the next four years, sensing God's call on my life, I went to college at night. I received an associate's degree and a bachelor's degree during that period and completed one year of seminary at Bethel Seminary in San Diego. I decided to leave the navy in 1980, much to the displeasure of my commanding officer. I remember his saying, "Are you crazy? You could be the youngest master chief in the navy. You're throwing it all away to go into ministry?" I was determined to do just that. Later on, I would apply for and receive a commission as a naval intelligence officer in the reserves. I would hold my commission as a Lt. Commander until retirement in January 2000.

I completed seminary, expecting to go into ministry directly. I didn't realize at the time that God had other plans. I worked for a series of companies, wondering all the while why I wasn't formally in ministry. I taught in several churches during this time and mentored many men in the process. I was promoted regularly and selected for competitive development. General Electric selected me as a "high potential" and trained me in the leadership/ management school at Croutinville on the Hudson. I was later selected for advanced leadership development and placed on the executive track. If someone was successful, GE would sponsor that person's continued development for executive-level positions throughout the company.

I lived, however, with a spirit of discontent, wondering if I had been set aside by the Lord and feeling like I was on the backside of the desert. While GE was trying to decide where to place me, I met a man on the basketball court of our church, whose family was in the automobile business. I remember saying to him, "How can you be a Christian and sell cars at the same time?" He decided to show me his company of thirteen franchises on my days off over the next several months. I quickly realized that this company was the first organization that applied biblical principles in its business with success, without compromising those principles. I wondered why this man was taking so much time with me. One night, after a racquetball game, he took me aside and told me that a consultant had advised his family to go to unrelated industries to find people who were known as excellent leaders. He would them bring those people into his company and train them in skills and competencies that would lead to assignment as a general manager of one of his franchises. He asked if I was interested.

I left GE and began a two-year training program, working in various automobile dealerships and learning the trade. I was told that I had to excel in all positions before a dealership would be turned over to me. I eventually was given a dealership that was struggling. In little over a year, we were profitable. I believe to this day that the reason was because I used leadership lessons from the Bible to develop personnel who produced remarkable results. Still, I was discontented. A friend of mine was being considered for an executive-level position at a leading church in San Diego, and he'd used me as a reference. I must admit that I was a bit jealous, as I longed for such an opportunity myself. He eventually declined the position and, unknown to me at the time, recommended me for the same position.

My Opportunity

The senior pastor of the church called me, and to my shock, he asked if I would be interested. He gave four reasons for choosing me: 1) I was successful in business, and many members of the church were businessmen; 2) I was a military officer, and many members were in the military; 3) I was a graduate of their denominational seminary; and 4) I was formerly a member of their church when I was stationed in San Diego.

Finally, I was in full-time ministry. Three months into the job I was praying and reading Acts 7. In that chapter, the story of Moses is presented. He was a contender for the throne of Egypt. According to Acts 7:25, "Moses thought that his own people would realize that God was using him to rescue them, but they did not."

After the death of the Egyptian by Moses' hand became public knowledge, Moses escaped into the desert. I tried to imagine what his thoughts must have been at the time: "I could have been God's leader to help Israel. Now, what am I leading? Sheep!" But I thought, *If God was going to develop a leader who would lead six million Hebrews through the desert to the promised land, what would His training plan look like?* Well, it might consist of the following training modules: how to live off the land; how to dress for the climate; how to take advantage of the topography, and care for livestock, and find one's way in the wilderness. What Moses didn't realize was that he was on a forty-year training program, which would culminate in a burning bush experience that would drastically alter the direction of his life.

I felt similar to Moses. I had been on a multiple-year journey that didn't make a lot of sense until now. As I looked over the landscape of my life, a pattern of God's activity emerged. I was finally able to connect the dots and realize that God had His plan for me all along. Those years "in the desert" were meant to train me in a variety of skills and competencies that could be applied with effectiveness in a ministry setting. I got up from my chair and wrote a phrase on the whiteboard in my office: "There is no waste in the economy of God."

I left that phrase on my board for several months, and I believe it to this day. I served as pastor of adult ministries and staff coordinator for almost four years. The role and its functions were similar to those of an executive pastor. I began my doctoral studies in that setting. Three years and seven months into the job (1995), I left to accept a call to Bethel Seminary in St. Paul. Several promotions later, I continued to serve at Bethel Seminary and Bethel University. And more currently, after completing two earned doctorates, I founded the Heart of a Warrior Ministries (www.heartofawarrior.typepad.com). This ministry helps men live lives of integrity and honor under God's authority.

Conclusion

Through it all, I remain a committed evangelical in my theology and practice. Aside from investing in the lives of my six grandchildren, I have found the greatest joy is in developing future leaders. I completed two and one-half years of mentoring nine Christian businessmen to develop a heart after God's heart. Since then, some one thousand men have completed a journey designed to calibrate their internal compass—the heart. A second phase helps men determine God's trajectory for their lives. I would be remiss if I did not acknowledge another significant mentor in my life, Dr. J. Robert Clinton. God used him to develop me as a Bible-centered leader. Bobby, as he prefers to be called, was first introduced to me through his writings. I was captivated by the literature based squarely on the word of God. *Leadership Emergence Theory* has dramatically shaped my understanding and practice of leadership. Bobby also has been a personal mentor to me through the years, helping me to make many difficult decisions along the way. I believe that Bobby has been a special gift from God to me. Now, I'm looking to the next chapter in my life in terms of where I can best serve the Father in accordance with my wiring. I want to finish well and leave a legacy for His glory and honor.

CHAPTER 3
GOD'S PREFERRED LIFESTYLE

[We are called] to live self-controlled,
upright, and godly lives. ...

Titus 2:11

In the last chapter I identified five situational lifestyles that we tend to adopt to deal with life's difficulties, frustrations, problems, and crises. These are unhealthy patterns that can, at best, only deliver temporary relief of the pressure. As you may recall, they are consciously selected initially but become a part of our nature over time. These lifestyles accommodate our weaknesses and patterns of behavior that are developed early in life to cope with life's difficulties. They do not offer any lasting solution; instead, they further complicate our lives and create more problems than they were employed to solve.

Now let me suggest a better lifestyle strategy, a clear target that will:

- help to bring focus to your life
- help you avoid the misery of a misspent life
- keep you from living in the misty lowlands of mediocrity
- bring honor and glory to God

When I was a boy, I lived vicariously through movies. One of my favorite movies was *Robin Hood*. I longed to be an archer, like the movie's hero, and rid the world of all that was evil. My first attempt at archery consisted of making a bow from of a bent branch with a string tied to both ends. My arrows were crooked sticks with slits on one end. My target was whatever struck my imagination, but even my best attempts at hitting the target met with little success. One Christmas, I finally got that for which I had been asking for so long—a fiberglass bow with a 35-pound pull and a quiver full of target arrows. I set up a makeshift target in the basement, but my first tries met with dismal failure. I couldn't understand why the inside of my forearm was being beat to shreds—until I realized that I had to wear a special guard on my arm. Still, no matter how long I stayed at it, I could only hit the target randomly. When I decided to take lessons, my aim improved markedly. I had to practice regularly, however, to maintain my edge.

Spiritual Archery

A variation on a common theme is: "If we don't have a clear target, we are bound to hit it, no matter where we aim"; that is, the only time we are guaranteed 100 percent accuracy is when we aim at nothing—we are bound to hit it. Our best intentions, our most focused efforts, a sincere desire, or our complete commitment may not amount to anything without a clear target, an effective strategy to get the arrow to the target, good equipment to deliver the arrow, and proper training.

Not long ago, a gathering for men who were involved in a journey to calibrate their hearts to God's heart was held. We met in a large room, set up with armor, a shield, swords, and banners. In the corner of the room was an archery target. Men are visually stimulated, so you can imagine the curiosity sparked by the target sitting off by itself. I stressed the importance of having a target—an objective we hope to obtain, something at which to aim. As I finished my introductory comments, an arrow pierced the air and struck the center of the target—the bull's-eye. Imagine the gasps in the air. As the men looked for the source, they saw a man with a compound archery bow standing on the other side of the room; he was smiling.

I reached for my equipment behind the shield—a plastic bow and plastic arrows with rubber suction cups, the type a small child would use. The men laughed as I stepped up to deliver my plastic arrow to the same target. I turned to face the men. "What are you laughing at?" I asked. "I can hit the target. It's not that hard." Muffled smirks revealed growing scepticism. I pulled the string back and released my arrow, only to have it drop to the floor in front of the target. Laughter exploded. Undeterred, I picked up the arrow and positioned myself closer to the target. I released the arrow, only to have it bounce off the target. Laughter erupted again. I turned to the audience and said in mock disdain, "What are you laughing at? We do the same thing in our spiritual journeys. We bring toys to the battle and believe good intentions will win the day. We approach our spiritual walks with little if any training and we play along the way. When faced with a crisis, we initiate a feeble response, only to meet with failure. We are ill-prepared for the battle."

I then interviewed the archer, whose arrow was deeply embedded in the center of the target. I asked how he had become such a good archer. He pointed out that to become successful archers, we must do the following:

1. Invest in good *equipment*. We can't expect to hit the center of our target without proper equipment. We must maintain our equipment in the best working order possible.

2. Determine which *target* we wish to pursue. Are we after live game? Do we intend to compete in contests? What do we want to hit?

3. Develop a positive *attitude*. We must believe that we will hit the center of the target; we must *will* the arrow to the bull's-eye.

4. Engage in the best *training* available. Take as many lessons as needed to perfect the skill.

5. *Assess* our surroundings—this is critical for accuracy—and adjust as necessary. What are the shooting conditions, in terms of wind, light, topography, distance, height, etc.?

6. *Practice*, practice, practice!

These tips apply to our spiritual journey as well.

Proper Equipment

We can't expect to grow in the Lord, engage the Enemy, and prevail in battle without good equipment. The Bible lists the proper equipment for every warrior.[128] The armor includes the belt of truth, the breastplate of righteousness, feet properly fitted with the Gospel, the shield of faith (which will help us lean into our fear), and the helmet of salvation. Our feet should be properly fitted with the Gospel. And we should carry the sword of the Spirit—God's word, the Bible.

Two important preliminary conditions are required if we are to be successful on the battlefield. First, prolonged engagement in battle requires great

---

128 Ephesians 6:10–17

strength and stamina. Our strength is in the Lord. Ephesians 6:10–17 describes the armor, but before we are told what armor to wear, we are reminded to "be strong in the Lord and in his mighty power." We don't go to the battle in our own strength.

> *The Sovereign LORD is my strength; he makes my feet like the feet of a deer, he enables me to go on the heights.*[129]

> *I can do everything through Him [Christ] who gives me strength.*[130]

> *And what more shall I say? I do not have time to tell about Gideon, Barak, Samson, Jephthah, David, Samuel, and the prophets, who through faith conquered kingdoms, administered justice, and gained what was promised; who shut the mouths of lions, quenched the fury of the flames, and escaped the edge of the sword; whose weakness was turned to strength; and who became powerful in battle and routed foreign armies.*[131]

Second, we are to put on "the full armor of God." If we go to the battle lines half-dressed, we open ourselves to becoming a casualty early on. We must not become needlessly vulnerable by wearing less than a full set of armor. Only with proper armor are we equipped to "take our stand against the devil's schemes." We are informed that our struggle is not "against flesh and blood but against the rulers, against the authorities, against the powers of this dark world and against the spiritual forces of evil in the heavenly realms."[132] A full set of armor will help us stand our ground for the duration of the battle. Roman soldiers often ran to battle, fully clothed in their armor. They trained to fight for long periods of time—the training was arduous and unrelenting. Their stamina and endurance was widely known and respected by their enemies. The Roman centurions who led them into battle were not known for their sensitivity and gentleness.

---

129 Habakkuk 3:19
130 Philippians 4:13
131 Hebrews 11:32–34
132 Ephesians 6:12

Proper Target

How can we hope to succeed in the battles, now and in the future, if we don't have a clear idea of our ultimate objective? What chance do we have to succeed if we haven't got a clue as to an effective strategy, aren't properly equipped to engage the Enemy, or haven't submitted to proper training?

It may be helpful to envision God's preferred lifestyle strategy as an archery target with a bull's-eye and several concentric circles extending outward from that bull's-eye. Each concentric circle from the outside in helps the archer zero in on the bull's-eye. In our walk with God, certain truths and their implications, when lived out in bold relief, help us zero  in on the bull's-eye—a godly life. This target stands in utter contrast to the situational lifestyles we described earlier. God's preferred lifestyle is the real target that we must strive to hit. By God's grace and mercy, the abiding presence of Jesus Christ in our lives, and the ongoing empowerment of the Holy Spirit, we will become master archers, and our lives will bear the spiritual benefits accordingly.

Proper Attitude

Before we look at the target in detail we need to understand God's attitude toward us. Many of us live our lives waiting for the hammer to drop. Or our worldview suggests a kind of "carrot and stick" persona for God. He offers a carrot and smacks us with the stick instead. Yet others believe we have been set aside, put on the shelf, or banished to the backside of the desert. Something we did or didn't do has placed us in the doghouse with God.

Some of us believe we have committed an unpardonable sin. Others believe the sins we have committed are so despicable that if any of our friends found out, we would be ostracized. Many of us live with continual anxiety and guilt over a sin that we deem utterly unredeemable. Living with the shame, we assume the posture of a wounded soldier and drift into the background, always on the periphery of activity. This position of defeat is just where the Enemy wants us. If he can convince us that our behavior is unpardonable or that we are under lifelong discipline, he wins. He can focus his attention on others who are on the edge and who lack the courage of their convictions.

These misperceptions about God and ourselves will keep us out of the battle unless they are replaced with the truth. God is not a bully or a cosmic killjoy, as the Enemy wants us to believe. He is a loving Father who doesn't give up on us.

> *"For I know the plans I have for you," declares the LORD,*
> *"plans to prosper you and not to harm you, plans to give you*
> *hope and a future."*[133]

Some spend their whole lives trying to discover God's will. If they don't marry the right person, attend the right school, go to the right church, or choose the right occupation, they will miss God's perfect will for their lives. So they choose to live with their bags packed, waiting for the day when they can go home to be with the Lord. Until then, life is to be endured. How tragic. How unnecessary.

First of all, we couldn't miss God's *perfect will* if we tried. It's not up to us. No human being can thwart God's perfect will. It will happen, regardless. We didn't choose the family that brought us to life. We didn't choose the era. We didn't choose our intellect, our physical appearance, our natural talents, or our temperament. We didn't choose; God did.[134]

Second, under the umbrella of God's *permissive will*, we have options that require the exercise of our free will. Did you notice that God has plans—plural—for us? True, we can choose God's better versus His best. We can choose to violate His moral will for our lives, the framework He has given us for an abundant life. Or we can choose not to choose. The point is that we are free to choose. Within the boundary of God's perfect will resides the region of free will. Picture it as a circle with a curved line around its perimeter. Inside the circle you are free to move. In concert with His permissive will, God may have preferred that you go to the left but for whatever reason, you chose to go to the right. There may be consequences to either decision, but they do not disqualify us for the future. God simply

---

133 Jeremiah 29:11
134 Psalm 139:1–18

provides a whole new set of options on the path we have chosen. God is the God of second, third, and fourth chances. No one will ever be able to snatch us out of His hand.

> *"I am the good shepherd; I know my sheep and my sheep know me—just as the Father knows me and I know the Father—and I lay down my life for the sheep. I have other sheep that are not of this sheep pen. I must bring them also. They too will listen to my voice, and there shall be one flock and one shepherd. The reason my Father loves me is that I lay down my life—only to take it up again. No one takes it from me, but I lay it down of my own accord. I have authority to lay it down and authority to take it up again. This command I received from my Father."*[135]

God knows what we have done in the past, what we are doing now, and what we will do in the future. Nothing catches Him by surprise. What are you concerned about? He loves us anyway; He loves us regardless. He loves us in spite of what we have done. Remember, it is never too late or too early to begin living a legacy worth leaving in the lives of others. It is never too late and never too early to begin living life abundantly. God is not finished with you.

Proper Training

Training that leads to the development of spiritual skill should include the following considerations:

1. *A good trainer is crucial.*

   > *It is God who arms me with strength and makes my way perfect. He makes my feet like the feet of a deer; he enables me to stand on the heights. He trains my hands for battle; my arms can bend a bow of bronze. You give me your shield of victory, and your right hand sustains me; you stoop down to make me great. You broaden the path beneath me, so that my ankles do not turn. I pursued my enemies and overtook them; I did not turn back till they were destroyed. I crushed them so that they could not rise; they fell beneath my feet. You armed me with strength for battle; you made my adversaries bow at*

---

135 John 10:14–18

my feet. You made my enemies turn their backs in flight, and I destroyed my foes. [136]

A student is not above his teacher, but everyone who is fully trained will be like his teacher.[137]

A poor trainer will produce a poor trainee. Who have you permitted to give input to your life? Who do you allow to advise you? What are their credentials? What experience do they have in training others? How have their trainees performed?

Who is investing in your life? To whom are you accountable? What are the parameters of that accountability? Dr. J. Robert Clinton, professor of leadership at Fuller Seminary, identified key characteristics of leaders who finished well. One characteristic was that the leader had anywhere from ten to fifteen significant mentors in his life. Another characteristic of those who finished the race well was that they were lifelong learners. They were open to change. They were also careful about choosing their mentors.[138]

2. ***A clear goal is important.***

Have nothing to do with godless myths and old wives' tales; rather, train yourself to be godly. For physical training is of some value, but godliness has value for all things, holding promise for both the present life and the life to come.[139]

There is no end to the amassing of goals. But what stands over all others? *Star Trek's* Jean Luc Picard, the fictional seasoned captain of the *Enterprise*, repeatedly told his crew that they could not violate the primary objective. In essence, they were not to interfere with the structure of cultures they encountered. What primary objective

136 Psalm 18:32–40
137 Luke 6:40
138 J. Robert Clinton. *The Mantle of a Mentor: An Exhortation to Finish Well.* Barnabas Publishers, 1993, pp. 9–12.
139 1 Timothy 4:7, 8

informs your training? What must you never forget as you train?

3. ***Proper guidelines must be followed.***

All Scripture is God-breathed and is useful for teaching, rebuking, correcting, and training in righteousness, so that the man of God may be thoroughly equipped for every good work.[140]

The rule book for spiritual archery is the Bible. Commands, precepts, principles, and guidelines abound to help us live life to the fullest; to live life in such a way as to bring glory and honor to our Creator; to live as a testimony to those God has called us to influence for His sake; to model Christ-likeness to others; and to bring congruity to our fractured lives.

4. ***No gain without pain.***

Do you not know that in a race all the runners run, but only one gets the prize? Run in such a way as to get the prize. Everyone who competes in the games goes into strict training. They do it to get a crown that will not last; but we do it to get a crown that will last forever. Therefore I do not run like a man running aimlessly; I do not fight like a man beating the air. No, I beat my body and make it my slave so that after I have preached to others, I myself will not be disqualified for the prize.[141]

Spiritual formation and transformation is hard work. There are no free passes to spiritual maturity. You cannot wish it to be, pay for it, or ask others to be it for you. Excellence requires energy and effort. Sometimes it will require all we have to give; other times it will seem tedious and repetitive. At other times it will require us to act opposite to our natural inclinations. When you were a child, it took concerted effort and focus to learn how to tie your shoelaces. After someone taught you how to do

140 2 Timothy 3:16, 17
141 1 Corinthians 9:24–27

it, you had to "train" to be able to do it without further instruction. Over time, it became second nature to you, but it didn't start out that way.

5. ***Training takes time.***

We have much to say about this, but it is hard to explain because you are slow to learn. In fact, though by this time you ought to be teachers, you need someone to teach you the elementary truths of God's word all over again. You need milk, not solid food! Anyone who lives on milk, being still an infant, is not acquainted with the teaching about righteousness. But solid food is for the mature, who by constant use have trained themselves to distinguish good from evil.[142]

You don't get up one morning and decide to run a marathon. You may have the desire and passion to do it, but if you don't train before attempting it, you will soon be painfully aware that you should have trained. When I was in the navy, I dreaded the physical training requirements we had to meet twice a year. We were warned well in advance about the trials and were given advice on how to prepare for the mile and a half run. Yet many of us waited to the last minute to get in shape for the run, and our performance was dismal. Some of us had to undergo remedial training as a result. It takes time to learn to run with endurance. We have to build up our stamina over time. The same is true regarding our ability to distinguish good from evil.

I understand that the training to become a treasury agent is long and tedious. Agents are trained to distinguish a counterfeit bill from the real thing, and often, agents don't see anything except legitimate currency until the end of their training. Working with the real thing for an extended period gave them the capability to determine a forgery quickly. Training takes time.

---

142 Hebrews 5:11–14

Proper Assessment

Just as an archer has to assess his surroundings to determine what can influence his accuracy, we must be able to do the same. What can influence the outcome of our efforts? What factors will contribute to or interfere with attaining our objective? How can these factors be mediated to counter their influence? What factors in our lives hinder us from becoming all God that intended for us to be? What unconfessed sin is there in our lives? What bad habits do we have that interfere with our spiritual growth? What outside influences can impact reaching God's objectives for our lives? How can they be removed? What holes are there in our armor? Where are we exposed? What has the Enemy used to get to us in the past? What stumbling blocks have hindered our spiritual advance? What dangers lie ahead? What we know can certainly hurt us but what we don't know can devastate us.

When soldiers are trained for battle, they are exposed to elements similar to those expected on the battlefield. They have to be trained for inclement weather, difficult terrain, possible equipment failure, breakdown in communications, and other possible scenarios.

In addition, accurate intelligence about the Enemy is crucial to victory on the battlefield. Many a battle has been lost because of inadequate intelligence. The tactics of the Enemy are many. We fear what we do not know. It pays to know the Enemy's tactics so that we can effectively counter them.

> *Submit yourselves, then, to God. Resist the devil, and he will flee from you. Come near to God, and he will come near to you. Wash your hands, you sinners, and purify your hearts, you double-minded.*[143] *Be self-controlled and alert. Your Enemy the devil prowls around like a roaring lion, looking for someone to devour. Resist him, standing firm in the faith, because you know that your brothers throughout the world are undergoing the same kind of sufferings.*[144]

To successfully resist the devil, we must know his strength and tactics. For instance, we should keep in mind that the devil is a created being. He does not possess the same attributes as God. He is not all-knowing, although he

143 James 4:7, 8
144 1 Peter 5:8, 9

has a superior intellect and the benefit of centuries of observing humans. He understands us quite well and can accurately predict our behavior. He is not all-powerful. There are many things he is not permitted to do. As an example, he was restricted regarding his persecution of Job.[145] He is not all-present. He cannot be everywhere at once. His minions, other fallen angels, do his bidding. No, Satan does not have God's attributes. God reserves the attributes of all-knowing, all-powerful, all-present for Himself.

Proper Practice

If only we could take a pill to produce instant spirituality, but there is no such pill for spiritual development; there is only hard, disciplined work under the authority of God and the empowerment of the Holy Spirit. The Scriptures tell us we have all we need for life and godliness.

> *His divine power has given us everything we need for life and godliness through our knowledge of Him who called us by His own glory and goodness. Through these He has given us His very great and precious promises, so that through them you may participate in the divine nature and escape the corruption in the world caused by evil desires.*[146]

Notice that we have been given everything we need, yet our active participation in the divine nature is necessary to appropriate the resources. In Hebrew philosophy, a belief was not a true belief until it was acted on.[147] Likewise, we have to have the courage to act on what we believe. Living for Christ requires practice. Godly behavior doesn't become a habit unless we act on it, repeatedly, over time. Lasting spiritual transformation is the result of a lifetime of practice. In the book of James we are told that faith by itself, if it is not accompanied by action, is dead.[148] He goes on to say that faith without deeds is dead.[149]

Our Target—God's Preferred Lifestyle

---

145 Job 1:6–12
146 2 Peter 1:3–4
147 Bill Thrall, et al. *The Ascent of a Leader*, p.101.
148 James 2:17
149 James 2:26

One of my favorite books in the Bible is the book of Ecclesiastes. Solomon, the author, is near the end of his life. The gift of wisdom given to him has been squandered. He has tasted all the world has to offer but concludes it was all vanity. He records his journey as a caution for the rest of us.

The book of Ecclesiastes is a powerful argument against self-centered, unbridled pursuits for wealth that don't share; pleasure for pleasure's sake; success instead of significance; materialism at the expense of biblically centered values; self-actualization instead of biblically informed purposes; the constant search for an intellectual understanding and comprehension of the world around us when the truth is found at the feet of Christ; and a desire for worldly wisdom instead of godly wisdom. Solomon reminds us over and over again that life lived on the horizontal plane of worldly affairs, apart from a vertical, empowering relationship with our Creator through a personal relationship with His Son, Jesus Christ, is utterly meaningless.

Have you ever felt that life is meaningless when you listen to the news, watch events on the TV, observe life as it passes you by, or watch politicians destroy each other for a perishable crown? We all question the meaning of things. When failure comes—as it inevitably will—our hopes and dreams go down the drain. A sense of emptiness descends on us like a black cloud.

Even more alarming, when our dreams and hopes have been realized, that same emptiness works its way back into our lives after a short period of elation. Once again, we are compelled to climb another mountain, only to find out that there is yet another mountain to conquer. Ultimate satisfaction is fleeting.

Apart from God, such activity is meaningless—vanities of vanity! We hunger for meaning but often look in all the wrong places. Life viewed and lived by human reason alone, apart from a personal relationship with God and an experiential relationship of God, is worthless, meaningless, vain, and unsatisfying. The world promises riches, fame, and power but only delivers progressive death and life-draining despair. Satan is the grand master of bait and switch!

The road to satisfaction and significance is not in what we acquire, what we sensuously enjoy, what we achieve, or the power we possess; it is in our relationship with God in Christ. Alignment with His purposes for our lives, alignment with how He has wired us, and involvement in activity directed by His purposes, and our divinely directed destiny is the only road to satisfaction and significance, to meaning and purpose.

There are only two choices before us:

1. Live life apart from God; the result is a meaningless existence.
2. Live life under God; the result is a meaningful existence.

True satisfaction is found in a life well-lived in obedience with God's divine direction, life-giving commands, and timeless purposes—for His world generally, and His people specifically. We are "a chosen people, a royal priesthood, a holy nation, a people belonging to God, that you may declare the praises of him who called you out of darkness into his wonderful light."[150]

The greatest tragedy that you and I will ever face will be when we get to the end of our lives, look back, and mournfully realize what we could have done in the Lord but chose not to—and that we never reached God's designed potential for us.

Instead, we settled for mediocrity. We make our way there through compromise and conformity to the pattern of this world. The Bible urges us to do just the opposite: "offer your bodies as living sacrifices, holy and pleasing to God—this is your spiritual act of worship. Do not conform any longer to the pattern of this world, but be transformed by the renewing of your mind. Then you will be able to test and approve what God's will is—His good, pleasing, and perfect will."[151]

God created us to be lean birds in the air, not fat birds on the ground. I am afraid many of us have forgotten what it's like to fly high and free, guided only by the internal conviction and power of the Holy Spirit.

How do we ensure that we have the right strategy in place for our lives? What does God's strategy for our lives look like? God's word gives us the pattern for our lives. Obedience to this pattern will help us realize our full potential in Christ. Proactive application will bring honor and glory to God.

---

150 1 Peter 2:9
151 Romans 12:1–2

God is very clear about His purposes for us. If we want to live a meaningful life, it must be aligned with His purposes. We will use a target as our visual symbol to represent God's preferred lifestyle for warriors after His own heart.

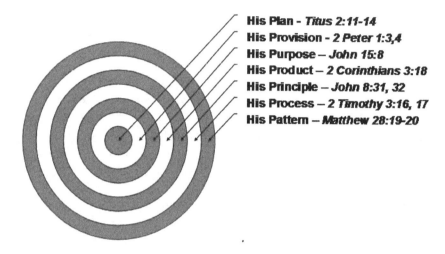

His Plan - *Titus 2:11-14*
His Provision - *2 Peter 1:3,4*
His Purpose – *John 15:8*
His Product – *2 Corinthians 3:18*
His Principle – *John 8:31, 32*
His Process – *2 Timothy 3:16, 17*
His Pattern – *Matthew 28:19-20*

The Bull's-eye—His Plan: Godliness

What does the center of the target—the bull's-eye—look like? What is the center of God's preferred lifestyle to which all spiritual activity is designed to point? To what end should a warrior after God's heart focus? To what circle of activity do all the other concentric circles of our target point?

What will provide clarity regarding the direction that our spiritual pursuit should take? In a phrase: *a life of godliness.*

Godliness Explained

One biblical resource defines godliness as "piety or reverence toward God. Godliness means more than religious profession and a godly conduct; it also means the reality and power of a vital union with God."[152] Another resource suggests godliness "supposes knowledge, veneration, affection, dependence, submission, gratitude, and obedience."[153] It speaks of a life marked by reverence for God and one committed to holiness. Of interesting note is the importance of truth as it relates to godliness. Knowledge of the truth, as opposed to knowledge only about the truth, leads to godliness.[154]

Godliness broadly means practical Christian piety, which includes holiness, goodness, devotion, and reverence to God. It finds its basis in a proper knowledge of God,[155] its outworking in a yielded life to God through Jesus Christ,[156] and its final goal as the development of the consciousness of God and of such similar traits as righteousness, faith, love, patience, and meekness.[157] It is the sum total of Christian values and duties.[158]

We also learn from Scripture that godly men who do God's will are heard by Him.[159] As followers of Christ, we are to live peaceful and quiet lives in all godliness and holiness.[160] We are commanded to train ourselves in godliness because it has value and holds promise, now and in the life to come.[161] Godliness with contentment is a high value in God's eyes.[162]

---

152 Nelson's Illustrated Bible Dictionary, Copyright 1986, Thomas Nelson Publishers.
153 McClintock and Strong Encyclopedia, Electronic Database 2000, 2003 by Biblesoft, Inc.
154 Titus 1:1
155 1 John 5:18
156 Romans 12:1
157 2 Peter 1:6
158 Wycliffe Bible Encyclopedia; New Unger's Bible Dictionary.
159 John 9:31-32
160 1 Timothy 2:1, 2
161 1 Timothy 4:7, 8
162 1 Timothy 6:6

In addition to fighting the good fight of faith, we are to pursue godliness.[163] Scripture tells us that there will be terrible times in the last days. People will be anything but godly in their behavior. They may have a form of godliness, but their lives will give true evidence of its powerlessness.[164] They may talk a good story; they may put on airs for all to see, but the substance of who they are will become apparent soon enough. Their profession of faith will not match their confession lived out. In those days, as it is now, "everyone who wants to live a godly life will be persecuted." [165] Look at the public figures running for political office or nominated for government positions that are shunted aside because of a declared commitment to their faith.

In the second letter from Peter, we are told God gave every Christ follower everything he needed to live a godly life.[166] Godliness also makes the list of biblical qualities essential for effectiveness and productivity in our knowledge of Christ. Those who don't possess godliness in addition to other key qualities mentioned are blind and ignorant.[167] Finally, we are urged to live holy and godly lives while we wait for God's final judgment on the world. We are not to be stagnant in our faith.[168]

Godliness Demonstrated

One passage in particular summarizes the sum total of godliness.

For the grace of God that brings salvation has appeared to all men. It teaches us to say no to ungodliness and worldly passions, and to live self-controlled, upright and godly lives in this present age, while we wait for the blessed hope—the glorious appearing of our great God and Savior, Jesus Christ, who gave Himself for us to redeem us from all wickedness and to purify for Himself a people that are His very own, eager to do what is good.[169]

This passage is the bull's-eye of our target. It also is the *beacon* by which we steer our lives, the *compass* by which we find our way, the *map* by which we plan our journey, the *scale* by which we weigh our lives, the *gyro* by

163 1 Timothy 6:11–13
164 2 Timothy 3:1–5
165 2 Timothy 3:12–13
166 2 Peter 1:3–4
167 2 Peter 1:5–9
168 2 Peter 3:11–13
169 Titus 2:11–14

which we pinpoint our location, the *balance* by which we determine our equilibrium, the *ruler* by which we measure our walk, the *tuning fork* to calibrate our lives, and the *buoy* by which we navigate the treacherous waters of our existence.

In this powerful passage, we find the beginning, ongoing, and completed Gospel as it plays out in our lives. The Gospel, in the person of Jesus Christ, brings salvation. The Gospel He preaches and the life He lived is a model for us, in that it teaches us to live differently than the world around us—to say no to ungodliness and worldly passions, and to live self-controlled, upright, and godly lives in this present age while we wait for the blessed hope—the glorious appearing of our great God and Savior, Jesus Christ. The fact that He is God, in the flesh, sets Him apart from all others who clamor for the worship and allegiance of mankind.

While pursuing my undergraduate degree in a secular institution, I took a class in religious philosophy. The instructor invited the class to the home of a psychiatrist, who was also a follower of an Indian guru named Sai Baba. In his testimonial of him, the psychiatrist said that Sai Baba was Jesus, Buddha, and Moses all wrapped up into one. I was incredulous and asked how this man, Sai Baba, could live with such opposing forces within him. When I was asked to explain, I said that Buddha didn't believe in God, Moses was a follower of God, and Jesus was God in the flesh. The instructor said that I just didn't understand, but the power of the Gospel is that Jesus is God and fully capable of saving mankind from their natural tendency for destruction of flesh and soul.

We are not to live in terror or as hermits separated from the world around us. No, we are to live our beliefs in boldness and power. No one wants to hear what we have to say about our faith until they observe how we live, as a result of our faith. Credibility comes with a life well lived, in congruity with what we declare we believe.

The passage before us goes on to say that in the living of life, we are not to forget the Giver of life. He has predetermined the roles we are to assume in His redemptive plan and purposes. We are not to sit by idly whiling away our time, waiting to go home to be with Him. No, we are to proactively do what is good and show the world what a redeemed sinner looks and acts like.

The remaining concentric rings emanating from our bull's-eye lead to the center of our target—a life of godliness.

First Ring—His Provision: Empowerment

The first ring of our target speaks to a passage we have cited earlier. It is one thing to be told to go to the battle lines; it is another thing to go ill-equipped. The Enemy would like us to believe that we go to our appointed places unarmed, so we shouldn't go. He'll spend much time trying to convince us not to go. He'll dredge up the past to remind us where we have failed, how many times we didn't complete our mission, how often we held back. He would like us to believe we are in the fight alone. Nothing could be farther from the truth. God's word says otherwise:

> *His divine power has given us everything we need for life and godliness through our knowledge of him who called us by his own glory and goodness. Through these he has given us his very great and precious promises, so that through them you may participate in the divine nature and escape the corruption in the world caused by evil desires. For this very reason, make every effort to add to your faith goodness; and to goodness, knowledge; and to knowledge, self-control; and to self-control, perseverance; and to perseverance, godliness; and to godliness, brotherly kindness; and to brotherly kindness, love. For if you possess these qualities in increasing measure, they will keep you from being ineffective and unproductive in your knowledge of our Lord Jesus Christ. But if anyone does not have them, he is nearsighted and blind, and has forgotten that he has been cleansed from his past sins.*[170]

His divine power is the fuel that propels us forward. Many of us spend our time ensuring everything is in working order, but we never turn the key and press on the gas. We are satisfied with polishing the fenders, checking the oil, tuning the engine, and cleaning the windshields. We may look fit and ready, but we never move.

The Work of the Holy Spirit

Our empowerment has always come from God's Spirit. One biblical resource helps us understand how the Holy Spirit empowers us:

---

170 2 Peter 1:3–9

The Holy Spirit transforms us from within. Jesus was soon going to leave the disciples, but he would remain with them. How could this be? The Counselor—the Spirit of God himself—would come after Jesus was gone to care for and guide the disciples. The Holy Spirit is the very presence of God within us and all believers, helping us live as God wants and building Christ's church on earth. By faith we can appropriate the Spirit's power each day.

The Holy Spirit works in every part of our life: he will be with us forever; the world at large cannot accept him; he lives with us and in us;[171] he teaches us; he reminds us of Jesus' words;[172] he convicts us of sin, shows us God's righteousness, and announces God's judgment on evil; he guides into truth and gives insight into future events; he brings glory to Christ.[173] The Holy Spirit has been active among people from the beginning of time, but after Pentecost he came to live in all believers. Many people are unaware of the Holy Spirit's activities, but to those who hear Christ's words and understand the Spirit's power, the Spirit gives a whole new way to look at life.[174]

The Holy Spirit provides the power to live a holy life. We have no legitimate excuse for non-engagement. We have everything we need.

Second Ring—His Purpose: To Demonstrate His Glory

What does it mean to bring glory to God? Simply this: to demonstrate His excellence in all we think, say, and do.

So whether you eat or drink or whatever you do, do it all for the glory of God. In the same way, let your light shine before men, that they may see your good deeds and praise your Father in heaven. We, who were the first to hope in Christ, might be for the praise of his glory. But you are a chosen people, a royal priesthood, a holy nation, a people belonging to God,

---

171 John 14:16–17

172 John 14:25; 15:26

173 John 16:8, 13–14

174 Neil S. Wilson, ed. *The Work of the Holy Spirit*, The Handbook of Bible Application, Tyndale House Publishers, 1992.

that you may declare the praises of him who called you out of darkness into his wonderful light. Now all has been heard; here is the conclusion of the matter: Fear God and keep his commandments, for this is the whole duty of man. This is to my Father's glory, that you bear much fruit, showing yourselves to be my disciples. Finally, brothers, whatever is true, whatever is noble, whatever is right, whatever is pure, whatever is lovely, whatever is admirable—if anything is excellent or praiseworthy—think about such things.[175]

We are to do it all for the glory of God. We are to let our light shine before men. We are to show the world how we live. We are to declare the praises of Him who called us out of darkness. We are to revere Him and keep His commandments. And we are to bear the fruit of His labors in us. We are to focus on whatever is excellent and praiseworthy.

He doesn't need us, but He has chosen us to be His testimony to a dying world nevertheless. We show His excellence by the way our lives represent and present His character. He desires us to model Christ-likeness every waking moment. We are to fulfill our duty against the backdrop of reverence for Him and in compliance with His moral will for our lives.

Third Ring—His Product: Progressive Christ-likeness

A well-lived life unfolds progressively over time. Growth is incremental and gradual. At times it will feel like there is no growth at all, although others may testify differently—those who observe us see the change more readily. God's objective in our transformation is Christ-likeness.

*And we, who with unveiled faces all reflect the Lord's glory, are being transformed into his likeness with **ever-increasing glory**, which comes from the Lord, who is the Spirit. It was he who gave some to be apostles, some to be prophets, some to be evangelists, and some to be pastors and teachers, to prepare God's people for works of service, so that the body of Christ may be built up until we all reach unity in the faith and in the knowledge of the Son of God and become mature, **attaining to the whole measure of the fullness of Christ.** Then we will no longer be infants, tossed back and forth by the*

175 1 Corinthians 10:31; Matthew 5:16; Ephesians 1:12; 1 Peter 2:9; Ecclesiastes 12:13; John 15:8; Philippians 4:8

*waves, and blown here and there by every wind of teaching and by the cunning and craftiness of men in their deceitful scheming. Instead, speaking the truth in love, we will in all things **grow up into him who is the Head, that is, Christ.** From him the whole body, joined and held together by every supporting ligament, **grows and builds itself up** in love, as each part does its work. For those God foreknew he also predestined to be **conformed to the likeness of his Son**, that he might be the firstborn among many brothers. Like newborn babies, crave pure spiritual milk, so that by it you may **grow up in your salvation**, now that you have tasted that the Lord is good.*[176]

Such transformation doesn't happen overnight. We are to grow up into Christ. We are to grow up in love. We are to grow up in our salvation. Salvation is not an event; it begins with conversion and continues through progressive sanctification (setting ourselves apart onto the things of God), and it concludes in ultimate glorification (completeness once we are in heaven).

Fourth Ring—His Principle: Live by Faith

What does it mean to live by faith? Close observation of the principles that follow indicate that the pattern of this world is completely, utterly, absolutely, totally, entirely, and wholly opposed to this pattern of life. The world wants freedom of action before obedience to standards, understanding of the details before commitment to any process, and realization of rewards before acceptance of regulation. For the believer, to live by faith means obedience before freedom, commitment before understanding, and acceptance before realization.

Obedience before Freedom

To the Jews who had believed him, Jesus said, "If you hold to my teaching, [then] you are really my disciples. Then you will know the truth, and the truth will set you free."[177]

Faith is needed to be able to obey before experiencing freedom. God can be trusted. We can't get around the requirement for faith; faith is simply

---

176 2 Corinthians 3:18; Ephesians 4:11–16; Romans 8:29; 1 Peter 2:2–3
177 John 8:31–32

informed trust. Any meaningful relationship is built on trust, and God has our best interests at heart. He has demonstrated His unconditional love for us at the cross. He shows mercy to us every day and his grace abounds.

The passage tells us real freedom is based on truth, and truth sets us free. Not just any truth but God's truth. Jesus is the truth.[178] The Bible is God's truth.[179] Notice the conditional clause, however, "If you hold to my teachings." Compliance with Christ's teachings makes us His disciples, first of all. Obedience precedes knowing, and knowing precedes freedom.

The world will never understand such faith. It is foolishness to them, but we know different: it's freedom to us.

Commitment before Understanding

Jesus answered, "My teaching is not my own. It comes from him who sent me. If anyone chooses to do God's will, [then] he will find out whether my teaching comes from God or whether I speak on my own. [180]

Once again a conditional clause precedes comprehension—"If anyone chooses to do God's will." Then and only then will we understand Christ's authority. He speaks for the Father. In fact, He and the Father are one.[181]

There is a touching scene in the Bible, when Jesus has just declared to those around Him that no one comes to the Father except through Him. He tells them, "If you really knew me, you would know my Father as well. From now on, you do know Him and have seen Him." Philip blurts out, "Lord, show us the Father and that will be enough for us." I can picture what followed. Jesus, with a tender voice and perhaps a hand on Philip's shoulder, would have said, "Don't you know me, Philip, even after I have been among you such a long time? Anyone who has seen me has seen the Father. How can you say, 'Show us the Father'? Don't you believe that I am in the Father, and that the Father is in me? The words I say to you are not just my own. Rather, it is the Father, living in me, who is doing His work.

---

178 John 14:6
179 2 Peter 1:20, 21
180 John 7:16, 17
181 John 10:25-30

Believe me when I say that I am in the Father and the Father is in me; or at least believe on the evidence of the miracles themselves."[182]

Faith is asked of us once again. Trust is required. The object we seek is only obtained when we trust, not before. That has always been the way of the world.

Acceptance before Realization

No discipline seems pleasant at the time, but painful. Later on, however, it produces a harvest of righteousness and peace for those who have been trained by it. [183]

According to this passage, what is the purpose of God's discipline in our lives? No one gets up in the morning and thinks, "Gee, I can't wait to be disciplined by God today. I'm really looking forward to His chastisement." Counseling might be in order if that is the case. No, we don't naturally look forward to rebuke, reproof, and discipline. Only after the fact do we appreciate what God needed to do to us, in us, and for us. Why? Because "it produces a harvest of righteousness and peace for those who have been trained by it."[184]

God knows what He is doing. He knows what it takes to shape us. Sometimes we have to discipline our children, not because we enjoy bringing misery into their lives but because we want them to learn now so that they won't have to suffer by learning the hard way later on. We do it because we love our children. God disciplines us because He loves us and wants the best for us.

Living by faith is not that uncommon. When you buy house plans, what must you do before a house is built? You must accept and abide by the plans; you trust in the plans.

In general, the world is completely opposed to this manner of trust. Just flip each statement: freedom before obedience, understanding before commitment, and realization before acceptance. The world wants a guarantee of freedom and open options before it is willing to submit and agree to give itself over to any authority. The world wants to know all the

---

182 John 14:6–11
183 Hebrews 12:11
184 Hebrews 12:11

details and what's going to be required of it before it commits. The world wants to know how it will benefit and what's in it for it before it accepts any restrictions on its behavior.

Being a member of God's family requires trust: obedience before freedom, commitment before understanding, and acceptance before realization. This is a life of informed faith in the One who is always faithful. He can be trusted because He has proven to be trustworthy.

Fifth Ring—His Process: Circle of Transformation

Transformation is not linear but circular. When we came to Christ and put our faith in Him, He began to work in us to transform us. He began with the most obvious issues. Maybe it was our language. Maybe it was a bad habit. Maybe it was our appearance. Maybe it was our health. As the obvious changes were made, He began to burrow deeper into the not-so-obvious issues. Maybe it was our attitude. Maybe it was our motives. Maybe it was our desires. The scalpel by which He performs transformational surgery on us is the Bible, His written word and in conjunction with the Holy Spirit. The Holy Spirit convicts the world of sin, righteousness, and judgment.[185] He diagnoses the problem, and the word is used to cut the sin out.

All Scripture is God-breathed and is useful for teaching, rebuking, correcting, and training in righteousness, so that the man of God may be thoroughly equipped for every good work.[186]

Notice the cycle of activity: teaching, rebuking, correcting and finally, training. When I joined the navy, I boarded a bus that took me to a location for processing. When I got there, it was late at night, and I thought someone would show me to my bed. Boy, was I wrong. They authorities brought me to a classroom, where my indoctrination began. They instructed me in how to stand at attention and respond to orders. They followed instruction with criticism of my posture and attitude. Then they told me how to correct my posture and my attitude. Finally, they told me how to get along in the navy and be a "righteous" sailor.

Now, I could have rebelled at the instruction phase. But I knew better. I could have rebelled at the criticism I received. But again, I knew better.

185 John 16:8–11
186 2 Timothy 3:16–17

I could have rebelled at correction. Once again, I knew better. Once I submitted to instruction, criticism, and correction I was ready for training in righteousness. That circular cycle repeated itself throughout my navy career. Those who resisted the cycle of transformation didn't make it very far in the navy.

The same is true in spiritual transformation. We must submit to the complete cycle before we can realize positive change in our lives. Notice the order of activity necessary before "the man of God may be thoroughly equipped for every good work." It looks something like this.

Multiply the process over your life and you will see how God uses the scalpel of His word to perform surgery on your soul. Submission to teaching means being willing to be redirected in accordance with the Bible. Submission to rebuke means being open to criticism from the Bible as the Holy Spirit convicts. Submission to correction means being obedient to God's solutions for change. And training in righteousness means acceptance of His guidelines for living in accordance with what we already are—righteous through Christ. We can stop the process of transformation at any point, but God will point out the areas of our lives that need attention.

Of course, you must be willing to hear God's voice when He speaks. At the turn of the twentieth century, people built icehouses to preserve perishable foods. In small communities, a large icehouse was built, made of thick walls, no windows, and two doors—one at the front, and one at the back. As winter began and slow-moving rivers and lakes began to freeze, the men of the community would cut large chunks of ice and transport them to the icehouse using horse-drawn sleds. Straw or sawdust would cover the ice, and people would store meats and other items for use during the winter and spring.

The ice would often last well into the summer because of the construction of the icehouse. Sooner or later, though, the ice would melt. The men of the community would then gather to clean out the icehouse. Because of the lack of ventilation and heat of summer, they could only work in the icehouse for short periods of time. One summer, a boy was observing the cleaning operation from a nearby hill. His curiosity peaked when he noticed the commotion caused by the frantic gestures of one of the men as he came out of the icehouse. The boy moved closer and overheard the agitated man complaining that he had lost his family heirloom, a priceless watch, in the debris.

The boy quickly disappeared into the icehouse, emerging a few minutes later holding the watch. The men were amazed and inquired how he found the watch. The boy responded, "Oh, it was easy. I lay down in the straw until I heard the ticking."

When is the last time you "lay down in the straw" to hear the Lord's voice speak into your life? After a great victory for the Lord against the prophets of Baal, Elijah ran away in fear of the threats of Jezebel. He hid in a cave in the mountains and pouted The Lord said to him, "'Go out and stand on the mountain in the presence of the LORD, for the LORD is about to pass by.' Then a great and powerful wind tore the mountains apart and shattered the rocks before the LORD, but the LORD was not in the wind. After the wind there was an earthquake, but the LORD was not in the earthquake. After the earthquake came a fire, but the LORD was not in the fire. And after the fire came a gentle whisper. When Elijah heard it, he pulled his cloak over his face and went out and stood at the mouth of the cave."[187]

Do you know why God speaks so profoundly in a gentle whisper? It requires you and me to lean forward to hear it. We must focus on God if we hope to hear His voice in our lives. The tyranny of the urgent, with its competing priorities and agendas, often keeps us from standing still long enough to hear the voice of God.

Sixth Ring—His Pattern: As You Are Going, Make Disciples

Many of us believe we have to learn to serve before we actually serve. That may be true some of the time. At other times, however, we learn to serve as we are serving.

Therefore go and make disciples of all nations, baptizing them in the name of the Father and of the Son and of the Holy Spirit, and teaching them to obey

---

187 1 Kings 19:1–18

everything I have commanded you. And surely I am with you always, to the very end of the age.[188]

The only imperative command in this passage is "make disciples." In other words, as we are going, in the normal pattern of our activities, during the normal routines of our life, *make disciples.* And how do we do that? First, baptize them so that they recognize that they are under new management—the old has passed away, and the new has come. Then teach them to obey everything that Christ has commanded us to do. Remind ourselves we are not alone, the Lord is beside us all the way. He will be with us for the entire journey, even to the end of the age. His pattern of service is to go, make, baptize, teach, remember, and be courageous. We are not serving alone.

Conclusion

There you have it—the target; God's preferred lifestyle. We don't have to adopt situational lifestyles to make it through life. God has given us a clear objective. His preferred lifestyle is our internal compass so that we won't lose our way. It will always point to True North, Jesus Christ.

I often ask audiences to close their eyes and point to true north. When I tell them to open their eyes, they are amazed at the arms and hands pointing in all directions. We firmly believe that we know where true north is, but many of us are mistaken. God's word will help us always find true north, regardless of what the world says.

We know have our objective in focus. The target is clear, and we know what to aim for. We know what it's going to take to hit the bull's-eye, and we know the purpose for our engagement. The parts and accompanying chapters that follow will help us reach this objective.

---

188 Matthew 28:19–20

PART II

SURVEYING THE BATTLEFIELD

CHAPTER 4
THE BATTLE

Our behavior is a reflection of the condition of our heart.

Proverbs 4:23

Most men I have talked to are unclear about their identity, their role in life, their purpose for existence, and the trajectory they should take to reach their divinely ordained potential.

We have allowed society and culture to stand in a privileged vantage point of authority and influence over us, which has shaped our perceptions about these issues. This has created misperceptions and lack of clarity about what we are to believe and how we are to act.

Five Deadly Lies

Let me introduce you to the five deadly lies that will lead to insignificance and mediocrity. I am sure there are many more, but these corrupted beliefs seem common to men of all ages.

Their roots, however, are driven deep early in life, reinforced by society, and amplified by poor lifestyle choices and decisions throughout our lives, unless we decide to take a stand to do otherwise.

Lie # 1: Masculinity Must Be Restrained

Many TV commercials depict men as savage beasts, lustful lechers, and clumsy oafs who are mindless, clueless, and insensitive. One particular commercial for health insurance opens with a well-conditioned woman making her way up a steep mountain. She is sure-footed and confident, and all her climbing equipment is in the right place. We hear the rattling of tin implements, and the camera shifts to a bumbling male behind her, tripping over the rocks, seemingly unprepared for the difficult climb ahead. He is carrying outdated and sloppily arranged equipment, and his face has a look of exhaustion, confusion, and fear.

Such depictions only lead to a loss of identity and confused masculinity. Societal pressures have distorted our understanding of true masculinity. Our culture feminizes men and tries to make women more masculine; both lose. Men are encouraged to become softer, and women are admonished to become harder to get ahead in this world. Those divinely ordained qualities that celebrate the distinct differences between men and women are vilified and discouraged by a society that has lost its way.

The message is clear: Men are not as equipped for life as women, and they need support and assistance to put one step in front of the other. To be sure, we do need assistance and support, but we are not helpless. Expressions of maleness are not appreciated in our society and are often suppressed for the gentler, kinder model of masculinity. God made men for adventure, achievement, and challenge.[189] I stressed earlier that men are wired to seek out a cause to die for, a challenge to embrace, and loved ones to protect.

In the journey, we may be competitive when we engage, loud in our interactions, and overly boastful in our endeavors. We may act first and think later, and we may not be politically correct in doing so, but we are men all the same. Unfortunately, we also leave messes in our wake when more careful thought and planning could have precluded them.

Men value risk, reward, accomplishment, achievement, heroic exercise, action, and adventure.[190] Competence, respect, honor, valor, and courage mean a lot to men. Failing any immediate opportunity to exercise or pursue these virtues, men will become involved in competitive activities, either as a spectator or a participant. At the heart of a man's soul is a hero dying to get out.

Antarctic explorer **Ernest Shackleton** posted the following advertisement in 1913:

---

189 David Murrow. *Why Men Hate Going to Church.* Nelson Publishers, 2005, 11.
190 Ibid., 15.

Men wanted for hazardous journey. Small wages. Bitter cold. Long months of complete darkness. Constant danger. Safe return doubtful. Honor and recognition in case of success.

Who would respond to such an ad? More than five thousand men applied for twenty-six slots.

Taking risks is a part of life. Taking risks is a part of every man's DNA. What have you risked for the sake of another lately? What have you risked for the sake of God's kingdom lately?

The timid soul asks, "What do I stand to lose if I do it?" The fruit-bearing Christian asks, "What do I stand to lose if I don't do it?" Real life is lived on the cutting edge."

—Neil Anderson

Our society seems to value safety, stability, harmony, predictability, protection, comfort, nurturing, duty, support, and preservation. These qualities are appreciated by many men and are widely accepted and applauded. But men are also tuned into risk, change, conflict, variety, adventure, competition, daring, pleasure, independence, and expansion.[191] In the pursuit of such things, however, the kinder, gentler members of our society do not always appreciate the bolder dimensions expressed by men.

In reviewing the best-selling *Men are from Mars, Women are from Venus,* David Murrow, a television producer and writer, collected two sets of qualities. The first set included the following characteristics: love, communication, beauty, relationships, support, help, nurturing, feelings, sharing, relating, harmony, community, loving cooperation, and personal expression. The second set included competence, power, efficiency, achievement, skills, proving oneself, results, accomplishment, objects, technology, goal orientation, self-sufficiency, success, and competition.[192] Realizing there may be some crossover, which set best represents men's values, and which set best represents women's values? More intriguing, which set does our society value the most? Our society has essentially

191 Ibid., 19.
192 Ibid., 23.

discarded both for an amalgamation of the two, neither of which represents the uniqueness of each. Most men identify with the second set of values.

Men are confused about their maleness. They are conflicted about their masculinity. Many men do not know what is acceptable anymore. The phenomenal response to the ministry Men's Fraternity, under the leadership of Robert Lewis, underscores this issue. Dr. Lewis' clear depiction of authentic manhood has been widely received by men. Over one thousand men attend his men's groups about authentic manhood every year.[193]

Biblically informed masculinity should be promoted and encouraged, not suppressed and compromised under the banner of political correctness. Absent of the guidance from the Bible, manhood can take on sharp edges and may result in cutting those who are around it. Biblically centered, authentic manhood is to be celebrated and championed. Lewis' definition of authentic manhood bears repeating: An authentic man is one who rejects passivity, accepts responsibility, leads courageously, and expects God's reward.

Lie #2: Performance Is All That Matters

This lie leads to performance overload, an achievement orientation that is never satisfied. Most men get their sense of significance from what they accomplish. Our culture rewards that mentality. We have bought into the lie that success is determined by what we do. So we spend our lives "doing."

We rationalize our behavior by believing that the next promotion, the next closed deal, the next degree, the next whatever will permit us to focus our attention on what really matters. We fool ourselves. Once we have conquered the next thing, we find yet another thing we must do. Once we finally get off the treadmill, we find that there is no one left with whom to share our victories; we have only the awards that adorn the walls of our den or office.

There is nothing wrong with striving for success. But if our sense of worth is wrapped up in what we do and not in who we are in Christ, we can miss the opportunity to model the character of Christ in our work setting, community, and family. A devotion to one's chosen profession or

---

193 Specifics regarding Men's Fraternity can be found at www.mensfraternity. com.

dedication to becoming successful is commendable. However, when such devotion and dedication becomes an excuse for neglecting our obligation to be light to a lost world, we sacrifice our God-given purposes, talents, and potential on the altar of expediency.

Neil Anderson, author of *Victory Over Darkness* and *Bondage Breaker*, was absolutely right. It's not what we do that determines who we are; it's who we are in Christ that should determine what we do. In God's eyes "beingness" is more important that "doingness." The doingness becomes all the more powerful against a backdrop of beingness. Character matters.

Competencies may be the tools of effective leadership, but character has always been the power of effective leadership. I train leaders, and I have found that many gifted leaders implement required competencies and produce predictable results. If you exercise a given competency out of a biblically informed character, the exponential results are often realized. Man tends to admire performance. God, on the other hand, looks at our hearts.[194]

Lie #3: Consequences of Unresolved Conflicts Subside Over Time

The attitude is that "given enough time all problems go away." This lie leads to conflict compartmentalization or "siloing." When it comes to resolving conflicts, men and women respond differently. As men, we have a tendency to compartmentalize conflicts—we stuff them until we're ready to deal with them.

The trouble is that we often leave these toxic issues in their compartments. They ultimately seep out and contaminate our relationships with the opposite sex. We think the issues that gave rise to the original argument are over and are astonished that the residual affects still linger in our loved one's mind and heart. Our attitude is "The argument is over. What's her problem?" When we are ready to move on to another course in the meal of our relationship, we find out that our wives are still trying to get the taste of conflict out of their mouths. Men, we changed the taste of the salad dressing, and that taste will linger for some time until we deal with it; until the bitterness goes away. Women have long memories. When we are ready to move on, they are still struggling with the distasteful relational details of the conflict. We may think it's over, but it's not.

194 1 Samuel 16:7

Spousal conflict is not the only arena with this phenomenon. Men have a tendency to compartmentalize all conflicting situations they cannot resolve immediately. They are jammed into a sealed compartment and set aside for later disposition. The toxic residuals make themselves felt on the periphery of our lives. They seep into every relational area and leave a nasty stain.

Compartmentalization is a sure formula for time-released toxic poison for your character, your relationships, and your God-ordained potential. Remember, men compartmentalize, but women absorb. We need to learn to deal with such problems head-on, no matter how long they take to resolve. Setting them aside only allows them to fester. Once we do get to them, we may find they have morphed into a much greater problem that we are not equipped to correct without professional help.

Lie #4: Real Men Don't Need Anyone

This lie leads to relational isolation and produces a withdrawal mentality when difficulties arise. When we men face conflict or criticism or failure, we have a tendency to either confront the issue aggressively or withdraw. Withdrawal will certainly be our final option, if not the first. We isolate ourselves to sweat out the consequences until we regain our equilibrium. Once the storm passes, we re-engage. Many of us never regain our balance; we remain isolated and open to the influence of the Enemy.

When men face conflict or are struggling with a difficult issue, they believe they need to step away from commitments or responsibilities until they resolve the issue. We see it all the time in Heart of a Warrior Ministries.[195] A man facing the threat of divorce feels he needs to step out of his group to deal with it. Another man struggling with sexual immorality feels he needs to deal with it alone. A man facing the threat of losing his job is embarrassed and leaves his accountability partners until his job stabilizes.

Women generally seek solace in relationships with other women when they are dealing with a crisis. Men, on the other hand, tend to want to deal with their problems alone. Most of the time it's a pride issue. Men have to be trained to act counter-intuitively to their natural inclination to climb into their caves and lick their wounds. They have to be taught to act opposite to what they normally do and to seek out other men to

195 See website www.heartofawarrior.org for specifics about this ministry.

help them in their time of need. Men need each other in the midst of a struggle, not in the absence of struggles.

The Enemy knows if he can isolate a man who is in trouble, he can devour him. Like most predators, a carnivore waits until the weak prey separates itself from the herd. Once separated, it cannot effectively defend itself. If a dumb animal knows this, why are we so oblivious to this tactic? The Enemy knows that as iron sharpens iron, one man sharpens another.[196] Back to one my favorite books in the Bible, Ecclesiastes:

> *Two are better than one, because they have a good return for their work: If one falls down, his friend can help him up. But pity the man who falls and has no one to help him up! Also, if two lie down together, they will keep warm. But how can one keep warm alone? Though one may be overpowered, two can defend themselves. A cord of three strands is not quickly broken.*[197]

The Scriptures also urge us to encourage one another and build each other up,[198] to spur one another on toward love and good deeds,[199] and to carry each other's burdens, and in this way we will fulfill the law of Christ.[200] These Scriptures are clear about the need to stay together, when at all possible. The worst thing a man can do is separate himself from sources of strength and encouragement as he tries, on his own, to work things out. The Enemy wins, and the weak sheep loses. That is the way it has been for ages.

In our Heart of a Warrior small groups, we require each man to sign a covenant. In that covenant is a stipulation that if a member desires to leave the group, he must meet with the group personally and explain why he wants to leave. We do not permit him to call in and leave a message. Our purpose is accountability, but we also want to come alongside a struggling brother to help him in his time of need. There may be legitimate reasons for stepping away, and in such instances, we pledge to meet with him informally while he is away from the group.

---

196 Proverbs 27:17
197 Ecclesiastes 4:9–12
198 1 Thessalonians 5:11
199 Hebrews 10:24
200 Galatians 6:2–3

Lie #5: Spiritual Growth Requires Behavior Modification

This final lie often leads to incongruence between what we say we believe and how we act. Spiritual impotence is the result. We might proclaim a biblically informed belief system, but it bears little resemblance to our actual behavior. What we verbally affirm as our beliefs may have little relationship to how we behave. What we say we are does not always align with who we really are. The Enemy has convinced us that the real battlefield is our behavior, so we spend a great deal of energy trying to adapt our behavior to acceptable standards.

Men instinctively know when they are out of alignment with their beliefs and values. Christ followers have the added conviction of the Holy Spirit. We live with the frustration of the inconsistency. We may rationalize the incongruity with regular proclamations to the contrary, but deep down inside, we feel it—and we don't like it.

Yet we practice sanctified behavior modification to constrain our dishonorable behavior. We do everything we can, it seems, to keep our lives from unraveling and exploding. We tough it out until we are beaten down by the sheer weight of it all. In an unguarded moment, the problem oozes to the surface once again.

When I was a boy, I was given a toy designed to keep me busy. It was a wooden bench with several objects embedded in the structure. Every time I used the wooden mallet to pound one down, another would pop up. I would spend hours trying to knock them all down flat but to no avail. And that is the way it is with behavior modification techniques. When we address the observable symptoms without getting to the root cause we are doomed to endless and fruitless activity.

Men want to be men of integrity. They want to be the same in all situations. They want to stand firm and not betray their beliefs. Many of us to wilt due to lack of courage, values confusion, pressures of life, the Enemy's stronghold in our lives, the burden of our responsibilities, repeated sin that plagues us, and the heat of battle. We act in ways that are not how we desire to be. Apart from Christ, the struggle is hopeless. In Christ, victory is possible. The road to congruence begins on the inside.[201]

---

201 Proverbs 4:23

Our Dilemma

Why do we do what we do? Why do we do the very things we say we hate to do? Why do we repeatedly sin in certain areas of our lives, while at the same time detesting these actions each time they surface in our lives? It's like an out-of-body experience as we witness these events—we feel helpless as we watch the sin cycle repeat itself, over and over again.

Newspaper headlines, news on TV, in the tabloids in the grocery store, and articles in popular magazines remind us daily of the incongruity between what we say we believe and how we act:

A young mother stands at the end of a boat ramp as she watches her car, carrying her two small boys; descend into the water to certain death.

A popular teacher, respected for his grasp of God's word, is arrested for soliciting child pornography on the Internet.

A religious leader of the largest African-American denomination in the world is indicted, convicted, and sentenced for fraud and embezzlement.

A renowned and respected heart surgeon dies of a heart attack, after which two families come forward, claiming him as their family head.

A student who leads a Bible study on campus is caught by his teacher, cheating on a math exam.

A well-known pastor is exposed for carrying on a long-term affair with one of his church members.

A young man, affable and well liked by all who know him, is indicted and convicted for the murder of at least seventeen boys and young men.

A revered leader of a nation commits adultery and compounds his sin by arranging the death of his partner's husband.

A gifted missionary is removed from his mission field and his denomination for repeated sexual liaisons with prostitutes overseas.

A music director of a large church is found to have an addiction for marijuana and pornography, the frequent use of which has resulted in great financial loss to his family.

A mother known for her public displays of affection for her children is convicted of gross physical abuse that led to their untimely deaths.

And it goes on, and on, and on.

What do these tragic stories have in common? The behavior of the individuals in these accounts is out of alignment with who we thought they were. They're not who they seemed to be or who they said they were.

We may not be involved in such horrific behaviors as those just described, but we share a common problem—we do not always act in accordance with what we say we believe. Behavior like this is not uncommon in the world. And, to our embarrassment, it is not uncommon in the church.

Take a few moments and truthfully consider the following scenario: If you knew you wouldn't get caught, that no one would find out, that your reputation would not be tarnished, no one could trace your activity back to you, and no one would ever know, what would you be open to do?

Once again, Paul, in his letter to the Romans, paints a clear picture of our dilemma:

> *I do not understand what I do. For what I want to do I do not do, but what I hate I do. And if I do what I do not want to do, I agree that the law is good. As it is, it is no longer I myself who do it, but it is sin living in me. I know that nothing good lives in me, that is, in my sinful nature. For I have the desire to do what is good, but I cannot carry it out. For what I do is not the good I want to do; no, the evil I do*

not want to do-this I keep on doing. Now if I do what I do not want to do, it is no longer I who do it, but it is sin living in me that does it.

So I find this law at work: When I want to do good, evil is right there with me. For in my inner being I delight in God's law; but I see another law at work in the members of my body, waging war against the law of my mind and making me a prisoner of the law of sin at work within my members. What a wretched man I am! Who will rescue me from this body of death? Thanks be to God—through Jesus Christ our Lord![202]

Paul's dilemma is our dilemma. Why do we do the very things we hate to do? He knows the source of his problem and so should we—sin at work within us! Sin, the Bible says, leads to death—not only spiritual death but physical death. The Scriptures remind us: "Don't you know that when you offer yourselves to someone to obey him as slaves, you are slaves to the one whom you obey—whether you are slaves to sin, which leads to death, or to obedience, which leads to righteousness?"[203] The hope for believers is found in the verses that follow: "But thanks be to God that, though you used to be slaves to sin, you wholeheartedly obeyed the form of teaching to which you were entrusted. You have been set free from sin and have become slaves to righteousness."[204] For many of us, this hope remains a dream—an aspiration but not a reality.

Same Old Song

We learned in previous chapters that following unhealthy lifestyle patterns instead of God's preferred lifestyle can produce behavior that brings discredit on God. We adopt these situational lifestyles to navigate our way through problems and crises. In every instance, we address our perceptions of reality, rather than reality itself. Our situational lifestyles simply accommodate the corruption within us and will never get to the heart of the problem.

---

202 Romans 7:15–25
203 Romans 6:16
204 Romans 6:17–20

Leadership theorists and medical experts both agree that solving a problem depends on a correct diagnosis of the symptoms. Sometimes, we treat the symptoms and not the real cause of the problem.

For example, suppose you develop a rash on your arm. It looks like dry skin to you, so you apply ointment to the area, and the rash disappears for a time. When it reappears, you apply the same ointment, resulting in its disappearance once more. You wonder if it might be an allergy. After a third occurrence, you decide to go to a doctor. To your surprise, you have scarlet fever. You have been treating the symptoms rather than the real cause of the rash.

Spiritually speaking, we often treat the symptoms of our spiritual problems and not the cause. More specifically, our behavior does not always reflect positively on our declared Christian beliefs. When our behavior is out of alignment with our beliefs, we assume that we are not reading our Bibles enough, going to church enough, giving testimony of our faith enough, or praying enough. Perhaps we repeatedly sin in a specific area of our lives. We despise the sin but seem helpless every time we are tempted in the same area.

The Bible promises victory but somehow victory continually escapes us. We remove the apparent sources of temptation from our lives or stop hanging around with those who encourage the behavior, but nothing seems to work.

The problem may be that we are treating the symptoms and not the cause of the sin problem in our life. Often, dysfunctional, despicable behaviors seemingly erupt in our lives. We didn't plan for it to happen, it just did—or did it? We're startled by it, as we thought we had control over such behavior—until now. How could this happen?

Predictable Patterns of Defeat

Well-meaning efforts to control our behavior last as long as the strength of our discipline. We effectively bind ourselves, with steel cables of discipline around our behavior, to conform to what we know is right. For example, we may put adult locks on certain cable TV channels—I know one man who did just that. When the TV prompt asked him to put in an alphanumeric code to lock the channel, he quickly entered random numbers by passing his fingers over his remote control with his eyes closed. He believed that because he didn't know the code, he wouldn't be plagued with falling for the temptation.

We will go to extremes to win the battle, only to find out there are myriad ways to get around the controls. The accountability measures we employ, or the rules and regulations by which we try to abide, or the mechanisms we bring to bear on the problem may work for a while—but only for a while. We may honestly intend not to surf the Internet again, or not to get involved in chat rooms, or not to go to the beach where we have been tempted before, or not to submit to the urges of our addiction. The sin in us, however, and the temptation we receive in our areas of weakness continue to be an unholy, potent source for further degradation—until we replace it with something far more powerful.

In an unguarded moment, we relax our man-made restraints and succumb to the sin that so easily knocks us off course. We lapse back into behavior we despise. While we are around other Christians, we're fine. But sooner or later, we find ourselves in places where no one can see us or where we are not known. It may be while we are staying in a hotel in another city. We turn on the TV and immediately, the TV menu beckons us to the adult movies. We experience the weight of temptation, with every intention of honoring God, but we linger nevertheless. Before we know it, we are ordering a movie that we know is not good for our soul. You might wonder why I am focusing on sexual temptation and sin. It's because it is the number one area in which most men are tempted.

This pattern, regardless of its nature, repeats itself in a variety of ways in the lives of well-intentioned and committed Christians. It may be associated with substance abuse, chronic lying, infidelity and other related immoral behaviors, financial improprieties, or some other manifestation of repeated patterns of sin in our lives. Once engaged in dishonoring behavior, we fall into remorse, making promises not to do it again. Trouble is, we have done it before and we'll probably do it again, unless something changes at the core of who we are.

We become discouraged because our well-intentioned efforts meet with such little success. In desperation, we make sincere commitments to do more of what we know we should be doing: spending more time reading the Bible, more time in service at church, more time thinking about healthy things, more spent time with good friends—all worthwhile, to be sure. But unless we deal with the root causes of our problems and replace the corruption with something designed to set us free, we are doomed to be repeat offenders.

Over time, we begin to wonder if we will ever see lasting victory over these debilitating patterns of behavior that are subtly destroying us. As a defense, we may rationalize our behavior as the sad lot of our humanity, the consequential by-product of our sinful natures. Lasting victory, we surmise, is only possible in heaven, not on earth. We get used to living on a lower level of mediocre Christianity. Over time, we forget what it was like to fly "like the eagles," figuratively and spiritually.

As Vance Havner, the quotable man of God now home with the Lord, suggests, "We were meant for the crags and not the cage."[205] The perspective from the crags is much clearer. He tells the story of a flock of geese, heading south for the winter. While passing over a barnyard, one of the geese looked down and decided to see what was going on. He flew down for a closer look and to his delight, he noticed how well the barnyard animals were taken care of. They had shelter from the elements, plenty of food to eat, and a safe place to live. So he decided to stay for the winter. He liked it so much that he stayed through the spring and into the summer. When fall came once again, the honking of geese flying south for the winter disturbed his slumber. His eyes moistened; his wings flapped. He made it as high as the top of the barn. But once again, he settled down into the comfort of the barnyard. When fall came once again and geese flew south for the winter, he didn't even notice their honking.

How many of us have gotten so used to living in the barnyard of convenience and compromise that we take little notice of what we are designed to be. We have become complacent and would rather be fed and housed. As Havner poignantly states, "We have become fat birds in a cage." Our lack of victory over sin has made us skeptical of anyone who would suggest that victory is possible and attainable this side of heaven. Living at that level is only for the "mystics," we believe. A mystic in many respects is simply an individual who has decided to proactively live by embracing God's promises and acting on them as facts. Its rarity suggests that such a person is a mystic. Such a person inspires mystery and wonder. He seems strange because he is so uncommon, it seems.

205 Vance Havner. *In Times Like These*, 96.

Back to the Question

We are back to our fundamental question. When it comes to human nature, why do people do what they do? Why do people do despicable things, sometimes over and over again?

In 1997, Israeli Prime Minister Binyamin Netanyahu spoke to The Washington Institute's Policy Forum about the nature of the conflicts between Arabs and Israelis. "Real peace," he said, "does not come from the hand that signs the treaties; it comes from the head and the heart that formulates them and then forms the attitude towards these treaties, because true peace comes from the heart, or more precisely, it comes from a change of heart." [206]

Netanyahu's comment compels us to consider how fundamental change is effected in our lives. How does lasting behavioral change take place? What factors contribute to effect or hinder change? Netanyahu suggests that real peace can only be attained by a "change of heart." Is he right?

The Bible agrees with his supposition. "Above all else, guard your heart, for it is the wellspring of life." [207] According to this passage, behavior flows from the heart. So much of our effort to conform our behavior to God's standards is simply employment of behavior modification techniques. We "do" things to become something instead of to "be" someone who does godly things. We spend inordinate effort on conforming our behavior to what we believe is godly behavior. The focus is on appearances.

Saul was the first king of Israel selected by God and anointed by the prophet Samuel. But because of repeated disobedience, a penchant for taking things into his own hands, susceptibility to external influences, waffling between right and wrong, and inconsistent character, he lost God's favor. The Lord said to Samuel, "How long will you mourn for Saul, since I have rejected him as king over Israel? Fill your horn with oil and be on your way; I am sending you to Jesse of Bethlehem. I have chosen one of his sons to be king." [208]

---

206 Rachel Ingber. *Israel's Vision of Security and Peace,* in <u>Peacewatch,</u> Number 121 (February 1997).
207 Proverbs 4:23
208 1 Samuel 16:1

Samuel proceeded to the house of Jesse to anoint the next king of Israel. The first to be paraded before Samuel was Eliab. He bore in his person a regal nature. Samuel thought he must be the one. But God stopped his musing right there. God said to Samuel, "Do not consider his appearance or his height, for I have rejected him. The LORD does not look at the things man looks at. Man looks at the outward appearance, but the LORD looks at the heart."[209]

Ultimately, seven sons were paraded before Samuel, all of whom God rejected. He asked Jesse if these were all of his sons. Jesse responded that an eighth son, the youngest, was tending sheep. He was sent for and brought in before Samuel. God told Samuel to anoint David; he was the one.[210]

The Source of the Dilemma

In God's own words, we hear what is the true source of our dilemma—the heart. Proverbs 4:23 tells us that our heart is "the wellspring of Life." In 1 Samuel 16:7, God tells us that man looks at the outward appearance, or behavior, but He looks at the heart. The world looks at behavior; God has always looked at the heart.

Scripture tells us that the Enemy prowls about, looking to gain a foothold, looking for someone to devour.[211] There is a battle going on for our hearts; there's a battleground where the success of the daily Christian life is determined. Understanding and winning the battle for the heart is essential to Christian maturity, freedom from bondage, and godliness.

The Enemy wants us to believe the battleground is our behavior. He knows, however, that it has always been the heart. If he can get us to focus our efforts on our behavior, the true battlefield of the heart will be relatively open to his manipulation and control. He is employing the proverbial "bait and switch" tactic. He wants us to focus our attention on the battlefield of behavior, while he focuses his attention on the battlefield of the heart.

What is his objective? He is not really interested in you or me as his objective. His real objective is to bring dishonor to God so that no one who observes our behavior will be attracted to His Son, Jesus Christ. He

---

209 1 Samuel 16:7
210 1 Samuel 16:6–12
211 1 Peter 5:8

uses us as a means to an end—to dishonor the Father. Such corrupted behavior, he knows, will keep others from coming to a saving knowledge of Christ. After all, if our behavior is no different from the world, why would the world be interested in our faith?

The Heart of the Matter

Let's examine Proverbs 4:23 a little closer.

"Above all else, guard your heart, for it is the wellspring of life."

The writer of Proverbs emphasizes the necessity of paying attention to our hearts. "Above all else," he says. Of singular importance, of utmost urgency, when all is said and done, we are to make sure we pay attention to our hearts. Not only are we to focus on the heart, we are to "guard" it. In other words, we are to maintain our vigilance, stay alert, to protect and defend against intrusion, to shield and fortify, and keep from harm. This is not passive activity. Many a castle, fort, and city have fallen to the Enemy because someone fell asleep on guard or wasn't paying attention to his duties. The writer underscores the importance and urgency of standing guard over our hearts.

Too many of us are complacent and apathetic about what we permit to invade our hearts. By our passiveness, we allow the corruption of the world to make its way to our hearts. When we let our guard down, all manner of filth finds its way to the deep recesses of our being. Some of us live our lives with careless ease, oblivious to the destructive forces vying for control of our lives.

What would the following personal audit reveal with regard to what may be influencing the heart and which results in ungodly behavior? Honest reflection may give us a clue about what lies in residence within our hearts.

- What are you reading?
- What are you watching?
- Who are you listening to?
- What are you listening to?
- How do you spend your free time?
- Who do you hang around with?
- What are your values?

Once again, "Above all else, guard your heart, for it is the wellspring of your life." Webster's defines "wellspring" as a fountainhead, a source of continual supply, a feeder that flows out from a source. Other terms that collectively capture the meaning of this phrase include headwater, headstream, springhead, and source. The implication for wellspring, then, is a source from which something flows; in this case, a source that flows out into life.

What we store in our hearts gushes forth and manifests itself overtly in our behavior, for good or for bad, depending on the quality of what is stored within. If our hearts are filled with the corruption of the world, unconfessed sin, dysfunctionality, distortions, or any other pollutants, our behavior will reflect this pollution. Oh, we may fool others and ourselves for a time by seemingly living our lives circumspectly, but eventually, our true selves will become evident in what we say and do. Watch someone's behavior over time, and you will see who he really is. What you observe may have little resemblance to who he claims to be or what he proclaims to believe.

If I were to close my fist and hold the grip tightly, it wouldn't be long before the strength of my grip would start to subside. We can keep up appearances for a time, but our true selves will eventually emerge.

Sources of Influence

The Bible indicates three primary sources of negative influence in our lives: the world, the flesh, and the devil. All three can corrupt our hearts, if we let them.

We are told not to fall in love with the world because anyone who is in love with the world and for what it stands does not have the love of the Father in him. Furthermore, "everything in the world, the cravings of sinful man, the lust of his eyes and the boasting of what he has and does, comes not from the Father but from the world."[212] Peter further states that we have been given promises to participate in the divine nature and escape the corruption in the world caused by evil desires.[213] Finally, he warns us when he says, "Don't you know that friendship with the world is hatred

212 1 John 2:15–17
213 2 Peter 2:3–4

toward God? Anyone who chooses to be a friend of the world becomes an Enemy of God.[214]

With regard to the "flesh," the Bible means the residual effects of sin in us. Before a person becomes a believer, he struggles with a sinful nature, inherited from Adam.[215] We are helpless against this sinful nature and subject to its power in our lives. Once a person comes to a saving knowledge of Jesus Christ, the sinful nature is replaced with a new spiritual nature.[216] The Christian is no longer helpless. The penalty of sin has been paid, and the power of sin has been broken. We are new creations in Christ.[217]

We struggle, however, with our predisposition to sin in certain areas; with sin strongholds within us; with bad habits learned and formed before we were saved; with consequences of poor decisions in the past—these issues comprise what the Bible calls the "flesh."[218] Through the power of the Holy Spirit, these last footholds of the Enemy can be demolished. The process of eliminating these influences in our lives is called sanctification, the progressive cleansing of remaining sin patterns in our life.

The flesh is the metaphorical repository of residual patterns toward sin that we developed while still unsaved. The penalty for our sin was paid at the cross. The power of sin was defeated in Christ, and its influence is mediated by the work of the Spirit. When we are in heaven, the very presence of sin will be eliminated forever. Yet many of us are still living as if we are chained to our old natures.

So, with what are we now struggling on this side of Christ's finished work on the cross? What have we brought with us into our relationship with Christ?

- Predispositions toward certain engrained types of sin
- Corrupted patterns of behavior that we learned over time
- Patterns of faulty thinking, reasoning, and emoting
- Biases and weaknesses cultivated by our sinfulness prior to Christ

214 James 4:4
215 Romans 5:12–21
216 Ephesians 4:22–24; Galatians 5:13–26
217 1 Corinthians 5:17
218 Galatians 5:16–17

- Dysfunctional attitudes and behaviors developed over a lifetime

For example, if you were a manipulative person in the past, driven by self-centeredness and greed, the sinful nature that gave rise to such sin is gone. However, the practice of manipulation to get your way may remain; the pattern may still be there. But now, in Christ, you have the power through His Holy Spirit to have victory over the inclination to manipulate others.

The following analogy may help: In the past, baby elephants were chained to iron stakes early in their lives. Every time they tried to pull away from the stake, the iron clasp around their leg, connected to an iron chain tied to an iron stake embedded deep in the ground, prevented their escape. They grew to learn that struggle was futile, so that when mature, an adult elephant could be held in place by a simple rope around its ankle, tied to a wooden stake in the ground. Certainly elephants are strong enough to break free from a simple rope, but in their minds, they still believe it's futile.

Before we came to Christ, we were bound to our sinful nature by a metal clasp, chain, and stake—our sinful nature. After we come to Christ, the metal restrictions are gone. What holds us to the wooden stake is a flimsy rope called the "flesh." These dysfunctional patterns of living represent the rope. Now, however, we can snap the rope easily through Christ. Many of us still believe we are held to the stake by an immovable tether.[219] That is exactly what the Enemy wants us to believe, and it isn't true.

We can break these patterns of dysfunctionality with God's help. The power that held us in the past has been removed at the cross. What binds us now can be broken.[220] We are told to abstain from the passions of the flesh that wage war against our soul.[221] What binds us now need no longer hold us back.[222] Yet many of us live as if we are held to our sinful nature by immovable restraints. We have forgotten that we are free in Christ, no longer bound to our past. We can now embrace our God-ordained future.

The Bible clearly describes our new nature:

219 1 Corinthians 3:1–4; Galatians 3:3–4
220 Galatians 5:16–24; Galatians 6:8–9
221 1 Peter 2:11
222 Romans 8:5–8, 13:14

Therefore, there is now no condemnation for those who are in Christ Jesus, because through Christ Jesus the law of the Spirit of life set me free from the law of sin and death. For what the law was powerless to do in that it was weakened by the sinful nature, God did by sending his own Son in the likeness of sinful man to be a sin offering. And so he condemned sin in sinful man, in order that the righteous requirements of the law might be fully met in us, who do not live according to the sinful nature but according to the Spirit.

Those who live according to the sinful nature have their minds set on what that nature desires; but those who live in accordance with the Spirit have their minds set on what the Spirit desires. The mind of sinful man is death, but the mind controlled by the Spirit is life and peace; the sinful mind is hostile to God. It does not submit to God's law, nor can it do so. Those controlled by the sinful nature cannot please God.

You, however, are controlled not by the sinful nature but by the Spirit, if the Spirit of God lives in you. And if anyone does not have the Spirit of Christ, he does not belong to Christ. But if Christ is in you, your body is dead because of sin, yet your spirit is alive because of righteousness. And if the Spirit of him who raised Jesus from the dead is living in you, he who raised Christ from the dead will also give life to your mortal bodies through his Spirit, who lives in you.[223]

An ongoing struggle exists between the "flesh" and the "Spirit." That is why we progressively grow in Christ.[224] That is why we must "work out [the ramifications] of salvation daily."[225] The power of sin over us has been broken, yet we must avail ourselves of the power of the Holy Spirit to deal with patterns of behavior we learned over a lifetime that made us susceptible to sin in the first place. Before Christ, we were at the mercy of our sinful nature. But through Christ, we "put off" our old natures and "put on" our new natures.[226] These were one-time events. The same

---

223 Romans 8:1–11
224 2 Corinthians 3:18
225 Philippians 2:12
226 Ephesians 4:22–24

passage, as well as others,[227] tells us to renew ourselves daily—that is God's plan for gradual purification, called sanctification in this life. We are now a new creation, not a remade old one.[228]

We are without excuse. Sometimes, we blame the world or the devil and forget about our own complicity. The Bible says, "For from within, out of men's hearts, come evil thoughts, sexual immorality, theft, murder, adultery, greed, malice, deceit, lewdness, envy, slander, arrogance and folly. All these evils come from inside and make a man 'unclean.'"[229]

With regard to the Enemy, the Bible says he prowls about looking for someone to devour.[230] He uses several tactics to get to our hearts, including equivocation,[231] distortion,[232] sifting,[233] compromise,[234] delusion,[235] deprivation,[236] revenge,[237] outwitting,[238] masquerading,[239] thorn in the flesh,[240] struggle,[241] confrontation,[242] worldliness,[243] infiltration,[244] deceit,[245] and overpowering.[246] Part of winning a battle is to know which tactics your Enemy uses. We fear what we don't know and become vulnerable. Understanding how the Enemy operates will give us an advantage in dealing with him.

The influences of the world, the flesh, and the devil are constantly trying to make their way to our hearts. Corrupted hearts produce corrupted

---

227 Romans 12:1–2
228 2 Corinthians 5:17; Colossians 3:9–10
229 Mark 7:21–23
230 1 Peter 5:8
231 Matthew 5:37
232 Matthew 13:19
233 Luke 22:31
234 Acts 5:3
235 Acts 26:18
236 1 Corinthians 7:5
237 2 Corinthians 2:10
238 2 Corinthians 2:11
239 2 Corinthians 11:14
240 2 Corinthians 12:7
241 Ephesians 6:12
242 Ephesians 6:13, 16
243 1 John 5:18–19
244 Mathew 13:25, 39
245 Acts 13:10
246 1 Peter 5:8

behavior. The Bible is clear—our behavior is essentially a reflection of the health of our heart. And our character is a portrait or snapshot of what's in our heart.

Character is the combination of natural and acquired features and traits that constitute a person's nature or fundamental disposition, from which specific moral responses issue.[247] Merriam-Webster Dictionary adds that character is one of the attributes or features that make up or distinguish an individual; the complex of mental and ethical traits marking an individual; his main or essential nature.

Your character is what and who you are at the core, all illusions, pretension, posturing, and adopted personas aside. It is not the ideal you wish you were. It's not what others say or think you are. It is who you *really* are, when the layers of carefully constructed hypocrisies are removed. The home of one's true character is what the Bible refers to as the heart.

The Final Frontier

Our lawmakers are afraid to go there, our judges don't want to interfere, and our politicians are confused about its dominion—the final frontier, the heart. We attach to it love, depth, organ, essence. But what does the Bible mean by it? It's the final frontier, the last place for exploration. It should be the first place we explore to determine the underlying cause of behavior, but we'd rather deal with the obvious, not the hidden. Which came first: behavior or the heart? Behavior is much easier to see. But it's what we don't see that determines what we do see.

The Heart Defined

So what do we mean by the heart? Bible scholars are nearly unanimous about what the Bible means when it refers to the heart. The word heart—or one of its derivatives—is found more than 820 times in the Bible; approximately 80 percent of the references are found in the Old Testament and 20 percent in the New Testament.

Vine's Expository Dictionary of Biblical Words is very helpful with this point. In the New Testament, the Bible describes the heart as the "seat

---

247 David Clark and Robert Rakestraw, eds. *Readings in Christian Ethics: Theory and Method (Vol. 1)*, Baker Books, 1994, 276.

of physical life,[248] joy,[249] desires,[250] affections,[251] perceptions,[252] thoughts and motives,[253] understanding,[254] reasoning powers;[255] imagination;[256] conscience;[257] intentions;[258] purpose;[259] the will;[260] and faith."[261] It is the seat of morality—that dimension of life related to right conduct, including virtuous character, honorable intentions, and right actions.[262]

Vine's also states "the heart, in its moral significance in the Old Testament, includes the emotions, the reason, and the will. The *heart* stands for the inner being of man, the man himself." As such, it is the fountain of all he does.[263] All his thoughts, desires, words, and actions flow from deep within him. Yet a man cannot understand his own "heart."[264]

Nelson's Illustrated Bible Dictionary adds to this definition. The heart is "the inner self that thinks, feels, and decides. In the Bible, the word heart has a much broader meaning than it does to the modern mind. The heart is that which is central to man. Nearly all the references to the heart in the Bible refer to some aspect of human personality. Finally, heart often means someone's true character or personality. Purity or evil;[265] sincerity or hardness;[266] and maturity or rebelliousness[267]—all these describe the heart or true character of individuals."

---

248 Acts 14:17; James 5:5
249 John 16:22; Ephesians 5:19
250 Matthew 5:28; 2 Peter 2:14
251 Luke 24:32; Acts 21:13
252 John 12:40; Ephesians 4:18
253 Matthew 9:4; Hebrews 4:12
254 Matthew 13:15; Romans 1:21
255 Mark 2:6; Luke 24:28
256 Luke 1:51
257 Acts 2:37; 1 John 3:20
258 Hebrews 4:12; 1 Peter 4:1
259 Acts 11:23; 2 Corinthians 9:7
260 Romans 6:17; Colossians 3:15
261 Mark 11:23; Romans 10:10; Hebrews 3:12
262 Clark and Rakestraw, 64.
263 Proverbs 4:4
264 Jeremiah 17:9
265 Jeremiah 3:17; Matthew 5:8
266 Exodus 4:21; Colossians 3:22
267 Psalm 101:2; Jeremiah 5:23

What about the mind? The mind is the control center of the heart. It is the gateway to our heart. It is the gatekeeper of our soul. The mind decides what will pass through to the heart. Apathy and complacency compromise the integrity of the gate of the mind.

Another way to look at the mind is that it acts as the operating software for the hard drive of the heart, and the mind can be dulled. Mini-compromises that originate in our mind can lead to the hardening of our heart, to ignorance and darkened understanding, to separation from life in God, a loss of sin sensitivity, and a life based on sensuality.[268]

In summary, the heart is the inner being of man, the core and essence of who we are, the unvarnished receptacle of our being, the irreducible minimum. It is where the impetus for our actions arises. It is the repository of what we truly trust in, rely on and cling to. It is the filter through which we process all life's decisions. It is the lens through which we make judgments regarding our observations of the world around us. It is what moves us to action. It is worth guarding; it must be guarded.

Heart Explained

Scripture yields five primary findings related to the heart:

1. Out of the heart comes evil.

The Bible tells us that every inclination of our heart is evil from childhood. Out of our hearts come immorality, deceit, arrogance, adultery and murder.[269] Good things come from a good heart; bad things from a bad heart;[270] an unbelieving heart turns away from God.[271] Out of the overflow of our hearts, our mouth speaks.[272] Apart from Christ in us, nothing good dwells within us, for we have all sinned and fall short of God's glory.[273] Just look at the behavior of the world. Better yet, look at our own behavior.

---

268 Ephesians 4:17–19
269 Mark 7:21–23
270 Matthew 12:35
271 Hebrews 3:12
272 Luke 6:45
273 Romans 3:23

2. God is concerned about the hearts of humanity.

The Bible tells us that men and women look at the appearance, but God looks at the heart.[274] Life-transforming belief comes from the heart.[275] He answers our prayers for a cleansed heart.[276] God's laws are written on our hearts,[277] and a man after God's own heart does what God wants him to do.[278] The world will always look at appearances. Our significance is often assessed by what the world thinks of us, our appearances, or our behavior. God, however, looks at our hearts and is concerned about its condition. He is looking for men after His own heart.

3. God desires a pure heart and pure motives.

The Bible tells us that a man or woman who pleases God has clean hands and a pure heart.[279] David enjoyed kindness from God because of his faithfulness and his righteous heart.[280] At conversion, God gave us a new heart.[281] God expects us to operate out of a sincere heart.[282] We are to do the will of God from our heart.[283] The Bible judges the thoughts and attitudes of our heart.[284] And we are to guard our heart, for it is the wellspring of life.[285] God appreciates wholesome thinking.[286]

God expects nothing less from His followers. In fact, He is explicit about it. "For the grace of God that brings salvation has appeared to all men. It teaches us to say no to ungodliness and worldly passions and to live self-controlled, upright, and godly lives in this present age, while we wait for the blessed hope—the glorious appearing of our great God and Savior, Jesus Christ,

---

274 1 Samuel 16:7
275 Romans 10:9–, 10
276 Psalm 51:10; 86:11–, 12
277 1 Corinthians 3:3; Hebrews 8:10
278 Acts 13:22
279 Psalm 24:4
280 1 Kings 3:6, 9
281 Ezekiel 36:26
282 2 Corinthians 9:7
283 Ephesians 6:5–6
284 Hebrews 4:12
285 Proverbs 4:23
286 2 Peter 3:1

who gave himself for us, to redeem us from all wickedness and to purify for himself a people that are his very own, eager to do what is good."[287]

4. The Enemy doesn't want the heart to be transformed.

The Bible tells us that the evil one continuously tries to snatch away what is sown in the heart.[288] The heart can become calloused, resulting in darkness and futile thinking.[289] We are not to give the devil a foothold in our hearts.[290] The Enemy prefers futile thinking and darkened understanding.[291] The Enemy prowls about, looking for an entry into our hearts to devour us,[292] and Satan's tactics include sowing lies in place of God's truth in our hearts.[293] Lasting transformational change is the last thing the Enemy wants. He would rather we struggle with our behavior and leave the heart to him. A transformed heart is his worst foe. When we live transformed lives, we become a formidable foe of the Enemy.

5. God wants our hearts to be transformed.

The Bible tells us that we are to think on those things that are excellent and praiseworthy.[294] We are predestined to be conformed to the image of Christ.[295] We are being transformed into His likeness, one step at a time.[296] God wants our behavior to be Christ-like.[297] He has given us everything we need to live a godly life.[298] We can understand and experientially know Christ,[299] and we are not alone or powerless. He has given us His Spirit to be with us.[300] If our lives are to bring honor and glory to the Father, our

---

287 Titus 2:11–14
288 Matthew 13:19
289 Matthew 13:15
290 Ephesians 4:27
291 Romans 1:21; Ephesians 4:17–19
292 1 Peter 5:8
293 John 8:44
294 Philippians 4:8
295 Romans 8:29
296 2 Corinthians 3:18
297 Ephesians 4:13, 15
298 2 Peter 1:3–4
299 Jeremiah 9:24
300 John 14:16–17

hearts must be tuned to Him. To change our behavior, we must have a change of heart.

Conclusion

The heart is the real battlefield, where defeat or victory is attained. God looks at the hearts of mankind. He evaluates us based on what is in our hearts. The Enemy also knows that if we win and control the heart, behavior will follow. Behavior can galvanize, enhance, embolden, animate, electrify, incite, fire up, stimulate, rouse, spur on, bolster, and reinforce what is already in the heart. Our mind chooses how we will respond.

Behavior simply strikes a resonate cord with what already is there. The heart, stimulated by situations, incidents, or circumstances, determines behavior. Behavior may appear to determine what is in our hearts but, in fact, it merely strikes a responsive note with what is already stored in our hearts.

Behavior can solidify what is stored in our hearts, kind of like a feedback loop to the heart. Behavior, however, does not happen in a vacuum. It is activated by the heart and put into play by the mind. Susceptibility to behavioral influences is determined by the degree of accessibility to the heart. Our passivity or unguardedness can make our hearts vulnerable to outside influences.

If our convictions within our heart are not strongly held, and if we do not allow the Spirit of God to control, inform, and condition the heart, then it can and will be shaped by other influences, such as friends, circumstances, the world, and Satan himself.

The point is to be so controlled and influenced by the Spirit of God as to have the mind and character of Christ in our hearts. The resulting behavior will be Christ-like and bring glory to God. To change behavior, we must have a change of heart.

Satan and his underlings want to corrupt our hearts; God wants us to have pure hearts. The battle rages, and you and I have the final decision. Who is going to win this struggle: Satan or God? We tip the scales. We decide with our mind who and what will influence our heart. We determine what will control our behavior. One sure way to let the Enemy win the struggle is to do nothing at all. Passivity is the oil on the slippery slope of destruction. Our lack of concern or lack of proactive involvement speeds up the process of decay in our soul. Edmund Burke, an eighteenth-century Irish statesman, said, "The only thing necessary for the triumph of evil is for good men to do nothing."

From God's point of view, character matters! The Bible is clear—our behavior (or performance) is essentially a reflection of the health of our heart. And our character is a portrait of what's in our heart. In other words, what is stored in our heart determines and conditions our behavior.

In the next chapter, we will examine the concept of heart more closely. Four components of the heart are defined and illustrated. The inter-relatedness of the components is explained. The relationship between behavior and what is stored in our hearts is discussed. The question "Does behavior determine what is in our hearts, or does what's in our hearts determine behavior?" is examined. The goal of the next chapter is to understand what generates our behaviors and the role each component plays.

BATTLE PLAN

1. Read 1 Samuel 16:1–13. Pay particular attention to verse 7. What does this passage reveal about God's perspective? How does this passage apply to your relationship with God?

2. Identify a behavior that you would like victory over. If behavior is a reflection of what is stored in our hearts, what might be the root cause of this behavior?

3. Ask God to reveal what's in your heart that reproduces dishonorable behaviors in your life. What did God reveal to you?

4. Confess what God has revealed to you and ask for His empowerment to remove it from your heart.

Remember, confession is acknowledging sin in your life, recognizing that sin is what drove Christ to the cross, receiving God's forgiveness through the finished work of Christ, and asking for empowerment through the Holy Spirit to have victory over this area of sin.

CHAPTER 5
THE BATTLEFIELD

After removing Saul, he made David their king.
He testified concerning him: "I have found
David, son of Jesse, a man after my own heart;
he will do everything I want him to do."

Acts 13:22

So far, we have accomplished the following:

- We have stressed the point that there is a battle going on all around us. Spiritual warfare is a reality. We have outlined twelve characteristics of a warrior after God's heart.

- We have identified five situational lifestyles that we adopt to make our way through our earthly journey. These dysfunctional lifestyles never quite deliver what they promise.

- We have described God's preferred lifestyle—the target for which we are aiming; the objective we are striving to reach.

- We have located the real battlefield, where a battle rages for the souls of humankind. The battlefield is the heart. The control center for the heart is the mind. Our behavior reflects the condition of our heart.

- We now will look at the heart in more detail. Our purpose is to investigate the battlefield more closely before we strategize how to win the battle for our soul.

The Battleground

The battlefield or battleground represents the primary area of conflict. Many battles are fought on more than one battlefront at a time. Battlefronts are military sectors in which actual combat takes place. Such was the case in the bloodiest conflict of the Civil War, the clash at Gettysburg, Pennsylvania. General Robert E. Lee's Army of North Virginia faced General George Meade's Army of the Potomac. Sixty-five thousand Confederate troops faced eighty-five thousand Union troops across an expansive battleground around Gettysburg in July 1863. The battle raged over several battlefronts, each impacted by what was happening on the other fronts, including Seminary Ridge, Cemetery Hill, Little Round Top, and Big Round Top. In three days, forty-three thousand men lost their lives. This battle effectively ended Lee's second invasion of the North and signaled the end of the Confederacy's domination of the war.

The battleground, where spiritual victory or defeat is determined, is the heart of men. For most men, the battle for their souls is fought over unfamiliar ground. The battle for the hearts of men, like Gettysburg, is also fought on several battlefronts, each impacting the other. A careful study of the Bible on the battlefield of the heart would produce the following conclusion: ***The heart is composed of essentially four battlefronts—beliefs, values, attitudes, and motives.*** Collectively, these four locations comprise the battlefield on which victory or defeat is decided, where winning or losing the war for our souls takes place.

In Scripture, terms used for the heart are best understood in a metaphorical sense. Gary Carpenter's concordance study of the Hebrew and Greek words for heart suggests that the term "refers to the true self, the whole inner man, or to the specific aspects that make up the inner man." He adds, "When employed to detail particular components of the true self, the heart can refer to our intellects (what we think), our emotions (what we feel), our wills (what we resolve to do), and our spirits or souls (what enables us to relate to God)."[301] From his point of view, the battleground is fought on four fronts: our intellect, emotions, will, and spirit.

I find it helpful to envision the battleground as covering these four specific battlefronts. Each has its unique challenges, strengths and weaknesses; dangers and threats; and skirmishes and pitched battles; and each its place of significance in the battle plan for winning the war. Each front, when lost or won, impacts the others. The Enemy fights on all four fronts, and we must be prepared to confront him on each front.

---

301 Gary Carpenter. *What the Bible Says About the Heart.* College Press Publishing Company, 1990, 19.

The Battlefronts

Having examined the related verses and passages on heart, I would describe the battleground as having four primary fronts: beliefs, values, attitudes or worldview (the set of perceptual attitudes we have about life, what we rely on to make sense of observed life), and motives.[302]

Beliefs—Our Foundation

Beliefs are not merely facts we affirm. Beliefs are what we trust in, rely on, and cling to at the core of our being.

Our central beliefs are the foundation for all behavior. The word *believe* in Greek translates as what we trust in, rely on, and cling to. These are more than verbal affirmations of beliefs. At our deepest core, these are what we really believe, so much so that they are a part of our being. They determine our values, affect our attitudes, and influence our motives. They ultimately determine how we behave in a given situation.

A word of caution: what we verbally affirm as our beliefs may have little relationship to how we behave. In many instances, what we say about ourselves bears little resemblance to what we actually do. Talk is cheap, as the saying goes.

We have become very good at rhetoric that has little or no relationship to who we are at the core of our being. We use skillful verbiage to hold others at a distance because if they get too close and observe our behavior, over time they will know what a fraud we are.

So the verbal statements we make are not proof perfect. If our behavior were observed over time, disregarding what we say about ourselves in the process, a pattern would soon emerge that would give us a clearer picture of who we really are and what we really believe. Behavior observed over time will reflect who we really are at the core of our being.

---

302 See *Appendix A: Categorization of Heart Scriptures.*

Hebrew scholars attest to the fact that real faith is beliefs in action. They see no separation between one's beliefs and one's actions. More specifically, a belief doesn't become an ingrained belief until it's acted upon.[303] Repeated application of one's beliefs indicates what one really believes. If there is a disconnect between the one's beliefs and one's actions then they are not really beliefs—they are simply affirmations or aspirations.

A biblical belief system might include things like the following.

- Ten Commandments; loving others as ourselves;
- We are created in the image of God;
- Man is sinful;
- Human nature is corrupt;
- God loves us;
- Apart from God life is meaningless;
- Salvation is the only means to wholeness;
- God has plans for our lives;
- Man's chief purpose is to demonstrate God's excellence in all that we do;
- Human life is to be cherished;
- Widows and orphans are to be taken care of; or
- Christ is the only means of salvation.

Corrupted or distorted beliefs might include the following topics.

- Homosexuality is genetically determined;
- Truth is relative;
- My body is my own;
- There is no God;
- There are no absolutes;
- Power is success;
- All lifestyles are to be accepted;
- Performance is all that matters; or
- The ends justify the means.

The verses that follow underscore the importance and the place of biblical beliefs in our life:

Proverbs 6:20–23 *O my son, keep your father's commands and do not forsake your mother's teaching.* ***Bind them upon your heart forever; fasten***

---

303 James 2:14–26

111

them around your neck. When you walk, they will guide you; when you sleep, they will watch over you; when you awake, they will speak to you. **For these commands are a lamp, this teaching is a light, and the corrections of discipline are the way to life** ...

John 8:31–32 *To the Jews who had believed him, Jesus said,* **"If you hold to my teaching, you are really my disciples. Then you will know the truth, and the truth will set you free."**

James 2:14–26 *What good is it, my brothers, if a man claims to have faith but has no deeds? Can such faith save him? Suppose a brother or sister is without clothes and daily food. If one of you says to him, "Go, I wish you well; keep warm and well fed," but does nothing about his physical needs, what good is it? In the same way,* **faith by itself, if it is not accompanied by action, is dead.** *But someone will say, "You have faith; I have deeds." Show me your faith without deeds, and I will show you my faith by what I do. You believe that there is one God. Good! Even the demons believe that—and shudder. You foolish man, do you want evidence that faith without deeds is useless? Was not our ancestor Abraham considered righteous for what he did when he offered his son Isaac on the altar?* **You see that his faith and his actions were working together, and his faith was made complete by what he did.** *And the Scripture was fulfilled that says, "Abraham believed God, and it was credited to him as righteousness," and he was called God's friend.* **You see that a person is justified by what he does and not by faith alone.** *In the same way, was not even Rahab the prostitute considered righteous for what she did when she gave lodging to the spies and sent them off in a different direction?* **As the body without the spirit is dead, so faith without deeds is dead.**

1 John 2:3–6 *We know that we have come to know him if we obey his commands. The man who says, "I know him," but does not do what he commands is a liar, and the truth is not in him.* **But if anyone obeys his Word, God's love is truly made complete in him.** *This is how we know we are in him: Whoever claims to live in him must walk as Jesus did.*

1 John 3:18–19 *Dear children,* **let us not love with words or tongue but with actions and in truth.** *This then is how we know that we belong to the truth, and how we set our hearts at rest in his presence...*

1 John 5:2–5 *This is how we know that we love the children of God: by loving God and carrying out his commands.* **This is love for God: to obey his commands.** *And his commands are not burdensome, for everyone born of*

God overcomes the world. This is the victory that has overcome the world, even our faith. Who is it that overcomes the world? Only he who believes that Jesus is the Son of God.

1 John 5:9–12 *Anyone who believes in the Son of God has this testimony in his heart. Anyone who does not believe God has made him out to be a liar, because he has not believed the testimony God has given about his Son. And this is the testimony: God has given us eternal life, and this life is in his Son. He who has the Son has life; he who does not have the Son of God does not have life.*

1 Peter 2:9 *But you are a chosen people, a royal priesthood, a holy nation, a people belonging to God, that you may declare the praises of him who called you out of darkness into his wonderful light.*

1 Peter 3:15–16 *But in your hearts set apart Christ as Lord. Always be prepared to give an answer to everyone who asks you to give the reason for the hope that you have. But do this with gentleness and respect, keeping a clear conscience, so that those who speak maliciously against your good behavior in Christ may be ashamed of their slander.*

Values—Our Filter

Values are what we hold in esteem. Values are the hills on which we will die; the principles by which we live. They comprise our morality. Values are the filter through which life is processed and decisions are made. No decision is made without reference to a value system, even if we cannot articulate those values. Values are what we esteem; we find it hard to understand why others may not hold them in that same esteem. Related terms would include morality, virtues, ethics, principles, rules, standards, and norms.

A value becomes a virtue when it is an ingrained habit that one applies without really thinking much about it.

Examples of biblically informed values might include centered living; devotion to God; family first; loyalty; justice; mercy; honesty; fairness; hard work; punctuality; self-discipline; courage; submission to the authority of God's word; being a man of integrity.

Examples of corrupted values might include that any form of sex is permissible; self-satisfaction; cunning; euthanasia; deception; that my race is superior to all others; if it feels good, do it; pornography is art; tolerance first and always; cheating is okay.

The verses that follow underscore the importance and the place of biblical values in our life:

Proverbs 4:7 *Wisdom is supreme; therefore get wisdom. Though it cost all you have, get understanding.*

Jeremiah 9:23–24 *This is what the LORD says: "Let not the wise man boast of his wisdom or the strong man boast of his strength or the rich man boast of his riches, but let him who boasts boast about this: that he understands and knows me, that I am the LORD, who exercises* **kindness**, **justice** *and* **righteousness** *on earth, for in these I delight," declares the LORD.*

Philippians 4:8 *Finally, brothers, whatever is* **true**, *whatever is* **noble**, *whatever is* **right**, *whatever is* **pure**, *whatever is* **lovely**, *whatever is* **admirable**—*if anything is excellent or praiseworthy—think about such things.*

Hebrews 8:10 *This is the covenant I will make with the house of Israel after that time, declares the Lord.* **I will put my laws in their minds and write them on their hearts.** *I will be their God, and they will be my people.*

Galatians 5:22–24 *But the fruit of the Spirit is* **love, joy, peace, patience, kindness, goodness, faithfulness, gentleness** *and* **self-control**. *Against such things there is no law. Those who belong to Christ Jesus have crucified the sinful nature with its passions and desires.*

2 Peter 1:3 *His divine power has given us* **everything we need for life and godliness** *through our knowledge of him who called us by his own glory and goodness.*

2 Peter 1:5–9 *For this very reason, make every effort to add to your faith* **goodness**; *and to goodness,* **knowledge**; *and to knowledge,* **self-control**; *and to self-control,* **perseverance**; *and to perseverance,* **godliness**; *and to godliness,* **brotherly kindness**; *and to brotherly kindness,* **love**. *For if you possess these*

qualities *in increasing measure, they will keep you from being ineffective and unproductive in your knowledge of our Lord Jesus Christ. But if anyone does not have them, he is nearsighted and blind, and has forgotten that he has been cleansed from his past sins.*

Attitudes—Our Lens

What we think—our perceptions and worldview—is the lens through which we view and understand the world around us.

If beliefs are the foundation for our behavior, and values are the filter through which we process life's decisions, then attitudes are the lens through which we observe life around us. Our perceptions about life are shaped by our attitudes. Our system of attitudes is also called our worldview.

The term worldview refers to any ideology, philosophy, theology, movement, or religion that provides an overarching approach to understanding God, the world, and man's relations to God and the world.

Our set of perceptual attitudes or worldview determines how we perceive and interpret our observations of the world around us. In *The Myth of Certainty* (2000), author Dan Taylor states that *"every person has a way of making sense out of the world. We have a compulsion for ordering and explaining our experiences. We belong to communities of belief which help shape, whether we are conscious of it or not, our views of the world and our actions in it. ... Most people thoughtlessly adapt an inherited worldview, or one absorbed from their surroundings. Even those who explicitly work one out often operate in daily life by a different, less conscious system than the one they carefully construct."*

How we interpret events, draw conclusions about what we read, evaluate what we observe, assess what we hear, process arguments, all depend on the worldview we hold at the time.

An example of biblically informed worldviews might include the following: the Beatitudes (Matthew 5:3–12); God is involved in history; humans bear God's imprint; something good can be found in every human being;

all things work together for good; theism; all creation is divinely inspired; the world is corrupted by sin; or being pro-life.

Examples of corrupted or distorted worldviews might include the following.

- White supremacy
- Humanism (man is the final authority)
- Post-modernism (there is no absolute truth)
- Racism
- Pro-choice
- Sense of entitlement;
- Predatory mentality (strength rules)
- Pluralism (all views, values, and practices are equally correct and acceptable)
- "The world is my oyster"
- Relativism (situational ethics)
- Hedonism (pleasure is pre-eminent)

The verses that follow underscore the importance and the place of a biblical worldview in our life.

Matthew 5:3–12 *"**Blessed are the poor in spirit**, for theirs is the kingdom of heaven. **Blessed are those who mourn**, for they will be comforted. **Blessed are the meek**, for they will inherit the earth. **Blessed are those who hunger and thirst for righteousness**, for they will be filled. **Blessed are the merciful**, for they will be shown mercy. **Blessed are the pure in heart**, for they will see God. **Blessed are the peacemakers**, for they will be called sons of God. **Blessed are those who are persecuted because of righteousness**, for theirs is the kingdom of heaven. **Blessed are you when people insult you, persecute you and falsely say all kinds of evil against you because of me.** Rejoice and be glad, because great is your reward in heaven, for in the same way they persecuted the prophets who were before you. ...."*

Ephesians 4:22–24 *You were taught, with regard to your former way of life, to **put off your old self, which is being corrupted by its deceitful desires; to be made new in the attitude of your minds; and to put on the new self**, created to be like God in true righteousness and holiness.*

Philippians 2:5–8 *Your attitude should be the same as that of Christ Jesus: Who, being in very nature God, did not consider equality with God* *something to be grasped, but made himself nothing, taking the very nature of a servant, being made in human likeness. And being found in appearance as a man, he humbled himself and became obedient to death—even death on a cross!*

Hebrews 4:12 *For the word of God is living and active. Sharper than any double-edged sword, it penetrates even to dividing soul and spirit, joints and marrow;* ***it judges the thoughts and attitudes of the heart***.

James 3:14–16 *But if you harbor bitter envy and selfish ambition in your hearts, do not boast about it or deny the truth.* ***Such "wisdom" does not come down from heaven but is earthly, unspiritual, of the devil.*** *For where you have envy and selfish ambition, there you find disorder and every evil practice.*

Motives—Our Stimulus

Motives stimulate our activity and behavior and mobilize us to act. Daniel McGuire, a biblical scholar, suggests that "motive gives essential and constitutive meaning to human action." Webster's defines motive as something, such as a need or desire, which causes a person to act. It might take the form of an impulse, an inducement, or goading—something that "spurs" us on. It can be seen as a driving force that arises from our predisposition, bias, or habitual inclination.

Motives compel us to take action and may arise from an external stimulus, such as an opportunity, circumstance, or event. Motives provide the bridge from thoughts (temptation) to action (behavior). Some people, for instance, are motivated by greed or jealousy. Others are motivated by love or desire. Still others might be motivated by idealism or self-interest.

Examples of biblically informed motives might be unconditional love, commitment to God, a vow, Christ-centered desires, commitment to a certain value, devotion, diligence, love of others, or self-preservation in the face of danger.

Examples of distorted or corrupted values might include greed, lust, self-gratification, gluttony, hatred, domination, conquest, anger, or pride.

The verses that follow underscore the importance and the place of biblical motives in our lives.

John 13:34–35 *"A new command I give you: **Love one another**. As I have loved you, so you must love one another. By this all men will know that you are my disciples, if you love one another."*

1 Corinthians 4:5 *Therefore judge nothing before the appointed time; wait till the Lord comes. **He will bring to light what is hidden in darkness and will expose the motives of men's hearts.** At that time each will receive his praise from God.*

1 Corinthians 13:4–8 ***Love is*** *patient, love is kind. It does not envy, it does not boast, it is not proud. It is not rude, it is not self-seeking, it is not easily angered, it keeps no record of wrongs. **Love does not** delight in evil but rejoices with the truth. It always protects, always trusts, always hopes, always perseveres. **Love never fails**. But where there are prophecies, they will cease; where there are tongues, they will be stilled; where there is knowledge, it will pass away.*

James 4.3 ***When you ask, you do not receive, because you ask with wrong motives,*** *that you may spend what you get on your pleasures.*

1 John 2:3–6 *We know that we have come to know him if we obey his commands. The man who says, "I know him," but does not do what he commands is a liar, and the truth is not in him. **But if anyone obeys his Word, God's love is truly made complete in him.** This is how we know we are in him: Whoever claims to live in him must walk as Jesus did.*

Unconditional love has always been the greatest motive for behavior that brings glory to God.[304]

Composition of the Heart

Beliefs, values, attitudes, and motives stimulated by situations, incidents, or circumstances determine behavior. Behavior may appear to determine our beliefs, values, attitudes, and motives but, in fact, it merely strikes a responsive and resonant chord with what is already stored in our hearts.

---

304 1 Peter 1:22; 1 Corinthians 13:4–6; 1 John 3:16–18

Behavior simply reinforces our existing beliefs, values, attitudes, and motives.

Behavior can act as a galvanizing influence on the heart. It can solidify what is stored in our hearts, kind of like a feedback loop. Behavior, however, does not happen in a vacuum. It is activated by the interaction of our beliefs, values, attitudes, and motives in the heart. Susceptibility to behavioral influences is determined by the degree of accessibility to the heart. Our passivity or un-guardedness can make our hearts vulnerable to outside influences.

If our beliefs, values, attitudes, and motives are not strongly held, and if we do not allow the Spirit of God to control them, then they can and will be shaped by other influences, including friends, circumstances, the world, and Satan himself.

The point is to be so controlled and influenced by the Spirit of God as to have the mind of Christ in our beliefs, values, attitudes, and motives, so that our character is Christ-like and our behavior brings glory to God. To change behavior, we must have a change of heart; in other words, to change our behavior we must have a change in our beliefs, values, attitudes, and motives. Behavior that brings glory to God is based on these factors, which must be influenced by the Spirit.

Relationship between the Components

There is a relationship between the components of the heart. The relationship is stated as a principle.

Although it is depicted as a straightforward cause-and-effect model, it is more like a circular interactive loop. Using the blood circulation in the heart as metaphor, we can visualize the connection and flow of beliefs to values, values to worldview, worldview to motives, and motives to behavior.

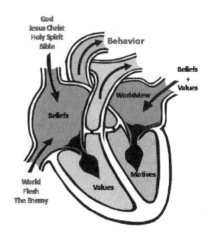

Our central beliefs are formed by certain influences—the world,[305] the flesh,[306] the Enemy,[307] or God.[308]

It matters what you allow to stand in a privileged vantage point of authority over your beliefs, or for that matter, over your values, attitudes, and motives. The behavior produced as a result of the interaction between these components will be directly related to what stands as an authority over them.

It matters which belief system you embrace. Our beliefs provide the foundation for our values, our worldview, and our motives.

The Principle

Our central beliefs *establish* *our core values. Our core values* *inform* *our perceptual attitudes, our worldview. Our worldview,* *conditions* *our motives. And our motives* *energize* *our behavior. Our behavior* *reflects* *what is stored in our heart.*

To demonstrate how this relationship plays out in a real-life scenario, let's look at a dysfunctional family led by an abusive, alcoholic father. He has four sons; one of whom is a devoted follower of Christ. The father comes home in a drunken rage. Each brother responds or behaves differently.

PERSON	CORE BELIEF	VALUE	ATTITUDE	MOTIVE	BEHAVIOR
Brother #1	Power rules.	No one gets in my way.	Intimidation	Safety/Survival	Fight
Brother #2	Peace at all cost.	I just do what people like.	Appeasement	Safety/Survival	Pacify
Brother #3	Pain should be avoided.	I just stay out of the way.	Flight	Safety/Survival	Flee
Brother #4	God so loved the world.	God can change anyone.	Understanding	Unconditional Love	Intervention

Notice the interplay between beliefs, values, attitudes, and motives of each son. The point to be made is that habitual reactions to circumstances early

305 1 John 2:15–17; 1 Peter 2:11
306 Mark 7:20–23
307 1 Peter 5:8–9
308 Titus 2:11–14

in life can become acting behavior when conflict arises later in life. If you are predisposed to fight, flight, or appeasement, you will behave similarly in any conflictive situation.

1. Brother #1—Intimidation (Fight)

He responds to his father by facing up to him. When confronted by his father, he pushes back, if not physically then verbally. His motive is safety and survival. His attitude is one of intimidation. The value that feeds this mix is one on which he acts—"No one gets in my way." The central belief that feeds his value, attitude, and motive and which results in his standing his ground, prepared to fight, is a belief that, in the end, power rules. His perception is that if he is confronted with conflict—or in this case, danger—it is better to fight.

A variety of causes could lead to acting on this particular belief. A person's temperament, environment, and circumstances may make this particular belief the most viable option for him. Let's not forget the power of willful sin that feeds this belief system has a negative impact which can lead to a dysfunctional behavioral lifestyle. In any case, this belief is deeply embedded, and his behavior is driven by it.

If the trajectory of this son's life is not intercepted by the grace of God and changed, he will continue to operate in this fashion any time he is confronted with conflict or a perceived danger. When his position is threatened in a boardroom, for example, his response will be to aggressively confront the conflict through intimidation and force.

2. Brother #2—Pacification (Appeasement)

When faced with the specter of an abusive father, brother #2 responds by appeasing his father. He offers some form of service that might appeal to his father and, he hopes, quell his father's anger or diminish its affects. His behavior is one of pacification. His motive is the same as brother #1—safety and survival. Appeasement is the lens through which he tries to make sense of something he cannot control.

Compromise becomes his tool of choice to dissipate the force of his father's aggressive behavior. He may fawn over his father or provide a distraction that might appeal to him and reduce his anger. The value that likely conditions his attitude and motivates him to pacify suggests the importance of finding some means that is acceptable to the father. In other words, "If I do what people like, life will be easier for me. Conflicts will be fewer."

The central belief underlying his value, attitude, and motive that results in such reactive behavior might be a belief that peace at all costs will win the day. Like brother #1, the reliance on this belief may be the result of personality predisposition, his environment, circumstances out of his control, abuse that has wounded him deeply, or sin.

When confronted with conflict in a boardroom setting, his behavioral pattern might be to compromise or pacify the aggressor or source of conflict. This could lead to a result that may be harmful to others or to the organization as a whole. It could also lead to withdrawal and resentment over time.

3. Brother # 3—Avoidance (Flight)

This brother responds to his father by fleeing and staying out of sight until the "storm" passes. His motive is the same as his two brothers—safety and survival—but his attitude is different. His worldview sees flight as the only viable option when danger is encountered. After all, isn't it better to flee and live another day than risk emotional danger by standing up to the problem or compromising one's identity in the process? These responses may not seem entirely rational, but they are certainly understandable.

His value in this situation may be the simple appreciation of staying out of the way to avoid the problem. He flees from conflict because his central belief may be that escaping pain is a natural response to danger, so it is all right and preferable to do so.

In the same boardroom situation, he meets conflict with absence—he is nowhere to be found, or he uses some excuse to leave. It is a pattern that happens every time he is faced with a potentially conflictive situation. It happens in his marriage when an argument arises. It will manifest itself in every arena of his life, until God intervenes and replaces his corrupted belief with truth.

4. Brother # 4—Intervention (Interaction)

This brother is a fully committed follower of Christ, whose belief system has been calibrated with God's truth. He believes and trusts that God loves the world—and that includes his abusive father. His father was created in the image of God, and God loves him, even though his despicable behavior has caused great pain in the family. The son does not condone his father's behavior, but he understands that it is the result of sin and corruption.

His value is "God can change anyone"—even his father. His attitude is one of understanding how his father has arrived at such a state; that alcohol was a poor substitute for what is really bothering his father. Now, alcohol is in control. The son's motive is born out of unconditional love—a natural result of his belief system, values, and perceptual attitudes. His behavior is not fight, pacification, or flight, but intervention. He knows his father's lifestyle choices can be changed, but first he must deal with his alcoholism by intervention methods.

Even though he has suffered like his brothers, his response is different because he has chosen to act on truth rather than lies. His source of truth is God.

The point ...

The point of this case study is to illustrate the power of redemption and the importance of operating from truth instead of corrupted beliefs, values, worldview, and motives. The organizing principle of brother # 4 is a Christ-centric belief system.

Conclusion

Change a person's central beliefs and his behavior will follow. In his book *Victory Over Darkness*, Neil T. Anderson said, "A productive behavior system is the by-product of a solid Christian belief system, not the other way around."

To change our behavior, we must have a change of heart.

- Our central beliefs must be tuned to the truth of God's Word.
- Our core values must reflect the character and person of Christ.

- Our attitudes about life must mirror God's perspective.
- Our motives must correlate with God's purposes.

When that happens ...

- The world can't help but take notice.
- Our character can't help but produce godliness.
- Our actions can't help but make a significant impact.
- Our behavior can't help but bring glory to God.

We choose who or what will control our lives—the world, the flesh, the devil, or the Spirit of God. We can stop the influence of the first three at the threshold.[309] It's our choice! Scripture tells us that we will reap what we sow in our heart.[310] "The one who sows to please his sinful nature, from that nature will reap destruction; the one who sows to please the Spirit, from the Spirit will reap eternal life."

BATTLE PLAN

1. Identify one **central belief** that can be validated as a belief through a concrete example of how it impacted your behavior.
2. Identify one **value** that resulted in a decision in a given situation. Give a concrete example.
3. Identify an **attitude** that helped you evaluate a given circumstance, situation, or event. Give a concrete example.
4. Identify a **motive** that stimulated you to act for good or bad. Give a concrete example.

309 2 Corinthians 10:3–5
310 Galatians 6:7–8

CHAPTER 6
THE BATTLEFRONT OF BELIEFS

To the Jews who had believed him, Jesus said, "If you hold to my teaching, you are really my disciples. Then you will know the truth, and the truth will set you free."

John 8:31–32

What do we truly believe?

What do we truly believe, as opposed to what we say we believe? Generally, it's easier to observe behavior over time to discover the underlying belief system that gives rise to behavior. When we ask someone what he believes, we may simply hear what he affirms or what he thinks we want to hear, but it bears little correlation with how he acts. Others can't tell you what they really believe. Some of our beliefs, good or bad, are the result of early life experiences.

For instance, a father, whose child loves him, divorces the child's mother and abandons the family. The child feels rejected and decides that no adult can be trusted. This initial belief becomes a generalized belief pattern—human beings are not to be trusted. He grows up distrusting others, resulting in isolation from others and the inability to form a loving and trusting bond.

In another example, an adolescent is exposed to pornography on the Internet and becomes enmeshed in its allure. Repeatedly giving into temptation in this area results in bondage to sexually explicit pictures. His idea of gratifying sex is distorted and corrupted as a result, and it impacts his relationships with the opposite sex.

In yet another example, an adult who has not proactively cultivated a healthy philosophy of life is exposed to a "get rich" scheme that promises wealth and power. Not having a counterbalance to this philosophy, he succumbs to its promises, realizes some financial return, and now believes the road to success is the accumulation of wealth by any means.

Many of us can't trace the circumstances that led to our ingrained beliefs. They may be the result of family of origin issues, personal tragedies, abuse, lack of discipline and restraint, influence by significant others, various crises in our lives, or compelling (but worldly) philosophies.

In most cases, it's just plain sin. Once we compromise our beliefs on the altar of expediency, it's simply a matter of time before a "stronghold" is established in our lives. Sin has a way of burrowing down into the deep places of our hearts and taking up residence to influence our behavior. You may have heard the following refrain:

> **Sow a thought, reap an attitude. Sow an attitude, reap an action.**
>
> **Sow an action, reap a habit. Sow a habit, reap a lifestyle.**

It is an apt description of how strongholds are established in our lives.

How we finish the following statements will reveal what we really believe, if we are honest about our responses.

- I would be more successful if …
- I would be more significant if …
- I would be more satisfied if …
- I would be happier if …
- I would be more at peace if …
- I would have more fun if …

If central beliefs indeed determine our behavior, what kind of behavior can we expect from those who may hold the following central beliefs?

- Might makes right.
- The end justifies the means.
- Truth is relative and personal.
- The Bible is merely ancient literature.
- Power is success.
- Success is significance.
- Performance is all that matters.

- Every person has the right to live as he or she chooses.
- We are a product of our environment.
- The majority or consensus should determine our course.
- There is no God.
- Man is an animal of a higher order.
- Luck and chance determines our fate.
- There are no absolutes.
- Image is everything.
- Money solves all problems.
- Life is a compromise.
- Time heals all wounds.
- People are untrustworthy.
- Life is threatening or hostile.
- Everything is right somewhere; nothing is right everywhere.
- No culture is better or worse than another.
- There are no objective morals, just differing opinions.
- Just go with the flow.
- Anything goes.
- Beauty is in the eye of the beholder.

If you hold to one or more of these beliefs, your behavior may result in activity that will lead you to places you may not want to go. For instance, if you believe that *power is success* you might behave in a manipulative or coercive manner by exercising authority over another person. Lord Acton once said, "Power corrupts. Absolute power corrupts absolutely."

If you believe that *performance is all that matters*, your identity as a person will be in what you can accomplish, instead of who you are in Christ. If you believe that *the end justifies the means*, you might be capable of despicable behavior, just to get what you want.

On the other hand, the Ten Commandments present a compelling central belief system. The first four commandments deal with our relationship with God. The remaining six commandments have to do with our relationship with others.

The Ten Commandments[311]

1. You shall have no other gods before Me.

---

311 Exodus 20:2–17

2. You shall not make yourself any graven image, or any likeness of anything that is in the heavens above, or that is in the earth beneath, or that is in the water under the earth.

3. You shall not take the name of the Lord your God in vain; for the Lord will not hold him guiltless who takes His name in vain.

4. Remember the Sabbath day to keep it holy.

5. Honor your father and mother, that your days may be long in the land the Lord your God gives you.

6. You shall not commit murder.

7. You shall not commit adultery.

8. You shall not steal.

9. You shall not bear witness falsely against your neighbor.

10. You shall not covet your neighbor's house, your neighbor's wife, or his manservant, or his maidservant, or his ox, or his donkey, or anything that is your neighbor's.

In the New Testament, Jesus summarizes the commandments as follows:

"Love the Lord your God with all your heart and with all your soul and with all your mind [the first four commandments]. *This is the first and greatest commandment. And the second is like it: Love your neighbor as yourself* [the remaining six commandments]. *All the Law and the Prophets hang on these two commandments."*[312]

These directives are still in force today for Christians. The difference is that the indwelling Holy Spirit empowers the believer to fulfill the commandments. We obey these commandments out of love for God, rather than obligation to God. We can choose to obey them or to disobey them. Obedience leads to an ordered life that will bring glory to God. If you were to adopt the Ten Commandments as your central belief system—that is, what you trust in, rely on, and cling to—how would your behavior change?

Our central beliefs must be tuned to the truth of God's word. When we analyze what we truly believe and compare it to God's truth, we will see if our beliefs are based on truth. We may be living our lives based on lies rather than God's truth. Our belief system may simply be the product of the world, our own desires, or the Enemy's lies.

---

312 Matthew 22:37–41

It matters what we allow to inform and have authority over our beliefs. Whatever influences our beliefs will influence our values, worldview, and motives. The

Privileged Vantage Point

- Tradition
- Heritage
- Reason
- Experience
- Some 'ism'
- Philosophy
- **Jesus Christ (bible)**

behavior that will result may or may not bring glory and honor to God. Such influences might include tradition, heritage, reason, experience, some "-isms" (such as humanism, secularism, or postmodernism), philosophy, ideology, religion, or culture. For the Christian, it must be Christ. *"To the Jews who had believed him, Jesus said, "If you hold to my teaching, you are really my disciples. Then you will know the truth, and the truth will set you free."*[313]

Implications of Beliefs

In an article titled "Doctrine and Ethics,"[314] Alister McGrath makes the following comments in response to questions I pose below:

1. From the author's point of view, why is the recovery of Christian doctrine (beliefs) fundamental to a recovery of Christian ethics?[315]

   Thinking people need to construct and inhabit mental worlds. They need to be able to discern some degree of ordering within their experience, to make sense of the riddles and enigmas. They need to be able to structure human existence in the world, to allow it to possess meaning and purpose, to allow decisions to be made concerning the future of their existence. In order for anyone—Christian, atheist, Marxist, Muslim—to make informed moral decisions, it is necessary to have a set of values concerning human life. Those

---

313 John 8:31–32

314 Alister McGrath. "Doctrine and Ethics." *Journal of the Evangelical Theological Society 34,2* (June 1991): 145–156.

315 Ethics: The discipline dealing with what is good and bad and with moral duty and obligation; a set of moral principles or values; a theory or system of moral values; the principles of conduct governing an individual or a group; a guiding philosophy; the study of human conduct and values (Merriam-Webster).

values are determined by beliefs, and those beliefs are stated as doctrines. Christian doctrine thus provides a fundamental framework for Christian living.[316]

2. What place should Christian doctrine (beliefs) have in Christian living?

The one thing I am here to say to you is this: that it is worse than useless for Christians to talk about the importance of Christian morality, unless they are prepared to take their stand upon the fundamentals of Christian theology. It is a lie to say that dogma does not matter; it matters enormously. It is fatal to let people suppose that Christianity is only a mode of feeling; it is virtually necessary to insist that it is first and foremost a rational explanation of the universe. It is hopeless to offer Christianity as a vaguely idealistic aspiration of a simple and consoling kind; it is, on the contrary, a hard, tough, exacting and complex doctrine, steeped in a drastic and uncompromising realism.[317]

3. What makes Jesus Christ different from any other notable moral or religious teacher in human history?

To allow that Jesus is a religious teacher is to raise the question of his authority. Why should we take him seriously? Although we have been fortunate enough to have had the advice of countless moral and religious teachers in human history, what makes Jesus different? What singles him out as commanding attention? It is untenable to suggest that Jesus' authority rests upon the excellence of his moral and religious teaching. To make this suggestion is to imply that Jesus has authority only when he happens to agree with us. We thus would have authority over Jesus.

In fact, however, the teaching of Jesus has authority on account of who Jesus is—and the identity and significance of Jesus can only be spelled out in doctrinal terms. It is doctrine that explains why and how Jesus' words and deeds have divine rather than purely human authority. It is doctrine that singles

---

316 McGrath, 84.
317 D. L. Sayers, *Creed or Chaos?* (London: Methuen, 1974), 28.

*out Jesus Christ, and none other, as being God incarnate ...
the authority of Jesus' moral and religious teaching thus rests
firmly upon a doctrinal foundation.*[318]

4. What role should truth play in one's belief system?

*Beneath all the rhetoric about relevance lies a profoundly
disturbing possibility: that people may base their lives upon
an illusion, upon a blatant lie. The attractiveness of a belief
is all too often inversely proportional to its truth. In the
sixteenth century, the radical writer and preacher Thomas
Muntzer led a revolt of German peasants against their
political masters. On the morning of the decisive encounter
between the peasants and the armies of the German princes,
Muntzer promised that those who followed him would be
unscathed by the weapons of their enemies. Encouraged by
this attractive and meaningful belief, the peasants stiffened
their resolve. The outcome was a catastrophe. Six thousand
peasants were slaughtered in the ensuing battle, and six
hundred were captured. Barely a handful escaped. Their
belief in invulnerability was relevant. It was attractive. It
was meaningful. It was also a crude and cruel lie, without
any foundation in truth. The last hours of that pathetic group
of trusting men rested on an utter illusion. It was only when
the first salvos cut some of their number to ribbons that they
realized they had been deceived."*

*Christian doctrine is concerned to declare that Christian
morality rests upon a secure foundation. An obedient
response to truth is a mark of intellectual integrity. It marks
a willingness to hear what purports to be truth, to judge it,
and—if it is found to be true—to accept it willingly. Truth
demands to be accepted because it inherently deserves to be
accepted and acted upon. Christianity recognizes a close link
between faith and obedience—making it imperative that
the ideas underlying and giving rise to attitudes and actions
should be judged and found to be right.*[319]

318 McGrath 86.
319 Ibid., 88–89.

5. What problems will the church encounter if it does not take doctrine (beliefs) seriously?

A church that takes doctrine seriously is a church that is obedient to and responsible for what God has entrusted to it. Doctrine gives substance and weight to what the Christian church has to offer the world. A church that despises or neglects doctrine comes perilously close to losing its reason for existence and may simply lapse into a comfortable conformity with the world—or whatever part of the world it happens to feel most at home with. Its agenda is set by the world; its presuppositions are influenced by the world; its outlook mirrors that of the world. There are few more pathetic sights than a church wandering aimlessly from one "meaningful" issue to another in a desperate search for relevance in the eyes of the world.[320]

6. What does the author mean by a "new dark age"? How would you assess the current status of morality in our country?

A crucial turning point in that earlier history occurred when men and women of good will turned aside from the task of shoring up the Roman imperia and ceased to identify the continuation of civility and moral community with the maintenance of the imperia. What they set themselves to achieve instead—often not recognizing fully what they were doing—was the construction of new forms of community within which the moral life could be sustained so that both morality and civility might survive the coming ages of barbarism and darkness. If my account of our moral condition is correct, we ought also to conclude that for some time now we too have reached that turning point. "

What matters at this stage is the construction of local forms of community within which civility and the intellectual and moral life can be sustained through the new dark ages which are already upon us. And if the tradition of the virtues was

---

320 Ibid., 89.

*able to survive the horrors of the last dark ages, we are not
entirely without ground for hope.*[321]

7. So what does this metaphor mean for us today?

The old Dark Ages was marked by fear of the unknown
and reliance upon the learned for exegesis of the world
around them. Knowledge and wisdom resided with the
aristocracy and the church. Individual study of God's
word was left to the so-called scholars with agendas.
Interpretation was under the sole purview of these
authorities. The common man and woman relied upon
others for truth. The reformation broke that bondage.
Luther's rebellion essentially gave the Scriptures back to
the people.

MacIntyre suggests we are in a *new dark age.* Living in
the fast lane and susceptible to the tyranny of the urgent
has compelled many of us to rely on new authorities for
knowledge and wisdom. These subject-matter experts can
be found on newscasts, talk shows, newsstands, and some
pulpits. Because of our hectic lifestyles, we turn to "sound
bites" from popular celebrities, inside and outside of the
church, for "truth." I agree with MacIntyre—we are
living in the new dark ages. When the organizing center
of our beliefs, values, worldview, and motives shifts from
the Bible to a pluralistic syncretism and amalgamation of
philosophies and ideologies, it won't be long before we
lose our way and fall into factions and special-interest
groups that fit our preconceived notions and whims.

The Bible tells us that we are to *"watch our lives and
doctrine closely."*[322] *Preach the Word; be prepared in season
and out of season; correct, rebuke and encourage-with great
patience and careful instruction. For the time will come (and
I believe is upon us now) when men will not put up with
sound doctrine. Instead, to suit their own desires, they will
gather around them a great number of teachers to say what*

---

321 Ibid., 89–90.
322 1 Timothy 4:16

their itching ears want to hear. They will turn their ears away from the truth and turn aside to myths. But you, keep your head in all situations, endure hardship, do the work of an evangelist, discharge all the duties of your ministry.[323]

8. What do you think of the author's concept of colonies of heaven?

Let us think of ourselves, our seminaries, our churches, and our families as colonies of heaven, as outposts of the real eternal city, who seek to keep its laws in the midst of alien territory. C. S. Lewis gave us many helpful ways of thinking about the Christian life, and one of the most helpful is that of the world as Enemy territory, territory occupied by invading forces. In the midst of this territory, as resistance groups, are the communities of faith. We must never be afraid to be different from the world around us. It is very easy for Christians to be depressed by the fact that the world scorns our values and standards. But the image of the colony sets this in its proper context. At Philippi the civilizing laws of Rome contrasted with the anarchy (a state of lawlessness) or political disorder of its hinterland (regions outside of Rome)."

And so our moral vision—grounded in Scripture, sustained by faith, given intellectual spine by Christian doctrine—stands as a civilizing influence in the midst of a world that seems to have lost its moral way. If a new dark age indeed lies ahead of us—indeed, if it is already upon us—then it is vital that the Christian moral vision, like the torch of liberty, is kept alight. Doctrine, I firmly and passionately believe, gives us the framework for doing precisely that. It can be done—and must be done.[324]

Matching Behaviors to Beliefs

It might prove helpful to suggest behaviors that might arise from certain beliefs. Many different behaviors could emanate from a given belief. The following are offered as possibilities:

323 2 Timothy 4:2–5
324 Ibid., 90–91.

Beliefs	Behaviors
There are no absolutes.	Ridicules universal truths
Might makes right.	Confrontational
I'm ugly.	Insecurity
The world is against me.	Always the victim
The environment sustains life.	Environmental activist
The wealth of the world belongs to everybody.	Overthrow of Russian monarchy
For God so loved the world.	Conducts an intervention with alcoholic father
Manifest Destiny: God wants the United States to own all land.	Subjugation of native tribes in the American West
Performance is all that matters.	Being a workaholic
Ethnic contamination breeds inferiority.	Jews are exterminated

When we look at behaviors, we can identify a possible underlying belief.

- Taking bribes might be supported by the belief that a greater good might occur or that I deserve remuneration for my efforts.

- An extramarital affair might be justified with a belief that sexual liaisons outside of marriage bring renewal to one's marriage or that man can't be expected to resist when someone offers sex, or that biological urges are meant to be satisfied.

- Cheating on our taxes could be warranted from a belief that the government gets more than its fair share or that it's all right if you can get away with it or everyone does it.

- Lying is a justifiable behavior when we believe everyone lies or that lying is acceptable when a human life is at risk, or that lying is all right if it doesn't really hurt anyone or if it produces a greater good.

- Honesty may be practiced because of a belief that honesty is the best policy, that you don't have to worry about it later, or that God wants us to be truthful.

Foundational Beliefs Versus Operational Beliefs

Foundational beliefs provide the stable platform of our existence. They are absolute truths that establish our relationship with our Creator and His created world. They are foundational in nature and give us confidence, hope, and orientation for our journey. They establish the fact that we are connected to our Creator, and they answer the fundamental questions of our existence, identity, purpose, and destiny. They inform our journey. They have to do with our *beingness*.

Operational beliefs are also absolute truths. The difference, however, is that they are actionable—they compel us to do something. They require a response and provide a general guideline for our behavior and actions. They provide the basis for our values—the filter through which we process our decisions; the hills on which we are prepared to die; the principles we intend to live out in our daily lives. They have to do with our *doingness*.

Foundational Beliefs

- All human beings carry the image of God in their person.
- The image of God in us is marred by sin.
- Human beings are moral creatures.
- Universal moral laws exist and are ordained by God.
- The chief purpose of man is to glorify God and enjoy Him forever.
- Sin alienates us from God and enslaves us.
- Man is created in the image of God (Gen 1:26–27).
- God has placed eternity in our hearts (Eccl 3:11).
- All human beings long for purpose, progress, and permanence.
- Human beings have a need for forgiveness and redemption.
- Christ's redemptive work is the basis for human salvation.
- Receiving Christ as Savior and Lord brings …
  - a new birth (John 3:3–21).
  - a new heart (Gal. 2:20).
  - a new relationship with God (Heb. 8:10a12).
  - a new power to live (1 John 3:1–2).

- The Christian has God's nature and Spirit within.
- The Bible is the Christian's ultimate authority for faith and practice (2 Tim. 3:16–17; Heb. 4:12).
- Physical death is not the end of our existence.[325]

Other Foundational Beliefs

- God created the heavens and the earth (Gen 1:1).
- God is our Creator (Gen 1:26–27).
- Jesus is God (John 1:1–4, 14).
- Jesus loves us unconditionally (1 John 4:13–19; Gal. 2:20).
- I am a permanent member of His family (Eph. 1:5).
- God's love knows no limits (John 3:16).
- God is not a God of confusion but a God of peace (1 Cor. 14:33).
- Jesus came so that He could die for sin (1 Cor. 15:3).
- Jesus will one day return (John 14:3; Acts 1:11; Rev. 22:7-21).
- The resurrection of the dead (1 Cor. 15:12-58).
- The final defeat of Satan (Rev. 20:7-10).
- There is one true God (Rom. 3:30; 1 Cor. 8:6; Eph. 4:6; 1 Tim. 2:5; Jam. 2:19).
- God reveals Himself in nature (Rom. 1:18–20).
- God reveals Himself in Christ (John 10:30; John 17:22–26).
- Human beings are born sinners (Rom. 7:5–17; Rom. 3:23).
- Jesus Christ is both God and man (Phil. 2:5–11).
- Salvation is through Christ alone (1 Tim. 2:5–6).
- Judgment is coming (Rev. 20:11-15).
- I am forgiven (Eph. 1:7).
- God ordained marriage between a man and a woman (Gen. 2:18–24; Matt. 19:4–5).
- The truth sets us free when we obey it (John 8:31–32).
- My highest purpose is to bring glory to God (1 Pet. 2:9; Eph. 1:12, 1 Cor. 10:31).
- I am to remember that God has raised me to a higher life (Eph. 2:1–7).
- Love is unconditional and others-oriented (1 Cor. 13:4–8).
- In everything, God works for good (Rom. 8:28).

325 Adapted from chapter 2 of *Worldviews in Conflict* by Ronald Nash (1992).

- All of creation suffers as a consequence of sin (Rom. 8:18–25).
- I will not be free of suffering here on earth (1 Pet. 1:6; 4:13; Rom. 5:3; 2 Tim. 1:8; Phil. 3:10).

Operational Beliefs

- I have a destiny to fulfill (Jer. 29:11).
- I have a contribution to make (1 Cor. 12:4-7).
- I have a ministry to complete (Eph. 4:11–16).
- I have a legacy to leave (2 Tim. 2:2; 1 Chron. 28:8).
- I am to love our neighbors as ourselves (Matt. 22:39).
- I am to keep God's commandments (Eccl. 12:13; Matt. 5:17–19; 1 John 5:2–3).
- I am to aim my life at righteousness and godliness (1 Tim. 6:11).
- I am to abstain from immorality (1 Thess. 4:3–8).
- My life should be an act of worship to God (Rom. 12:1–2; Col 3:17).
- I am to put to death that which is earthly in me (Col. 3:5–10).
- My thoughts should be honorable and pure (Phil. 4:8).
- I am to put on the whole armor of God (Eph. 6:10–18).
- I am to love my wife as God loves the church (Eph. 5:25).
- I am to love the Lord with all my heart, soul, and mind (Matt. 22:37).
- Christ-likeness is my objective (Eph. 4:13, 15; Rom. 8:29; 2 Cor. 3:18).
- I am to live a life worthy of His calling (Eph. 4:1–2; Col 1:10).
- I am to live a sober, upright, and godly life (Titus 2:11–14).
- The heart is to be guarded (Prov. 4:23).
- I am to make wise use of my time (Eph. 5:15–16).
- I am to expose the works of darkness (Eph. 5:11).
- I am to walk by the Spirit and not my flesh (Gal. 5:16–26).
- I am to be God's love letter to the world (2 Cor. 3:2–3).
- All things are to be done decently and in order (1 Cor. 14:40).
- I am to seek the good of my neighbor first (1 Cor. 10:24).
- My body is the temple of the Holy Spirit (1 Cor. 6:19–20).

- I am not to yield to wickedness (Rom 6:12–13).
- I am to never flag in zeal (Rom. 12:11).
- I am to live in harmony with others (Rom. 12:14–21).
- The truth sets us free when we obey it (John 8:31–32).
- My highest purpose is to bring glory to God (1 Pet. 2:9; Eph. 1:12, 1 Cor. 10:31).
- I am to remember that God has raised me to a higher life (Eph. 2:1–7).
- In everything, God works for good (Rom. 8:28).
- Spiritual warfare is our greatest battle (Eph. 6:10-17).[326]

Conclusion

There is good reason to state that beliefs are the foundation upon which all else is built. What you believe (trust in, rely on, and cling to) at the core of your being will influence your values, attitudes (worldview), and motives, the combination of which will result in behavior that will bring either glory and honor to the Lord or dishonor and shame. Look at it this way: if you begin a journey, and you start that journey one degree off your intended direction, how far might you be off by the time you've reached ten miles from your starting point? You could end up in the wrong place at the end of the journey—lost, trying to find your way.

What you believe is critical to your journey. McGrath once again helps us understand the importance of beliefs:

Beliefs are important because they claim to describe the way things are. They assert that they declare the truth about reality. But beliefs are not just ideas that are absorbed by our minds and that have no further effect upon us. They affect what we do and what we feel. They influence our hopes and fears. They determine the way we behave. A Japanese fighter pilot of the Second World War might [have believed] that destroying the enemies of his emperor ensured his immediate entry into paradise—and, as many American navy personnel discovered to their cost, this belief expressed itself in quite definite actions. Such pilots had no hesitation in launching suicide attacks on American warships. Doctrines are ideas—but they are more than mere ideas. They are the foundation of our understanding of the world and our place within it.[327]

---

326 Adapted from various sources.
327 McGrath, 87.

BATTLE PLAN

1. Identify five central beliefs you hold that can be verified by concrete examples of behaviors that arise from them.

2. Ask your spouse or the person closest to you what he or she thinks are your central beliefs and what he or she has observed about you in this regard.

3. What central beliefs do you hold that you would like to change? Why?

4. What "strongholds" of the Enemy are you struggling with? Find someone you trust and share your situation with him. Ask him to pray for you and hold you accountable by checking up on you from time to time in this area.

5. Of the operational beliefs identified earlier, which ones resonate with you? Why?

6. If the Ten Commandments (Exodus 20:1–17) were firmly established as your central belief system, what changes would happen in your life?

7. Identify an additional Christian belief system listed in this chapter that would condition your life in such a way as to produce God-honoring behavior.

CHAPTER 7
THE BATTLEFRONT OF VALUES

This is the covenant I will make with the house
of Israel after that time, declares the Lord.

I will put my laws in their minds and
write them on their hearts.

I will be their God, and they will be my people.

Hebrews 8:10

Once again, values are the hills on which we are prepared to die, the principles by which we intend to live, the filter through which we make life's decisions. Every decision we have made, are making, or will make is based on the values we hold, whether or not we can articulate them. It might be argued that only sociopaths, the insane, the addicted while under the influence, and babies have no value system.

Generally, however, the rest of us do have a value system from which we make decisions in life. For many of us, our system of values is an unordered set of qualities often in conflict with one another. One day, we make a decision of merit; the next day, a bad decision with negative consequences. For still others, the consistency of the decisions they make may indicate a congruent system of values.

Like beliefs, values can be aspirations rather than observable realities in our lives. Men and women often ask me to mentor them. They know I am big on values, so they often begin their comments by stating their values. I listen intently and respectfully. I then ask them the following question: "What decision have you made or what action have you taken within the last three months that gives evidence of the values you say you hold?" Many of them cannot give me any examples. This is due to the fact that the values they say they hold may simply be an interest, preference, or affirmation but not an actionable commitment as yet.

In *Readings and Christian Ethics, Volume 1: Theory and Method* Drs. David Clark and Bob Rakestraw of Bethel Seminary provided helpful information regarding values and associated terms, such as morality, character, virtues, ethics, principles, and rules.

> *Values*, in the moral sense, are qualities (such as loyalty, truthfulness, or justice) that human beings esteem and toward which they direct their moral behavior. When a value becomes an operational part of one's character, and [he acts] on it without deliberation or conscious consideration, it is called a *virtue*. Hunter Lewis describes values as personal commitments that propel us to action. Leith Anderson says that values explain why we do what we do. They govern our underlying thoughts, attitudes, and decisions that result in behavior.

> *Morality* is the dimension of life related to right conduct, including virtuous character, honorable intentions, and right actions. It can be seen as a system of moral conduct, particular moral principles or rules of conduct, or conformity to ideals of right human conduct.

> *Character* is the combination of natural and acquired features and traits that constitute a person's nature or fundamental disposition, from which specific moral responses issue.

> *Virtue* is the moral stance or constitution of an individual, consisting not merely of a collection of individual virtues, but the strength of character to coordinate and exercise the virtues in a way that makes him morally praiseworthy—a quality of character by which an individual habitually recognizes and does the right thing.

> *Virtues* are specific dispositions, skills, or qualities of excellence that together make up a person's character and that influence his or her way of life. Plato identified four cardinal virtues to which all mankind was to strive: prudence or wisdom, courage or fortitude, temperance or moderation or self-control, and justice. They are called cardinal virtues because all other virtues hinge on these

four. To these, Augustine added three Christian virtues: faith, hope, and love.

Ethics is the discipline that deals with what is good and bad and with moral duty and obligation; a set of moral principles or values; a theory or system of moral values; the principles of conduct that govern an individual or a group; a guiding philosophy; the study of human conduct and values.

Principles are broad moral guidelines and precepts that are more foundational and more general than rules. *Rules* are concrete and specific directives for conduct that derive from principles.

In *Readings in Christian Ethics*,[328] the following point is made: "Emphasis on virtue is prominent in ancient philosophers such as Plato and Aristotle, and Christian theologians like Augustine and Aquinas emphasized virtue. The focus of virtue is on the character of an individual rather than on the individual's obligations. Rather than developing principles by which we make decisions, the emphasis should be on the development of virtuous people who will then make decisions that lead to the good of the individual and society. The Bible emphasizes our duty to obey God. Virtue grows as a consequence of obedience."[329]

William May, in the same book, shows the relationship between beliefs and engrained values (virtues). He insists, and I agree, that virtues arise from beliefs. He makes the following points: 1) many virtues directly correlate with principles and ideals (beliefs); and 2) a society without commitment to principles (beliefs) would not allow virtues to flourish.[330] His comments give us insight into why our culture is disintegrating around us. We do not espouse a central belief system. Therefore, our values are widely divergent and often contradictory. Coherence, continuity, and unity of our souls depend on adoption of biblically centered beliefs and biblically informed values.

---

328 David Clark and Robert Rakestraw, eds. *Readings in Christian Ethics, Volume 1: Theory and Method.* Baker Academic, 1994.
329 Clark, 247–8.
330 Ibid., 249.

Why all the specifics? Simply because values are so important for navigating life. Within our character is a system of morality composed of values on which we act daily and virtues on which we act without thinking. These values may consist of principles, precepts, or rules that we employ as we interact with the world around us.

So what's the point? A biblically informed value system, established by biblical beliefs and consciously acted upon in a consistent and congruent way, will help us live a godly life—the primary objective of God's preferred lifestyle, as discussed in chapter 3.

Too many of us operate from an incongruent set of values informed by opposing authorities, such as tradition, experience, some ideology or philosophy, culture, or some "-isms," such as humanism, secularism or postmodernism. All too often, our values are suppressed in our subconscious. Yet we act in direct relation to them, even though we cannot identify them or describe them. Nevertheless, they have influence on our behavior.

A key point to remember: a value doesn't become a virtue until it becomes a habit in our life. A value must be practiced in the same direction over time before it becomes a part of our spiritual DNA. The Holy Spirit will empower us as we act on our value. Scenarios where our values may come into play are often set in motion by circumstances, events, and people. Added to this mix are God's periodic integrity-checks, which he uses to shape our character.

When I had been at the seminary for a little over six months, I was approached by a colleague one Sunday before services. He asked if I would like to go to lunch with him and his wife. There had been friction between us in the past, and I was glad I had an excuse not to accept his invitation—at least, that was my justification. I am embarrassed to say that my "excuse" was that I'd planned to go to the mall to look for motorized treadmills. I declined by saying that I had something I had to do. Not five minutes later, the president of the university approached me and asked if I could go to lunch with him and his wife. Without thinking, I said yes. As soon as the words were out of my mouth, I was convicted by the Holy Spirit. I wasn't going to give up that easily. I spent the entire time during the sermon arguing with God on why I should go to lunch with the president and not with my colleague. The sermon that day was on integrity. By the end of the pastor's sermon, I had lost the argument. I approached the president after the service and told him I couldn't go to lunch with him. If I did, I would not become the man of integrity that was spoken about in the sermon. I found my colleague and told him that what I had planned to do was not that important and that I would go to lunch with him.

One of my values is to be a man of integrity. God used this situation as a values-check for me. I failed the integrity-check initially. I chose to act on my value by swallowing my pride and setting things right. I want the value of integrity to be real in my life. God will send integrity-checks, obedience-checks, and faith-checks to help forge our character. It may simply be a situation where we were given too much change at the grocery store, or we found a wallet, or we're tempted to fudge on our taxes, embellish our résumé, slander an associate, call in sick when we are not, or some other test. If a value is to be real in our life, it must be consciously acted upon in the same direction over an extended period of time. Otherwise, it is only an interest, preference, or respected option, or not yet a commitment.

I often tell others that no one cares what we have to say until they observe how we live. If we live a value-centered life—a life of integrity and honor under God's authority—they will ultimately listen to what we have to say. What we declare that we value is not always how we live. There is, however, absolute congruence with who we are at the core and how we behave for good or for bad.

Knowing What We Value

Just as there are statements that, once completed, will indicate what we truly believe, there are questions we can ask ourselves to determine what we truly value:

1. What is it that I treasure so highly that I am irritated when other people don't also treasure it?
2. What are the things I respect so deeply that I tend to be resentful of those who treat them with disrespect?
3. If I knew that I had six months to live, what would become the most important to me? What would become unimportant to me?
4. What core value(s) do I hope my children will adopt?

145

If it were possible to follow you around without being noticed for the next three months, I would be able to tell you what you truly valued. Your behavior over time would reveal your values. If I could talk to people close to you—a wife or a brother or a father or a mother—and I asked them what your values were, they could probably tell me. If I were to ask your work associates what you valued, they could probably tell me.

I often give an exercise to the people I mentor. I instruct them to meet with their spouse or loved one or someone who really knows them. They are to assure that person that there will be no argument with or consequences to his or her response when they ask this person the following question: "Based on your observations of my behaviors over time, what would you say are my values?"

When I conduct pre-marital counseling, I require a specific exercise of the couple before I will officiate at their wedding. I ask both of them to spend time together and determine which five values they want to apply in leading their family. They are not to discuss the values with each other until they come back to see me. Sometimes their values agree but often, each chooses values different from his or her mate. I then require them to work together on the five values they want to influence their relationship with each other and the children they may have together.

Relationship between Beliefs and Values

For each value you hold, there is an underlying belief or beliefs that establish that value. For instance, if I have a value that life is sacred, the underlying belief may be that man is created in the image of God. If I have a value that the environment is to be protected at all costs, my underlying belief might be that the environment sustains life. Several other connections are included in the table below:

BELIEF	VALUE
I am the only one who can fix it.	There is always someone to fix.
All pain is bad.	All pain is to be avoided.
I am not good enough.	An ideal of good is out there.
Most decisions are bad decisions.	Avoid making decisions.
I don't want to be insignificant.	Achievement is everything.
There are no absolutes.	Truth is relative.
I'm ugly.	Thin is beautiful.

We are created in the image of God.	Everyone has value.
A healthy lifestyle is important.	Smoking is unhealthy.
Humans are simply higher animals.	Animals have rights.
Love one another.	Care for strangers.
Your faith will be tested.	Persevere.
The truth will set you free.	Honesty is the best policy.
Cleanliness is a sign of a civilized society.	Cleanliness is next to godliness.

One belief can establish multiple values. Several related beliefs can establish a single value. There is no single belief that can produce one specific value alone. Values are often easy to distinguish. Underlying beliefs, however, are often difficult to determine. It is easier to observe a person's behavior over time to determine what he values or what he may believe.

Again, it matters what we allow to stand as an authority over your values. For instance, a Christian can have a value for truth—and so can a humanist or atheist. What that value produces in one's behaviors will more than likely be different from the others. A Christian's underlying belief may be that Jesus is the way, *the truth*, and the life, and if he holds to His teaching, he will know the truth, and the truth will set him free. His behavior has the focus of living by God's truth, instead of the world's truth. For the humanist, having a value for truth may be favorable for business or the esteem of respected colleagues. The practice of truth for the atheist may be to promote his or her beliefs as the only truth. So you see, what informs your values makes all the difference.

When values are loosely acquired without attention to any ordering structure or congruent belief system, the values can produce conflictive results—they may be inconsistent from one day to the next.

For the Christian, God's word—the Bible—brings consistency to our beliefs and the values that arise from those beliefs. Jesus is the personification of the values we should hold as believers. Scripture tells us: *Whatever is true, whatever is noble, whatever is right, whatever is pure, whatever is lovely, whatever is admirable—if anything is excellent or praiseworthy—think about such things. Whatever you have learned or received or heard from me, or seen in me—put it into practice. And the God of peace will be with you.* [331]

Elsewhere in Scripture, other values are identified: *His divine power has given us everything we need for life and **godliness** through our knowledge of him who called us by his own glory and goodness. Through these he has given us his very great and precious promises, so that through them you may participate in the divine nature and escape the corruption in the world caused by evil desires. For this very reason, make every effort to add to your **faith** **goodness**; and to goodness, **knowledge**; and to knowledge, **self-control**; and to self-control, **perseverance**; and to perseverance, **godliness**; and to godliness, **brotherly kindness**; and to brotherly kindness, **love**. For if you possess these **qualities** [values] in increasing measure, they will keep you from being ineffective and unproductive in your knowledge of our Lord Jesus Christ. But if anyone does not have them, he is nearsighted and blind, and has forgotten that he has been cleansed from his past sins.* [332]

The Importance of Wisdom as a Value

Proverbs teaches moral and ethical principles (values). The book of Proverbs is an excellent source for selecting biblically informed values for your life. I would strongly urge you to read Proverbs and identify the values that God esteems. In many cases, they are described in contrast to an evil counterpart.

The primary author of the book of Proverbs is Solomon, third king of Israel and the son of King David. The first nine chapters deal essentially with the value of wisdom. Chapters 10 through 22 represent a collection of single-verse proverbs. Proverbs 22:16 through 24:44 offers thirty sayings, called the Words of the Wise. Proverbs 25 through 31:9 include Solomon's wise sayings, the words of Agur, and the words of Lemuel. Chapter 31:10–31 is an oft-quoted poem on the virtuous woman.

Did you ever wonder why Solomon, when given an opportunity to ask for anything from God, chose wisdom? Some scholars believe he was in his late teens at the time. Do you know any seventeen-year-olds who would ask for wisdom? Later in his life, Solomon gathered his sons to pass on to them what he had learned from his father. The following dialogue answers these questions.

331 Philippians 4:8–9
332 2 Peter 1:3–9

Listen, my sons, to a father's instruction; pay attention and gain understanding. I give you sound learning, so do not forsake my teaching. When I was a boy in my father's house, still tender, and an only child of my mother, he taught me and said, "Lay hold of my words with all your heart; keep my commands and you will live. Get wisdom, get understanding; do not forget my words or swerve from them. Do not forsake wisdom, and she will protect you; love her, and she will watch over you. Wisdom is supreme; therefore get wisdom. Though it cost all you have, get understanding. Esteem her, and she will exalt you; embrace her, and she will honor you. She will set a garland of grace on your head and present you with a crown of splendor.[333]

The answer is obvious: Solomon's father, David, impressed upon Solomon at an early age the importance of wisdom. So, when given the opportunity, Solomon chose wisdom because his father valued wisdom.

The Value of Wisdom

When I was a pastor at College Avenue Baptist Church in San Diego, John MacArthur, senior pastor of Grace Community Church, founder of Masters Seminary, and author of numerous books, visited our church. I asked John MacArthur what he thought was the biggest problem facing Christians for the foreseeable future. His answer came quickly and consisted of one word—discernment!

Why do so many Christians seem to lack wisdom today? As early as the fourth century BCE, Plato the philosopher identified wisdom (prudence) as one of the four cardinal (hinge) virtues man should aspire to. We are buried in data today. Many of us lack wisdom because we haven't processed the data through the grid of God's word. Biblical, godly wisdom should head the list of our values and, we hope, become a living virtue in our lives.

Education should lead to insight. The question is, what level of insight—information, knowledge, or wisdom—will it help us obtain?

Many of us are living at the *information level* that is simply the ordered understanding of raw data. We do not give enough time to reflection,

---

333 Proverbs 4:1–9

leading to comprehension. The tyranny of the urgent, frenzied activity of our daily lives and the constant bombardment of data (TV, faxes, newspapers, magazines, Internet, e-mail, radio, audiotapes, iPods, superficial conversations, etc.) rob us of an ordered analysis of our world. We operate off sound bites instead of measured and thoughtful examination.

Many others are stuck at the ***knowledge level***, satisfied with the acquisition and accumulation of information that is ordered in such a way as to produce an intellectual grasp of the essentials—enough to converse intelligently on the subject but little more. The trouble with remaining at this level is that our mental comprehension doesn't move to applied wisdom. It never reaches our hearts.

We need to move to the ***wisdom level*** by prioritizing the acquisition and accumulation of knowledge into godly wisdom. This is accomplished by processing gained knowledge through the filter of God's word, the Bible. Our ultimate goal should be to apply that wisdom to life, in general, and to our lives, specifically, so that we are equipped for every good work.

In summary, **information** is the ordered understanding of raw data. **Knowledge** is meaning derived through study, reflection, and comprehension. **Wisdom** is knowledge applied, based on one's core beliefs and value system.

An example of these levels of insight can be found in Exodus 20, where we are exposed to information, the existence of the Ten Commandments. We develop a knowledge about them when, through study and reflection, we comprehend their meaning (i.e., the first four commandments address our relationship with God, and the remaining six commandments address our relationship with others). Knowledge becomes wisdom when we understand the commandments' implications to us individually, and we personally apply them to our lives as we process them through a belief system that has established our values.

There is a vast distance between having knowledge *about* something and having a personal knowledge *of* something. The bridge from one to the other is godly wisdom applied to our lives.

One man was given an opportunity to ask for whatever he wanted. His request was motivated by his desire to justly rule his people. God gave him much more than he asked for!³³⁴ Godly wisdom is available to every believer who asks for it, in faith. Anyone who lacks wisdom should ask God, who gives generously to all without finding fault, and it will be given to him.³³⁵

What is godly wisdom? This wisdom, available to every believer, views and interprets the world from God's point of view, discerns truth from falsehood, and derives clarity and understanding from the word of God through the Spirit of God. Its source is God. This kind of wisdom is markedly different from worldly wisdom and the spiritual gift of wisdom. You see, a person in possession of worldly wisdom will be influenced by the wisdom the world offers, which may be diametrically opposed to the word of God.³³⁶ It may be the product of some ideology or philosophy at complete odds with the Gospel of Jesus Christ.³³⁷

If our life and the way we live it are to bring honor to God, we must see life as God sees life. We must interpret our experiences in the light of godly wisdom. Data, knowledge, and comprehension must be processed through a window of godly wisdom. Godly wisdom gives us the ability to see life as God sees it. Godly wisdom is a value that needs to become a virtue in our lives. The following guiding principles help us to understand the difference between worldly wisdom and godly wisdom.

- Godly wisdom is centered in Christ.³³⁸
- Godly wisdom consists in the knowledge of His will.³³⁹
- Godly wisdom is based on an exercise of faith.³⁴⁰
- Godly wisdom is not self-centered.³⁴¹
- Godly wisdom is based on the Bible, the word of God.³⁴²
- Godly wisdom is perfected through obedience.³⁴³
- Godly wisdom is available to believers.³⁴⁴

334 1 Kings 3:3–14
335 James 1:5
336 Colossians 3:16
337 James 3:17
338 1 Corinthians 1:30; 2:6–16
339 Colossians 1:9; Ephesians 1:8–10
340 James 1:5–7
341 James 3:13–17
342 Colossians 1:28; 3:16; Psalms 111:10
343 Deuteronomy 4:6; Jeremiah 8:8–9; Proverbs 10:8; 9:10
344 James 1:5–8; Hebrews 4:12; James 3:14–16

How do we know godly wisdom when we hear it? We'll know if we can answer affirmatively to the following questions. Is it centered in Christ? Is it based on the word of God? Is it an exercise of faith? Is it in conformance to His will? Is it pure, peaceable, and gentle? Is it open to reason, full of mercy and good fruits? Is it without uncertainty and insincerity?

God's Family Set of Values

At the moment of conversion, you were given a new heart.[345] He has put His laws in our minds and written them on our hearts.[346] In fact, He has given us the seed of His character, the values of His kingdom in our heart.

One evening, I was on my way to minister in a prison and was listening to a talk show. The guest was talking about tribes. He identified several—Native Americans, Zulus, and other such groups. He also mentioned the dark side of tribes—gangs in our communities and gangs in prisons. Regardless of the type of tribe, one common feature distinguishes them—they do not regulate or control their behavior by a system of laws and regulations. Instead, they live by a code of honor.

So, what is the seed of God's character and the values of His kingdom? What is the code of honor that marks a member of His kingdom—those qualities that distinguish us from the world around us? Before we answer that question specifically, we need to understand that we are different from the world around us.

At the moment of our conversion, we were transferred from our citizenship in this world to a new citizenship in heaven. We are no longer of this world. We are a representative, a citizen, of the kingdom of God in this world, until he calls us to our future home.[347]

Our king and new commander is Jesus, who appeared to all men, teaching us to say no to ungodliness and worldly passions, to live self-controlled, upright, and godly lives in this present age as we wait for the blessed hope—the glorious appearing of our great God and Savior, Jesus Christ,

345 Ezekiel 36:26–27
346 Hebrews 8:10–12
347 Philippians 3:20–21

who gave himself for us to redeem us from all wickedness and to purify for himself a people that are his very own, eager to do what is good.[348]

Our new citizenship is the kingdom of God, a future hope and a present reality. This changes everything. We are aliens and strangers in this temporary earthly place. While on earth, we are to abstain from sinful desires that war against our soul. We are to live in such a way among the fallen that although they may accuse us of many things, they will see our good deeds and glorify our King, whom we serve.[349]

As I write this, I am sitting at a table in the library of the home of C. S. Lewis in Headington, England. I was selected as a visiting scholar and will be here for three weeks to finish this book. It is fitting to recall what Lewis, author of *Mere Christianity*, said about this issue. He said that we, as Christians, should view the world "as Enemy territory; territory occupied by invading forces." Building on this theme, McGrath adds: "In the midst of this territory, as resistance groups are the communities of faith. We must never be afraid to be different from the world around us. It is very easy for Christians to be depressed by the fact that the world scorns our values and standards. But the image of the <u>colony</u> sets this in its proper perspective. At Philippi, the civilizing laws of Rome contrasted with the anarchy [a state of lawlessness or political disorder] of its hinterland [regions outside of Rome]."

"And so our moral vision—grounded in Scripture, sustained by faith, given intellectual spine by Christian doctrine—stands as a civilizing influence in the midst of a world that seems to have lost its moral way."[350]

We are not of this world; our citizenship is in the kingdom of God. What makes this kingdom distinct from all other kingdoms? Well, for one, we are not to "*conform any longer to the pattern of this world, but be transformed by the renewing of my mind. Then I will be able to test and approve what God's will is—His good, pleasing and perfect will.*"[351] Second, we are "*not to love the world or anything in the world. If anyone loves the world, the love of the Father is not in him. For everything in the world—the cravings of sinful man, the lust of his eyes and the boasting of what he has and does—comes not*

---

348 Titus 2:11–14
349 1 Peter 2:11–12
350 McGrath, 90–91.
351 Romans 12:2

from the Father but from the world. The world and its desires pass away, but the man who does the will of God lives forever."³⁵²

Third, "*Don't you know that friendship with the world is hatred toward God? Anyone who chooses to be a friend of the world becomes an Enemy of God.*"³⁵³

All right, we are aliens and strangers who are to live our lives in such a way that they boldly proclaim the kingdom to which we now belong; that we no longer live our lives in accordance with the dictates of this world; that we are careful not to embrace this world; and that friendship with this world is hatred to God.

So, what defines the kingdom of God?

Our *declaration of independence* is our acknowledgement that we stand in bold relief against the backdrop of our culture, prepared to give a defense for the hope that it in us—that we are separate from this world and the culture in which we exist. The only other option is to give in to our culture, becoming a willing partner in it, and not be distinguished apart from it. Dependence on God produces independence from the world. Independence from the world is only possible when we become dependent upon the King. Dependence on the world results in independence from God.

The *constitution* of the kingdom of God is the Ten Commandments—its *amendments* are the Beatitudes³⁵⁴, its *vision* is the Sermon on the Mount.³⁵⁵ Our *new identity* is our *Bill of Rights*, and it finds its focus in who we are in Christ.

1 Corinthians 6:19–20	I have been bought with a price, and I belong to God.
Ephesians 1:3–8	I have been chosen by God and adopted as His child.
Colossians 1:13–14	I have been redeemed and forgiven of all my sins.

352 1 John 2:15–17
353 James 4:4
354 Matthew 5:1–11
355 Matthew 5–7

Hebrews 4:14–16	I have direct access to the throne of grace through Jesus Christ.
Romans 8:1–2	I am free from condemnation.
2 Corinthians 1:21–22	I have been established, anointed and sealed by God.
Philippians 3:20	I am a citizen of heaven.
1 John 5:18	I am born of God and the evil one cannot touch me.
John 15:5	I am a branch of Jesus Christ, the true vine, and a channel of His life.
John 15:16	I have been chosen and appointed to bear fruit.
1 Corinthians 3:16	I am God's temple.
2 Corinthians 5:17–21	I am a minister of reconciliation for God.
Philippians 4:13	I can do all things through Christ, who strengthens me.

Our corporate set of values, which we received at conversion, is the fruit of the Spirit. It marks us as adopted sons into the family of God—the character of God imparted to us, His values embedded in us, the code of honor we are to live by.[356]

The Fruit of the Spirit

The term fruit is found fifty-two times in the New Testament. It is associated with conversion in only three instances. In all other instances it is associated with the character of God—the values that represent the heart of God, received at the moment of conversion in seed form. The obligation of believers is to nurture and cultivate the seed until the fruit is produced thirtyfold, sixtyfold or one hundredfold in the believer. We are called to bear this fruit in our lives.

Let me take you to Scripture that illustrates the importance of the fruit, for which the apostle John provides clarity. What does this passage tell us about the fruit of the Spirit?

---

356 Galatians 5:22–24

"I am the true vine, and my Father is the gardener. He cuts off every branch in me that bears no fruit, while every branch that does bear fruit he prunes so that it will be even more fruitful. You are already clean because of the word I have spoken to you. Remain in me, and I will remain in you. No branch can bear fruit by itself; it must remain in the vine. Neither can you bear fruit unless you remain in me. I am the vine; you are the branches. If a man remains in me and I in him, he will bear much fruit; apart from me you can do nothing. If anyone does not remain in me, he is like a branch that is thrown away and withers; such branches are picked up, thrown into the fire and burned. If you remain in me and my words remain in you, ask whatever you wish, and it will be given you. This is to my Father's glory, that you bear much fruit, showing yourselves to be my disciples."[357]

First, our nourishment and nutrition, for the fruit comes from the vine.

Jesus is the vine from which we are nurtured and sustained. We cannot exist in any healthy or holistic sense apart from the sustenance of the vine. The gardener, the Father, cares for and nurtures the growth. He prunes the vine and waters the vine. He ensures that the vine is exposed to the sun. The nutrients are supplied by the vine, Jesus Christ.

Sustenance comes from an intimate relationship with Christ. We cannot produce the fruit of the Spirit apart from Christ. Rebellion against Christ will result in disease in the fruit. The produce will be diminished as a result.

Second, it is possible to be attached to the vine but bear little or no fruit.

Every branch that does not bear fruit is pruned. My wife has a unique way of looking at this issue. She says you cannot fall back unless you have first moved forward. It is entirely possible that people can legitimately receive Christ but bear little or no fruit. I have two cherry trees in my backyard; pitted cherries from these trees make great cherry pies. I noticed something about the trees. A couple of branches connected to the trees bore no fruit at all. They had once done so but no longer. All though sustenance from the tree was available, the branches no longer drew life from the tree.

357 John 15:1–8

What causes a branch to bear little or no fruit? Here are a couple of examples: Worms can destroy the fruit. Unconfessed sin can result in disease that will ultimately destroy the fruit. A deep wound uncared for can reduce the production of the fruit. Unremitting grief over the loss of our innocence when we were young, or a deep emotional wound inflicted by others can produce an open wound in our soul. Only the salve of God's love and grace can heal the wound. Every branch that does not bear fruit is in need of being pruned.

It is possible to be grafted into the vine, yet bear little or no fruit. Sometimes, God will remove us before our time because our continued existence will draw others away from Christ. In other words, we will do considerable harm to others if we continue to exist. We can be taken out before our time. Think of Ananias and Sapphira who held back the proceeds of a sale of land promised as a donation.[358] Sustenance comes from an intimate relationship with Christ. We cannot produce the fruit of the Spirit apart from Christ. Rebellion from Christ will result in disease in the fruit. The produce will be diminished as a result.

Third, careful cultivation is required to produce healthy fruit.

Love, joy, and peace can only be produced as a by-product of an intimate, vibrant relationship with the God, the Father. Patience, kindness, and goodness can only be produced as a by-product of our interaction with others. Faithfulness, goodness, and self-control can only be produced as a by-product of internal discipline.

Love, joy, and peace are nurtured **upward**. Patience, kindness, and goodness are nurtured **outward**. Faithfulness, gentleness, and self-control are nurtured **inward**. In other words, the fruit of the Spirit is produced in the life of a believer as a direct result of a relationship with the Father, with others, and with ourselves. It must be exposed to the following.

- the sunshine of God's love *(worship)*
- the water of God's word *(study)*
- the fertilizer of God's Spirit *(prayer)*
- the pruning of discipline *(repentance)*
- the disease control of sin *(removal and replacement)*

358 Acts 5:1–11

This is fruit that can be appreciated and absorbed by the world in desperate need of a healthy diet to sustain wholesome life. If the fruit of God's Spirit is not evident in your life, if the character of God is not observable in your life, if the values of God's kingdom are not evident in your behavior, how will the world know you are an adopted son of God's kingdom?

What marks your life as evidence that you belong to the kingdom of God? To what degree does your life give evidence of the character of God? What sets you apart from the world? What distinguishes you from the rest of the world? What is there about your life that causes the world to take notice? To what degree is the fruit of the Spirit evident in your life?

Fourth, the product of your life will be evaluated.

While visiting my grandparents when I was a boy, I was very hungry and went into the kitchen, where I found a bowl of fruit. In that bowl were bananas, peaches, grapes, and apples. I grabbed an apple and bit into it, only to find out it was wax. Not only was I terribly disappointed, but I nearly lost my front tooth!

What kind of fruit are you producing in your life? Is it godly, spiritual fruit; ungodly, diseased fruit; or worldly, artificial fruit?

Godly Spiritual Fruit	*Worldly* Artificial Fruit	*Ungodly* Diseased Fruit
Love	Conditional Love	Hatred
Joy	Happiness	Despair
Peace	Apathy	Anxiety
Patience	Indifference	Impatience
Kindness	Self-interest	Cruelty
Goodness	Manipulation	Evil
Faithfulness	Half-heartedness	Unfaithfulness
Gentleness	False Modesty	Harshness
Self-control	Conditional Restraint	Self-indulgence

At the judgment seat of Christ we will give account for what we have done with what we have been given. When our efforts have been exposed to the holiness of God, some will remain while others will be burned up.[359] There is a day of reckoning coming.

What behaviors in your life bear testimony that your values are God's values? What values are the hills on which you are prepared to die? What values are the principles by which you intend to live? What values are the filters through which you process all the decisions of life?

To what degree are you defined by love, joy, and peace—a direct reflection of the quality of your relationship with God? As you interact with others, are you seen as patient, kind, and good—a direct reflection of your relationship with those who are within your sphere of influence? Does your life give ample evidence of gentleness, faithfulness, and self-control—a direct reflection of your internal discipline, diligence, and devotion? Do people see Jesus in you?

Satan's value preferences might consist of the following values.

- My needs are most important;
- Premarital sex is okay;
- Whatever meets my needs, no one will get in my way;
- Ethics are relative to my situation;
- If it feels good, do it;
- Same sex love is good;
- Abortion is a right;
- Manipulation serves a function;
- My race is superior to all others;
- Pornography is an art form; or women are to serve my needs.

These are not God's values, but love, joy, peace, patience, kindness, goodness, faithfulness, gentleness, and self-control are.

Personal Values

Besides the corporate, family set of values that we all receive at the moment of conversion in seed form—seed that must be cultivated, nourished, watered, pruned, and exposed to the Son—we can acquire other values. These values are unique to the believer and may differ from one believer to another, with differing results. These values define our uniqueness and shape us in accordance with our wiring and God's purposes.

---

359 1 Corinthians 3:10–15

The fruit of the Spirit is in our spiritual DNA; it's DNA that we all possess. Yet we look different, having different aptitudes, personality temperaments, and natural abilities. So the fruit of the Spirit marks us as spiritual beings, carrying in our person the character and values of God. Personal values are acquired over time and stimulate us to act in different ways, in accordance with God's redemptive plans and specific purpose for our life.

My personal core values are devotion to God, promise-keeper, truth-seeker, loyal servant, man of integrity, faithful to family, lifelong learner, Bible as the authority, responsible behavior, and strength and honor. I have acquired these values over a lifetime in Christ. Some of these values are more dominant than others. A few of these values have become virtues—I act on them without thinking.

Because of problems in our family, our daughter and her children came to live with us. My wife and I had been saving our money for some time to build a retirement home on a lake that would also provide a ministry setting after retirement. When our daughter and her three sons, with another son on the way, came to our home, I knew immediately what I was to do. We built a 1200-square foot addition onto our home, much to the surprise and counsel to the opposite of our realtor. My wife and I believed God was calling us to re-parent our daughter and act as surrogate parents to our grandchildren. They lived in our home for four years before God brought another man into my daughter's life along with two additional children.

Not once did I regret the decision. Not once did I think of doing anything different. As you may remember, *faithful to family* is one of my values that has become a virtue. I was mentoring a young man at the time this new journey began. When he asked me why I would give up a lifelong dream so quickly, I simply responded by saying, "It was the right thing to do." Our investment in the life of our daughter and our six grandchildren has been the joy of our life. It wasn't always easy, but it was always right.

God laid it on my heart early on that I was to give my grandchildren values to live by. Derrick is my peace and justice boy; Braedan is my strength and honor boy; Talisa is my love and joy girl; Kieran is my courage and valor boy; Gaelan is my goodness and integrity boy; and Lochlan is my truth and wisdom boy. I greet them with their values when I see them. "Strength and honor Braedan." He responds with "Strength and honor Papa."

When Braedan was younger, I was called to his teacher's office; I thought he had misbehaved. When I got to the school, I was asked to come into her office. I was *really* worried then, but she unfolded an amazing story. Braedan is very popular. All the kids love playing with him. While on the playground, he noticed that no one was playing with a certain little girl. Apparently, he stood up before his friends and said he wouldn't play with them unless they played with her. I was so proud.

When we got in the car and he explained what had happened on the playground that day, I said to him, "How does Papa greet you, Braedan?" He responded, "Strength and honor." "And how do you greet Papa?" He said, "Strength and honor." I then said, "What you did on the playground today took strength, and you did the honorable thing." Until that moment our greeting was a familiar and cherished way to connect with one another. Now, however, it took on a very different meaning. To this day, when we are together, he likes to tell me about the honorable things he has done since last we were together.

I am often asked how I chose the values for my grandchildren. Some I knew instinctively, but most came after long prayer and discussion with my wife. One day, my daughter made an amazing comment about the values I had given her children. She said, "How did you know that the values you gave my children were not who or what they are naturally? Instead, they are what they must grow into." I said, "I didn't know. Apparently, God knew." For instance, Kieran's values are courage and valor. At this stage of his life, he is afraid of the dark and of a whole series of things. Courage and valor is what he will grow into but not what he currently is. Remember, we often become what we are named.

Types of Values

There are different types of values you might consider: personal, spiritual, or relational. There are other categories, I am sure, but I hope that these three will get you started on thinking about what values God wants you to embrace, in addition to the fruit of the Spirit. Start small, possibly one or two, after prayer and contemplation. Commit to acting on these values at every chance or situation that presents itself.

Personal	Spiritual	Relational
Decency	Devotion	Compassion
Courage	Diligence	Forgiveness

Perseverance	Dedication	Friendliness
Self-discipline	Faithfulness	Honesty
Centeredness	Holiness	Loyalty
Wisdom	Joyfulness	Justice
Hard Work	Obedience	Fairness
Purity	Prayerfulness	Unselfishness
Gratefulness	Godliness	Helpfulness
Truthfulness	Servanthood	Support

Whichever values you choose, I would suggest you do the following:

1. Provide *focus* by identifying one or two Scriptures that inform and condition the value. That way you will ensure it is a biblical value, and the behavior that will follow will be God-honoring.
2. Select the *value* itself. For clarification, you might want to embed the value in a phrase that further describes it. Terry Walling, in his helpful manual *Perspective,* gives the following examples:

Value	Description
People first	My capacity to influence requires the maintaining of relationships.
Being before doing	It is easier to do, but it is more important to be. God cares about the process and the journey.
Team	Living life and working alone proves nothing.
Family	My wife and children is my significant ministry.
Learning	I value learning and a teachable spirit.
The Kingdom	Jesus desires more and better followers.
Primacy of local church	It is God's chosen vehicle for today. My involvement is critical.
Leadership	Everything rises and falls on leadership.
Change	Changeless Gospel continually must confront a changing world.
Faith	Life today requires both strength and courage.
Relevancy	Meaningful ministry at work and in my neighborhood.

3. Identify an immediate *context* in which you will practice the value. For instance, if truth is your value, and you have been lying to your wife, then obviously the context is the relationship with your wife.
4. Select a *time frame* in which you intend to practice the value. For example, you might pick a month, or two months—I wouldn't go longer than three months. When the time frame is completed, do an evaluation, and see where you need to go from there.

Six Levels of Resolve

A value does not result in correlated behavior until we commit ourselves to act on it repeatedly, in the same direction, over a period of time. Doing so under the empowerment of the Holy Spirit will ultimately move a value to a virtue. At this point, we act on it without much thought—it has become a part of our spiritual DNA.

Level 1: Aspiration—many of us aspire to values that are not in any way reflected in our behavior. We might esteem them, but they have no influence over us. They are an interest but little more.

Level 2: Preference—some of us have a distinct preference for one or more values over others. For instance, we might value loyalty over honesty, or mercy over justice. But in either case, they are simply preferences, having little impact on our behavior.

Level 3: Respect—we respect certain values to the degree that we can't understand why others don't respect the same value. When we see examples of these values played out in the lives of others, it immediately gets our attention. Yet respect for a certain value is no guarantee that it will influence our own behavior.

Level 4: Affirmation—this level may produce public proclamations of affirmation of one or more values. We go on record that these values are important to us. We are willing to declare it and defend it. But still, this level of resolve might produce little consistent and repeated reflection in our behavior.

Level 5: Commitment—it is at this stage that we are willing to act on a value we esteem. We proactively decide to intentionally live by this value. The evidence of commitment is in the number of instances to which we can testify its influence in our behavior. Habitually acting out the value becomes a high priority, to the degree that we are willing to be held accountable for it.

Level 6: Virtue—when the habitual practice of a particular value becomes a fixed part of our character, it is now a virtue in our lives. Again, virtues are "specific dispositions, skills, or qualities of excellence that together make up a person's character and that influence his or her way of life."

In the article "Christian Ethics and the Ethics of Virtue,"[360] Stephen S. Bilynskyj makes the following comments:

> *In the classical-medieval view, ethics is primarily the science of developing human character through the fostering of the virtues. Christian ethics is the practice of being a certain kind of people. It is to learn to embody a character which is defined in relation to the life of Jesus Christ. This kind of ethics still involves making decisions, but individual acts are placed in their context as the acts of people with a particular history and character. For instance, having already become the kind of person for whom an extramarital affair was not an option, a decision not to engage in such an affair simply manifests what kind of person we are. There is a kind of circularity in the acquisition of virtue. For it is by acting virtuously that we acquire a virtue; yet it is the possession of virtue which allows us to act virtuously. The question of what (and who) we are (should) precede the question of what we are to do."*

Conclusion

Simply showing an interest in a value will not necessarily result in conforming behavior. It takes more than interest, respect, and affirmation. It takes commitment and obedience to God's values to produce a character like Christ—Christ-likeness.[361]

360 Clark, 258–260.
361 Ephesians 4:11–16; Romans 8:28–29; Colossians 1:28–29; 2 Corinthians 3:18

Obedience in the same direction over an extended period of time will produce a character that will bring glory to the Father because it bears in the person who practices it the imprint of His Son. So, "*whatever is true, whatever is noble, whatever is right, whatever is pure, whatever is lovely, whatever is admirable—if anything is excellent or praiseworthy—think about such things.*"[362]

Obedient conformity to God's values, born out of meditative reflection on His word, will produce a virtuous life that will provide a testimony to all who come across your path. It shows them that you are a member of God's family, a testimony to the resurrected life of His Son in you. Declare this day that you will get your marching orders from Him alone and not the Enemy, the world, or your own selfish desires.

BATTLE PLAN

1. Throughout the next two weeks, read the book of Proverbs and identify God's value preferences for us. List them on a separate piece of paper. Be prepared to share some of your findings at the next meeting.
2. Identify any corrupted values in your life, renounce them before God, and replace them with biblically informed values.
3. Review where you are with regard to God's family values—the fruit of the Spirit—using the following scale. To what degree is the fruit of the Spirit (Galatians 5:22–24) evident in your behavior? Put a mark on the line that represents the degree to which each element of the fruit is observable in your life. What are you going to do about each value, depending on where you are on each line?

	Non-observable	Highly Visible
Love		
Joy		
Peace		
Patience		
Kindness		
Goodness		
Faithfulness		

362 Philippians 4:8

Gentleness   _____

Self-control   _____

          _____

1. In prayer, ask God to help you identify five biblical values by which He wants you to live. Record them in your journal or Bible and begin to make them a priority in your life. Over the next two weeks, proactively behave in accordance with these values. Be prepared to share testimonies of how you volitionally lived out one or more of these values.

2. If you are married, meet with your wife and tell her what you have been learning about the importance of values related to God-honoring behavior. Together, develop a list of five family values that will characterize your home from this point on. Commit them to the Lord in prayer, and display them in a prominent place in your home as a continual reminder of your commitment.

CHAPTER 8
THE BATTLEFRONT OF ATTITUDES

*For the word of God is living and active. Sharper than
any double-edged sword, it penetrates even to dividing
soul and spirit, joints and marrow; it judges the
thoughts and attitudes of the heart.*

Hebrews 4:12

On September 11, terrorists commandeered four separate flights carrying
266 passengers in total. Two planes were flown into the twin towers
of the World Trade Center in New York, another into the Pentagon in
Washington DC, and the fourth crashed in a field in Pennsylvania, short
of its intended target. The potential loss of life could have exceeded the
combined fatalities of all major terrorist events since 1941—2,752 people
lost their lives.

The nation was plunged into mourning, shocked from its smug sense of
security and complacency, and made painfully aware that our lives would
be dramatically changed from that day forward. Many hoped that we
Americans would be forced to rally around a common set of beliefs and
values that would serve to mobilize us and replace our lethargy with a
common vision for the future. Our worldview was changed.

What could have been the worldview of the perpetrators of this heinous
crime on innocents? A *Pioneer Press* article by David Drehle provides some
insight. He states: "Tuesday, September 11, 2001—a date which will live
in infamy—the United States of America was suddenly and deliberately
attacked by a faceless, stateless Enemy apparently lacking any conventional
political objective. ... This is a new kind of war." Drehle quotes Daniel
Benjamin, a leading antiterrorist expert, who said, "In this new era, the
threat is more explicitly religious. There is a desire to create mass casualties
among Americans. A particular strand of radical Islamic thinking holds
that the [United States] is the corrupting influence in the universe. The

point for these enemies is not to score a political point or to raise the political influence of one group or country; it is to kill Americans and undermine Americanism."

Drehle further comments: "The goals of the Enemy appear to be almost rhetorical, a terror founded on corpses but shaped by symbolism." This unparalleled attack, he says, is against "American influence around the world. Tuesday's targets were powerful symbols of that influence. The twin towers of the World Trade Center represented the financial supremacy of Wall Street (and all democratic economies), while the Pentagon is the center of America's world-dominating military. By damaging, even obliterating, these symbols, the attackers seek to explode the whole idea of American authority."

The "new kind of war," this "new era," this "new Enemy" represent a "new" worldview founded on Islamic beliefs and fueled by Islamic fundamentalist values that resulted in a fanatical commitment to drastic and dramatic actions, oblivious to the sanctity of life—their own or their victims. Let us not lose sight of the insidious primary cause of distorted and corrupted beliefs, values, and worldviews—sin! Sin, the Bible says, leads to death. In this case, it not only led to spiritual death but physical death. As Scripture reminds us: "Don't you know that when you offer yourselves to someone to obey him as slaves, you are slaves to the one whom you obey—whether you are slaves to sin, which leads to death, or to obedience, which leads to righteousness?"[363] The hope for believers is found in the verses that follow—"But thanks be to God that, though you used to be slaves to sin, you wholeheartedly obeyed the form of teaching to which you were entrusted. You have been set free from sin and have become slaves to righteousness."

Worldview is a composite and systematic ordering of our beliefs and values into a collective whole, a lens through which we view and interpret life. The question we need to answer is what is our worldview? How do we view and interpret life? How do we make sense of the world around us? How do we respond to the events to which we are exposed on a daily basis? How do we make order of the world around us? How do our attitudes, whatever they may be, shape the way we see our world? These questions specifically deal with our worldview, whether or not we can articulate it. Our worldview is shaped by our beliefs, values, and other pervasive influences, such as what

363 Romans 6:16–17

we read, who we listen to, the experiences we've had, the crises we've faced, and the world around us. A more subtle influence is Satan himself.

Our worldview is our beliefs plus our values!

Worldview

Each of us has a set of perceptual attitudes that help shape our outlook on life. If beliefs are the foundations for our behavior, and values are the filters through which we process life's decisions, then attitudes are the lens through which we observe life around us. Our perceptions about life are shaped by our attitudes. Our system of attitudes is also called our worldview.

Dan Taylor, in *Myth of Uncertainty*, said: "Most people thoughtlessly adapt an inherited worldview, or one absorbed from their surroundings. Even those who explicitly work one out often operate in daily life by a different, less conscious system than the one they carefully construct."[364]

As mentioned earlier, our worldview is the lens through which we view the world and try to make sense of what we observe. Godly wisdom is necessary to form a biblically centered worldview through which to process our world and personal events, situations, and circumstances that we face on a daily basis. Correct interpretation of our observations and the principles we bring to bear as we evaluate these observations is a precursor to understanding and effective resolution.

Examples of Worldviews

Secular Humanism: man is the center of the universe; no higher order exists

- *Ethical Humanism:* the human quest for being good through human efforts
- *Postmodernism:* truth is relative; rationalism and reason are subjective
- *Hedonism*: pleasure and self-gratification is our primary objective
- *White Supremacy*: the white race is superior to all others
- *Self-gratification*: a form of hedonism that focuses on sensuality

---

364 Dan Taylor. *Myth of Uncertainty*, 23.

- *Racism*: power and influence wielded on the basis of prejudice
- *Self-actualization*: sees life through the lens of self-interests and fulfillment
- *Pro-choice*: the right to decide, based on a personal agenda
- *Self-preservation*: anything that ensures that self is sustained is justifiable
- *Sense of Entitlement*: life owes me, and I deserve it
- *Alternative Lifestyles*: all sexual preferences and conduct are permissible
- *Predatory Mentality*: I deserve what I'm willing to take by force
- *"The World is My Oyster"*: everything is fair game for satisfying my wants
- *Freedom of Expression*: the right to say and do what I please.
- *Relativism*: truth is merely opinion; that which the majority says it is.
- *Pluralism*: the multitude of views, values, and practices in the world, with no justifiable way of choosing among them, are equally acceptable.

Other worldviews might include atheism, materialism, naturalism, communism, New Age, modernism, agnosticism, liberalism, conservatism, universalism, skepticism, socialism, pessimism, pantheism, pacifism, optimism, fascism, ecumenism, cynicism, multiculturalism, and any other -isms you might encounter.

Relationship between Beliefs, Values, and Worldview

For the sake of clarity, it will be helpful to show the relationship between beliefs, values, and worldview. Our worldview is a cohesive and interrelated conceptual system that includes our beliefs and values, as related to key issues such as our understanding of God, the world, and personhood. Beliefs by themselves are simply a collection of theological presuppositions and propositions. Values are simply a collection of principles and rules for decision-making and behavior. When they are integrated into a systematic whole, they become one's worldview.

The **Rosetta Stone**, discovered in 1799, included an inscription in three languages (Greek, Egyptian hieroglyphic, and Demotic) regarding an Egyptian decree of 196 BCE. The two known languages provided the key to the third, thereby providing the key to deciphering Egyptian hieroglyphics. Similarly, our worldview, comprising an integrated set of beliefs and values, provides the key to deciphering the world around us. Metaphorically, the right eyeglasses can put the world into clearer focus.

Ronald Nash, in *Worldviews in Conflict*, suggests that "our worldview beliefs are generally restricted to a relatively small set of significant issues. Two people could share similar views of God, the universe, ethics, and the Son. But they could disagree about many other issues." For instance, two Christians could essentially agree on fundamental beliefs about the person of God, the authority of the Bible, and the origins of our world but could disagree about the sovereignty of God and the free will of man, as is the case of proponents of Calvinism and Arminianism.

Notre Dame philosopher Thomas Morris, in his book *Francis Schaeffer's Apologetics*, explains that "the most important presuppositions in any person's system of beliefs [and values—their worldview] are the most basic and general beliefs about God, man, and the world that anyone can have. They are not usually consciously entertained but rather function as the perspective from which an individual sees and interprets both the events of his own life and the various circumstances of the world around him. These presuppositions, in conjunction with one another, delimit the boundaries within which all other less foundational beliefs are held." From a biblical perspective, the Beatitudes could be considered a worldview.[365]

---

365 Matthew 5:3–12

Critical Elements of a Worldview

According to Dr. David Clark, provost of Bethel University and renowned theologian, five essential issues must be addressed in the formation of a worldview:

1. The nature of ultimate reality
2. The nature of human personhood
3. The basic human dilemma
4. The solution to the human dilemma
5. Our human destiny

Worldviews Compared

	HUMANIST	BUDDHIST	CHRISTIAN
Reality	Natural world	Nothingness	God
Person	Highly evolved animals	Part of a whole	Image bearers
Dilemma	Lack of knowledge	Human desires	Sin
Solution	Education	Enlightenment	Christ
Destiny	"Living the dream"	Nirvana	Heaven or Hell

For instance, let's compare two worldviews—secular humanism and Buddhism. With regard to the nature of **ultimate reality**, the secular humanist views the natural world as the ultimate reality. The Buddhist, on the other hand, sees nothingness as the ultimate reality—that is, what is true reality.

When it comes to a theory about **personhood**, the secular humanist sees mankind as highly evolved animals. The Buddhist sees mankind as non-distinct; a simple part of a complex whole. Self-actualization is completely out of the picture because self-identity is an anathema (a taboo) to Buddhists.

The **human dilemma,** the essential problem of making it through life, is a lack of knowledge for the humanist. The Buddhist perception regarding the essential nature of the human dilemma is the problems that arise from human desires.

When it comes to the **solution** for the human dilemma, the humanist believes that education will solve any problem. The Buddhist believes we must experience enlightenment that presupposes an elimination of human desires.

Finally, the concept of our **human destiny** is "living the dream" for the humanist. In other words, taking full advantage of what the natural world has to offer requires knowledge that can only be produced by proper education. For the Buddhist, our human destiny is met when we reach Nirvana, a euphemism for "nothingness."

Ronald Nash, professor of philosophy and theology at Reformed Theological Seminary, suggests consideration of seven major elements for a "well-formed" worldview: God, ultimate reality, knowledge, ethics, humankind, a set of ideals that lays out how we think things should be, and an explanation for the disparity between the ways things are and the way they ought to be. "Christianity attributes the discrepancy between the ideal and actual existence to the pervasiveness of sin. An inadequate [or corrupted] worldview, like improper eyeglasses, hinders our efforts to understand God, the world, and ourselves."

Nash also states that each worldview has a cardinal or hinge presupposition —a touchstone, overarching presupposition that acts as an ordering influence for all other presuppositions—"a fundamental truth about reality [that] serves as a criterion to determine which other presuppositions may or may not count as candidates for belief [and values]."

In Nash's opinion—and I wholeheartedly agree—the following presupposition is the touchstone, overarching, ordering belief. "Human beings and the universe in which they reside are the creation of God who has revealed Himself in Scripture (and Christ)."[366]

Our Changing World

In his September 2002 address to a United Nations' prayer breakfast, Ravi Zacharias, noted Christian philosopher, summarized the thought trends by decade and provided insight into some of the issues involved.

In the 1950s, kids lost their innocence. They were liberated from their parents by well-paying jobs, cars, lyrics and music that gave rise to a new term, "the generation gap."

In the 1960s, kids lost their authority. It was a decade of protests. Church, state, and parents were all called into question and found wanting. Their authority was rejected, yet nothing ever replaced it.

In the 1970s, kids lost their love. It was the decade of nihilism, dominated by hyphenated words beginning with

366 Ronald M. Nash. *Worldviews in Conflict.* Zondervan, 1992, 51–52.

"self"—self-image, self-esteem, self-assertion. It made for a lonely world. Kids learned everything there was to know about love, and few had the nerve to tell them that there was indeed a difference.

In the 1980s, kids lost their hope. Stripped of innocence, authority, and love, and plagued by the horror of nuclear nightmare, large and growing numbers of this generation stopped believing in the future.

In the 1990s, we lost our ability to reason. The power of critical thinking has gone from induction to deduction and very few are able to think clearly anymore. I have often said the challenge of the truth speaker today is this: How do you reach a generation that listens with its eyes and thinks with its feelings?

To this I would add the following—in the first decade of the new millennium, we lost our moral and spiritual moorings. We are encouraged to tolerate everything. Compromise and political correctness is the rule of the day. Christianity is depicted as an intolerant faith. We are urged to be "for" everything and "against" nothing. Politically correct tolerance may be another worldview that affirms and accepts everything. The true definition of tolerance, however, is withholding whatever power you possess against what you find objectionable.

Competing Worldviews

Michael Armour and Don Browning, in *System-Sensitive Leadership*,[367] suggested six competing worldviews they have found in the church.

Worldview	Description	Primary Focus
1	The world is a dog-eat-dog place where only the tough survive.	Power over the Adversary

---

367 Michael C. Armour and Don Browning. *System-Sensitive Leadership: Empowering Diversity without Polarizing the Church*. College Press Publishing Company, 2000.

2	The world is governed by timeless principles and eternal absolutes.	Transcendent Truth and Principle
3	The world is teeming with unlimited potential for personal success and fulfillment.	Personal Achievement
4	The world is so interdependent that every life form and individual is a cherished treasure.	Egalitarianism and Ecology
5	The world is a vast network of complex, often paradoxical relationships, where ever-changing realities demand holistic approaches to life.	Systemic Health
6	The world is a single planetary organism, an integrated whole in which boundaries between mind, matter, and energy are elusive.	Holistic Identity and Convergence

Key Beliefs of a Christian Worldview[368]

- All human beings carry the image of God in their person.

  This image, marred by sin, makes us creatures capable of reasoning, love, and God-consciousness. It also explains why we are moral creatures.

- Universal moral laws exist and are ordained by God.

---

[368] Adapted from chapter 2 of *Worldviews in Conflict* by Ronald Nash, 1992.

- The chief purpose of man is to glorify God and enjoy Him forever.

- Sin alienates us from God and enslaves us.

- All human beings long for purpose, progress, and permanence.

- Human beings have a need for forgiveness and redemption.

- Christ's redemptive work is the basis of human salvation.

- Receiving Christ as Savior and Lord brings a new birth,[369] a new heart,[370] a new relationship with God,[371] and a new power to live.[372]

- The Christian has God's nature and Spirit within and is called to live a particular kind of life in obedience to God.

- The Bible is the Christian's ultimate authority for faith and practice.

- Physical death is not the end of our existence.

- What we do in life echoes in eternity.

Conclusion

Although it may be argued that there are multiple Christian worldviews, I would suggest the following statements comprise what most Christians agree is the essence of a Christian worldview—the set of perceptual attitudes that offer clarity about our world, both seen and unseen.

1. The nature of ultimate reality—God exists and is active in our lives.
2. The nature of human personhood—humans bear the image of God.
3. The basic human dilemma—the image of God is marred by sin.

---

369 John 3:3–21
370 Galatians 2:20
371 Hebrews 8:10–12
372 1 John 3:1–2

4. The solution to the human dilemma—the person and work of Christ.
5. Our human destiny—eternal life or eternal damnation.

BATTLE PLAN

1. What central beliefs and core values establish and inform your worldview? How can you justify your worldview in the light of the Bible? In other words, what key verses can you cite as justification?
2. How might Matthew, in the following passages, inform, influence, or condition one's worldview?

> **Matthew 22:37–40** *Jesus replied: "'Love the Lord your God with all your heart and with all your soul and with all your mind.' This is the first and greatest commandment. And the second is like it: 'Love your neighbor as yourself.' All the Law and the Prophets hang on these two commandments."*

> **Matthew 28:19–20** *"Therefore go and make disciples of all nations, baptizing them in the name of the Father and of the Son and of the Holy Spirit, and teaching them to obey everything I have commanded you. And surely I am with you always, to the very end of the age."*

3. The next time you view a favorite movie, try to identify the central beliefs, core values, and worldview of the primary actors.
4. When you are with others try to determine their worldview by asking the following question: *"What is your understanding, perception, or opinion of the following issues?"*

   a. Ultimate Reality: What is your opinion regarding reality?
   b. Human Personhood: What is your understanding regarding humanity?
   c. Basic Human Dilemma: What is the primary problem facing mankind?
   d. Solution to the Human Dilemma: What is the solution to this problem?
   e. Human Destiny: What happens to us after we die?

5. If the Beatitudes (Matthew 5:3–12) were firmly established as your worldview, how would your perception of the world around you change?

6. In prayer, ask God to help you calibrate your worldview to His worldview. As you read God's word ask the Holy Spirit to bring clarity to you regarding the essential components of a Christian worldview.

CHAPTER 9
THE BATTLEFRONT OF MOTIVES

Therefore judge nothing before the appointed time; wait till the Lord comes. He will bring to light what is hidden in darkness and will expose the motives of men's hearts. At that time each will receive his praise from God.

1 Corinthians 4:5

When a crime has been committed, a detective will try to determine the motive for the crime. That is about as far as most detectives go. The best detectives, however, try to determine the perpetrator's attitude, value system, and beliefs. Both start with observation of the crime site. Motives compel us to act and move us from thought and emotion to over the threshold to action. Motives stimulate us to respond to a given stimuli, such as a circumstance or event.

For instance, if you are motivated by lust, it might only take a glimpse of a beautiful woman to compel you to act on that impulse. Take King David, for example. It only took a glimpse of Bathsheba, bathing, to compel him to act on his lust. His sin was compounded when he ultimately had Uriah, her husband, killed in battle.[373]

We are told in Scripture that the Lord searches every heart and understands every motive behind the thoughts.[374] We also are told that He will bring to light what is hidden in darkness and will expose the motives of men's hearts.[375] All our ways may seem innocent to us but our motives are weighed by the Lord.[376] God's response to our requests may not be granted because we ask with wrong motivation.[377]

---

373 2 Samuel 11
374 1 Chronicles 29:9
375 1 Corinthians 4:5
376 Proverbs 16:2
377 James 4:3

Motives Defined

Motives compel us to act. Webster's Dictionary defines a motive as something that stimulates or causes a person to act; it implies an emotion or desire that operates on the will. Similar words to "motive" include impulse, incentive, or inducement. Impulse suggests a driving power arising from personal temperament or constitution. Incentive applies to an external influence inciting to action. Inducement suggests a motive prompted by the deliberate enticements or allurements of another.

Samuel A. Meier, associate professor of Hebrew at Ohio State University, offers the following clarification regarding motives. His comments appear in the Evangelical Dictionary of Biblical Theology:

> *Motives pose at least a twofold dilemma: (1) the status of a good deed done for the wrong reason or an evil deed done with good (or even without) intent; and (2) the effect of a motive (good or bad) that never has opportunity to find fulfillment. The fundamental issue prompting the dilemma is that there is not a one-to-one correspondence between a given action and the motive of its agent: the same action may be either censured or defended depending upon one's motive. For example, a difference between first- and second-degree murder resides in whether or not the homicide was intentional: the former is punishable by death, while the latter allows for clemency.*[378] *Offenses against God can become less heinous if they are accidental, as the sacrifices for accidental sins make clear.*[379] *An individual whose actions are, or result in, evil becomes less reprehensible when it is discovered that the person did not intend that consequence. This principle is apparent when Jesus does not want his executors condemned because their motives are not commensurate with the great crime they are committing: "Father, forgive them, for they do not know what they are doing."*[380] *Good motives can prompt people to actions that have unfortunate results,*[381] *a legal principle that has become the basis of much Western law:*

---

378 Exodus 21:12–14; Numbers 35:9–25; Deuteronomy 19:4–13; Joshua 20:1
379 Leviticus 4–5; Numbers 15:22–31
380 Luke 23:34; Acts 3:17
381 Matthew 13:28–30

the act itself does not make one a criminal unless done with criminal intent.

In the same way, otherwise acceptable deeds become less attractive, even repulsive, when base motives are behind them. Prayer, giving to the poor, and fasting are activities encouraged throughout the Bible, but Jesus underscores that God will not reward those who do them for selfish reasons.[382] *The ritual associated with the temple (sacrifices, prayer, holy days) was a legitimate expression of piety for the ancient Israelites, yet the prophets insisted that God was disgusted with the whole enterprise when the people did it without humility and repentance.*[383] *The most powerful symbols of spiritual identification (circumcision, baptism) can be undermined by one who submits to them but is not inwardly changed.*[384] *Good motives may result in conflicting actions: some early Christians did not, while others did, eat a special diet; some believers did not, while others did, observe certain days as sacred. In each case, it is the motive that makes these otherwise neutral actions acceptable: if one is seeking to please God (i.e., not other people or oneself), then the individual is exonerated.*[385]

So what can we deduce from his remarks? God is most concerned about our motives. Poor results can come from good motives, and similarly, good results can come from bad motives. Things don't always work out the way we hoped they would, even with proper motives. And sometimes great results are enjoyed from impure motives. For instance, we might lead a fund-raiser because we are motivated by a need to be seen as influential and respected. The fund-raiser may be a success, but our motives were impure. God will expose the motives of men's hearts. He may choose to be merciful and extend grace.[386] We might recommend that a friend confront a bully because we are motivated by concern for him. The bully then might physically attack our friend and put him in the hospital. Our motive was right, but the results were bad. God judges the motives of men's hearts.

---

382 Matthew 6:1–18
383 Isaiah 1:11–15; 29:13; 58:3–7; Amos 4:4–5; 5:21–24
384 Jeremiah 9:25–26; Matthew 3:7–8; Romans 2:25–29; 1 Peter 3:21
385 Romans 14:1–14; 1 Corinthians 10:31; Colossians 3:17
386 1 Corinthians 4:5

Motives Explained

Several scenarios are presented below. No one can be absolutely sure as to the motives of these individuals, but we can speculate as to what they might have been in each case.

- What was Cain's motive(s) in Genesis 4:1–16; 1 John 3:12? (Anger or hatred)
- What was Jacob's motive(s) in Genesis 27:1–9? (Greed)
- What was Moses' motive(s) in Exodus 2:11–12 and Acts 7:23–29? (Justice)
- What was Saul's motive(s) in 1 Samuel 18:1–30? (Jealousy)
- What was David's motive(s) in 2 Samuel 11:1–27? (Lust or guilt)
- What was Peter's motive(s) in Luke 22:39–62? (Fear)
- What was Jesus' motive(s) in John 2:13–25? (Indignation)
- What right and wrong motive(s) does Matthew 6:1–18 demonstrate? (Humility)
- What is God's motive(s) in Titus 2:11–14? (Save mankind; train in godliness; redemption; purification; do good)
- What were God's motives in sending His beloved Son to the cross? (Love)

The Enemy's Tactics

The Enemy prowls about, seeking those whom he can devour.[387] He seeks to corrupt our motives, thereby producing behavior that repels people from Christ and the Christian way of life. His tactics vary with each individual. He may use a variety of approaches to reach his objective, the dishonoring of the Father through His children. What tactics does he use on you?

Equivocation: The Enemy seeks to blur issues. "Simply let your yes be an unequivocal yes, and your no be an unequivocal no; anything beyond this comes from the evil one." [388]

387 1 Peter 5:8
388 Matthew 5:37

Distortion: "When anyone hears the message about the kingdom and does not understand it, the evil one comes and snatches away what was sown in his heart. This is the seed sown along the path." [389]

Sifting: "Simon, Simon, Satan has asked to sift you as wheat. In this tactic the Enemy is given the opportunity to test Simon." [390]

Compromise: Then Peter said, "Ananias, how is it that Satan has so filled your heart that you have lied to the Holy Spirit and have kept for yourself some of the money you received for the land?"[391] Ananias held back some of the proceeds he promised as a gift.

Delusion: This is one of the Enemy's favorite tactics. He seeks to confuse our understanding of truth and lead us into myths.[392]

Deprivation: "Do not deprive each other except by mutual consent and for a time, so that you may devote yourselves to prayer. Then come together again so that Satan will not tempt you because of your lack of self-control." [393]

Revenge: "If you forgive anyone, I also forgive him. And what I have forgiven—if there was anything to forgive—I have forgiven in the sight of Christ for your sake." [394] True forgiveness chooses not to seek revenge in thought, word, or deed.

Outwitting: The Enemy seeks to outwit us for we are not unaware of his schemes.[395]

Masquerading: He masquerades as an angel of light, seeking to deflect us from God's best.[396]

Thorn in the Flesh: We are sometimes given a cross to bear so that we will depend on God. Paul was given a thorn in the flesh: "to keep me from becoming conceited because of these surpassingly great revelations,

---

389 Matthew 13:19
390 Luke 22:31
391 Acts 5:3
392 Acts 26:18
393 1 Corinthians 7:5
394 2 Corinthians 2:10
395 2 Corinthians 2:11
396 2 Corinthians 11:14

there was given me a thorn in my flesh, a messenger of Satan, to torment me."[397]

Struggle: "For our struggle is not against flesh and blood but against the rulers, against the authorities, against the powers of this dark world, and against the spiritual forces of evil in the heavenly realms." [398] Facing struggles tests our allegiance to God.

Confrontation: Life is a battle. "Therefore put on the full armor of God, so that when the day of evil comes, you may be able to stand your ground, and after you have done everything, to stand. In addition to all this, take up the shield of faith, with which you can extinguish all the flaming arrows of the evil one."[399]

Worldliness: We continually run the risk of becoming worldly because we live in the world. The world rubs off on us. Only the word can cleanse us. "We know that anyone born of God does not continue to sin; the one who was born of God keeps him safe, and the evil one cannot harm him. We know that we are children of God, and that the whole world is under the control of the evil one."[400]

Infiltration: "But while everyone was sleeping, his Enemy came and sowed weeds among the wheat, and went away" … and the Enemy who sows them is the devil. The harvest is the end of the age, and the harvesters are angels.[401]

Deceit: "You are a child of the devil and an Enemy of everything that is right! You are full of all kinds of deceit and trickery. Will you never stop perverting the right ways of the Lord?"[402]

Overpower: "Be self-controlled and alert. Your Enemy the devil prowls around like a roaring lion looking for someone to devour." [403]

---

397 2 Corinthians 12:7
398 Ephesians 6:12
399 Ephesians 6:13, 16
400 1 John 5:18–19
401 Matthew 13:25, 29
402 Acts 13:10
403 1 Peter 5:8

Wrong Motives

Once again, motives are what stimulate our activity, mobilize us to act, and stimulate our behavior. The power of a motive is the desired payoff. The payoff is directly related to one's values.

Although not an exhaustive list, the following motives will produce behaviors that reflect badly on the family of God, in general, and our testimony—the way in which we live our faith, in particular. Although the world at large looks at our behavior, God looks at our motives. So even if the results appear noble and good, from God's perspective, the ends may not justify the means.

Anger	Blind Ambition	Conditional Love	Conquest	Control
Envy	Destruction	Domination	Gluttony	Greed
Hatred	Immorality	Jealousy	Lust	Materialism
Meanness	Possessiveness	Pride	Racism	Self-centeredness
Self-protection	Sense of Entitlement	Sexual Gratification	Superiority	Vengeance
Cruelty	Domination	Control		

Some motives lead to others. **Greed** may lead to coveting, embezzlement, gambling, robbery, stealing, love of money, or materialism. **Lust** may lead to adultery, debauchery, sexual immorality, sexual addiction, self-indulgence, carnality, masturbation, sensuality, unfaithfulness, fornication, promiscuity. **Envy** may lead to covetousness, jealousy, betrayal, bitterness, hatred, rage, resentment, or vengeance. **Pride** may lead to arrogance, boasting, conceit, ingratitude, insensitivity, judging others, mocking, self-centeredness, self-deception, self-justification, selfishness, self-love, self-reliance, self-righteousness, self-sufficiency, self-will, stubbornness, vanity, or slander.

Godly Motives

The number one godly motive is unconditional love. It is a love that is others-oriented; a love that is action not emotion; a love that seeks the better of the one loved; a love that desires another's well-being and welfare, even if they are unlikable.

1 Corinthians 13:4–8 is one of the most beloved passages in the Bible. It speaks of unconditional love and describes what love is, what love is not, and what love is, regardless. Love *is* patient, kind, and rejoices with the truth. Love *is not* envious, boastful, angry, keeping a record of wrongs, or delighting in evil. Love *never* fails. Love *always* protects, always trusts, always hopes, and always perseveres.

Elsewhere in Scripture we are commanded to love, which is only possible because such love is action-oriented and not based on emotions.[404] Words come easily, but action speaks louder than our words. Isn't it interesting to note that many believers come to Christ because of God's unconditional love for them? Yet once saved, many of the same believers make their love for God conditional in terms of what He can or will do for them. We often make our love for our spouse or children conditional on their performance. "I love you if …" or "I love you because …" instead of "I love you regardless."

When I speak to men, I confront them with a challenge—to out-serve their wives and expect nothing in return. When a man does that, he is generally surprised by his wife's response. After her initial shock or skepticism, most wives will be grateful and responsive. But regardless of her response, you should serve your wife anyway—view such service as an act of worship to God. I challenge you to do this for two weeks and see what happens.

We prove our love for God by our obedience.[405] How often have we heard a parent say to his children, "Will you just do what I tell you to do?" Obedience is a sign of our love for God. God said, "They honor me with their lips but their hearts are far from me."[406]

One Another

The phrase "one another" is found over fifty times in the New Testament. What does the exercise of unconditional love look like? Something like this—we are to be devoted to one another; honor one another; live in harmony with one another; stop passing judgment on one another; accept one another; instruct one another; greet one another; agree with one another; serve one another; bear with one another; be kind and compassionate to one another; submit to one another; admonish one another; encourage

404 John 13:34–35
405 1 John 2:3–6
406 Matthew 15:8

one another; not slander one another; live in harmony with one another; spur one another on to love; offer hospitality to one another; be humble to one another; forgive one another; and have fellowship with one another. Seems pretty clear, doesn't it?

What Motivates You

Several things cause people to act: to meet a need, solve problems, achieve, learn, grow, serve, compete, produce, win, or be noticed. These are internal motivations. External motivations also compel us to act, such as in a challenge, crisis, emergency, or opportunity.

Not all motivations are bad, not all are good; not all are pure, not all are impure. What motivates you? Is it achievement or advancement; recognition or status; honor or praise; success or wealth; significance or meaning; survival or perseverance; power or influence; control or dominance; discovery or knowledge; improvement or actualization; growth or development; notoriety or acclaim; danger or excitement; perfection or excellence; pleasure or satisfaction; happiness or exhilaration; newness or uniqueness; acquisition or possession; or spirituality or Christ-likeness?

Conclusion

What compels you to act? What motivates you to respond? What stimulates you to engage? What moves you from thought to action? Honest answers to these questions will reveal your true motives. To bring glory and honor to the Lord, only one motive rises to the top—unconditional love; the genuine concern for the welfare and well-being of another individual, even if he is unlikeable. Over time, you will find him likeable if you practice unconditional love. Such a motive will produce honorable, spiritually empowered behavior. The world takes notice of such love because it is so rare.

BATTLE PLAN

1. If you established unconditional love as your primary motive (John 13:34–35; 1 Corinthians 13:4–8; 1 John 2:3–6), how would you and others benefit?

2. Which of the following motives do you struggle with the most: self-centeredness, conditional love, anger, lust, racism, greed, envy, jealousy, materialism, control, ambition?
3. Examine your life before God. Where have you expressed conditional love? Where have you expressed unconditional love?
4. In the next two weeks, seek out opportunities to act out of a motivation of unconditional love.

PART III
WINNING THE BATTLE

CHAPTER 10
PUTTING IT TOGETHER

*You brood of vipers, how can you who are evil say
anything good? For out of the overflow of the heart the
mouth speaks. The good man brings good things out
of the good stored up in him, and the evil man brings
evil things out of the evil stored up in him.*

Matthew 12:34–35

We live in the tyranny of the urgent because life is hectic and complex. We employ systems, methods, strategies, and processes to bring some order out of the chaos of our life. We desperately look for balance amid competing priorities that press in on us. We might even attend time-management workshops, looking for a magic formula that will bring order to our lives. Just when we think we have a handle on these unceasing demands, something new is added to the mix—something we didn't plan or foresee. They say life happens in between plans. Unforeseen events cascade in on us, disturbing a rare equilibrium that we might be enjoying for a short season. Once again, we try to reprioritize our responsibilities and obligations. We try to simplify our lives. We wait for the next round of circumstances that will disturb our fragile world. Sound familiar?

Balance Versus Centeredness

Living a balanced life is impossible. Life does not happen in a balanced way. We can't prepare for every possibility or anticipate every crisis. Maintaining balance under these circumstances is futile. We are encouraged in Scripture: *"Be careful, then, how you live—not as unwise but as wise, making the most of every opportunity, because the days are evil."*[407] Does this mean we should constantly strive for balance? Is there another option? Stuff happens in our life that catches us by surprise and throws us for a loop—something we didn't know was coming, something that knocks us off balance.

---

407 Ephesians 5:15–16

Time is a precious resource. It cannot be saved or stored; it can only be used. Time that is not used is lost forever; it can never be recovered. Everyone has twenty-four hours per day.

The Bible says: "There is a time for everything, and a season for every activity under heaven:

- A time to be born and a time to die,
- A time to plant and a time to uproot,
- A time to kill and a time to heal,
- A time to tear down and a time to build,
- A time to weep and a time to laugh,
- A time to mourn and a time to dance,
- A time to scatter stones and a time to gather them,
- A time to embrace and a time to refrain,
- A time to search and a time to give up,
- A time to keep and a time to throw away,
- A time to tear and a time to mend,
- A time to be silent and a time to speak,
- A time to love and a time to hate,
- A time for war and a time for peace."[408]

Wouldn't it be nice if we knew exactly what season of life we were in so that we could reorder our lives accordingly? Is a balanced life really possible? Does life happen to us in a predictable manner? Is all of life under our control?

Life comes at us in unpredictable ways. Sometimes, we see it coming. Other times, it takes us by surprise. Sometimes we're prepared; other times we are not prepared.

Much of life is like walking a tightrope. Picture yourself there. What would your mind be focused on? What would be the state of your body? What would happen if a gust of wind hit you from the left or from the right? Would you be able to relax?

Maintaining balance in the midst of life's circumstances is difficult, if not

---

408 Ecclesiastes 3:1–8

impossible, to achieve. We are under constant tension and anxiety, hoping to maintain our balance on the high wire of our existence. When a crisis hits us from one side, we lean into it so that we won't lose our precarious balance. Is that the way to live? Is that what God expects of us?

Jesus modeled a different approach to the demands in His life. When we look at the earthly life of Jesus, we don't see a harried, haphazard, and reactive lifestyle. No, we see a proactive, centered life. Crowds pressed in on him, and people clamored for His attention. His disciples urged His involvement. The Bible says that He often withdrew to lonely places and prayed.[409] He was never harried, even when his friend, Lazarus, died.[410] He commended Mary, to her sister, Martha, for choosing the right thing to do while she was distracted by many things.[411] Christ was centered because He knew His priority—to do the will of His Father and to finish His work.[412] He knew His priorities and ordered His life to fulfill those priorities.

We have a choice how to live—reactively or proactively; in accordance with God's plans or our plans; in alignment with His purposes for us or others' purposes for us; living by the clock or living by the compass.

One strives for balance; the other strives for centeredness. One reacts to circumstances; the other responds to circumstances. One is often out of control; the other is often in control.

Stephen Covey popularized a matrix depicting four types of activity. Quadrants I, II, and IV are reactive activities, while quadrant II is proactive. Too much time spent in I, II, and IV results in a fast-moving treadmill existence. Spending sufficient time in IV limits and controls the effects of the other quadrant activities.

---

409 Luke 5:16
410 Luke 11:6
411 Luke 10:40–42
412 John 4:34

Quadrant II Time Management Matrix

	Urgent	Not Urgent
Important	**I** Ministry Crises Personal Crises Pressing Problems Deadline-driven Projects Job Responsibilities Important Meetings Some Phone Calls	**II** Prayer Spiritual Renewal Values Clarification Relationship Building True Re-creation Visioning, Planning, Training Preparation
Not Important	**III** Interruptions Some Mail, Some Email Some Phone Calls Other People's Crises Some Meetings Drop-in Visitors Popular Activities	**IV** Trivia, Busy Work Irrelevant Mail, Irrelevant Email Some Phone Calls Time Wasters Busy Work Excessive TV Escape Activities

Stephen R. Covey 1994

If we spend too much time in **Quadrant I** we are susceptible to stress, burnout, crisis management, and always needing to put out fires.

Too much time spent in **Quadrant III** results in short-term focus, crisis management, reactive leadership, little time or patience for goals and plans, feeling victimized and feeling out of control; it produces shallow or broken relationships.

Too much time spent in **Quadrant IV** results in total irresponsibility, being replaced or fired from jobs, and an unhealthy dependence on others or institutions for basics.

When sufficient time is spent in **Quadrant II,** the results are quite different: vision, perspective, centeredness, discipline, few crises, and control. Covey states: "In a successful company 20–25 percent of time is spent on Quadrant I activities, just 15 percent of time on urgent but not important (Quadrant III) activities, and 65–80 percent of time on Quadrant II activities. Quadrant II activities—important but not urgent activities—are present wherever success is present."

Quadrant II is the only proactive cell in the matrix—the others are all reactive. Quadrant II focuses on being centered; the others seek balance.

How does a "spinning top" maintain its equilibrium against opposing forces? When it is hit, it is momentarily knocked off its equilibrium but soon regains its upright posture. It instinctively finds its center of gravity.

What does a centered life look like? What is your spiritual center of gravity? Is it so strong that you're able to find your equilibrium, no matter what life throws at you?

Four Essential Elements

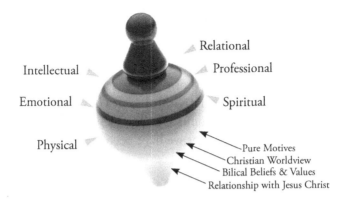

Relational

Intellectual

Professional

Emotional

Spiritual

Physical

Pure Motives
Christian Worldview
Bilical Beliefs & Values
Relationship with Jesus Christ

What do we know about this "spiritual center of gravity"? It has four essential elements that build on one another. The first is a *personal relationship with Christ.* The second essential element is *biblical beliefs and values.* The third is a *Christian worldview*, and the fourth essential element is *pure motives.* Clarity, at the core, includes Bible-centered beliefs, Christ-centered values, God-focused perceptual attitudes, and Holy Spirit-empowered motives.

Such a centered existence influences all life's activities and interactions. Once we know our personal "spiritual center of gravity," we should order our lives accordingly.

Foundation for Our Spiritual Center of Gravity

1. *We are wired at birth for God's purposes!*

The books of Psalms and Ecclesiastes offer some clarity on the issue. **Psalm 139** dispels the notion that life happens by chance—that it is unplanned, a matter of fate and circumstance. We are not here by mistake or by chance but by decree and deliberate intention.

> *For you created my inmost being; you knit me together in my mother's womb. I praise you because I am fearfully and wonderfully made; your works are wonderful, I know that full well. My frame was not hidden from you when I was made in the secret place. When I was woven together in the depths of the earth, your eyes saw my unformed body. All the days ordained for me were written in your book before one*

*of them came to be. How precious to me are your thoughts,
O God! How vast is the sum of them! Were I to count them,
they would outnumber the grains of sand. When I awake, I
am still with you.*[413]

Blasé Pascal, the seventeenth-century philosopher, scientist, and inventor, described a phenomenon we are born with called a "God-shaped void." Because each of us possesses this "God-shaped void," we are compelled to ask fundamental questions about life. The Bible brings this idea into biblical focus by informing us that we have been embedded with a sense of the eternal.

*He has made everything beautiful in its time. He has also set
eternity in the hearts of men; yet they cannot fathom what
God has done from beginning to end.*[414]

From this embedded sense of the eternal arises the uncontrollable necessity to find answers to three fundamental questions about life. These questions are asked in every culture and every generation: *Why am I here?* (purpose) *Where am I going?* (progress) *What is the significance of my life?* (permanence)

The Bible gives us a clear picture regarding these fundamental questions. God *does* have a purpose for our lives. We *are* here for a reason. Our life *can* count for something of lasting value.

2. *God has specific plans for our lives!*

We have a *destiny* to fulfill. God has plans for us!

*"For I know the plans I have for you," declares the LORD,
"plans to prosper you and not to harm you, plans to give you
hope and a future.*[415]

We have a *purpose* to engage. God has a purpose for our lives!

*For we are God's workmanship, created in Christ Jesus to do
good works, which God prepared in advance for us to do.*[416]

---

413 Psalm 139:13–18
414 Ecclesiastes 3:11
415 Jeremiah 29:11
416 Ephesians 2:10

We have a *contribution* to make. God has equipped us for our purpose!

> *There are different kinds of gifts, but the same Spirit. There are different kinds of service, but the same Lord. There are different kinds of working, but the same God works all of them in all men. Now to each one the manifestation of the Spirit is given for the common good.*[417]

We have a *ministry* to complete. Our objective is Christ-likeness!

> *It was he who gave some to be apostles, some to be prophets, some to be evangelists, and some to be pastors and teachers, to prepare God's people for works of service, so that the body of Christ may be built up until we all reach unity in the faith and in the knowledge of the Son of God and become mature, attaining to the whole measure of the fullness of Christ. Then we will no longer be infants, tossed back and forth by the waves, and blown here and there by every wind of teaching and by the cunning and craftiness of men in their deceitful scheming. Instead, speaking the truth in love, we will in all things grow up into him who is the Head, that is, Christ. From him the whole body, joined and held together by every supporting ligament, grows and builds itself up in love, as each part does its work.*[418]

We have a *legacy* to leave. God wants us to invest in others!

> *And the things you have heard me say in the presence of many witnesses entrust to reliable men who will also be qualified to teach others … So now I charge you in the sight of all Israel and of the assembly of the LORD, and in the hearing of our God: Be careful to follow all the commands of the LORD your God, that you may possess this good land and pass it on as an inheritance to your descendants forever.*[419]

---

417 1 Corinthians 12:4–7
418 Ephesians 4:11–16
419 2 Timothy 2:2; 1 Chronicles 28:8

3. *We have a legacy to live and leave in the lives of others!*

I think it is safe to say that everyone would like to leave a positive *legacy* for the sake of the Lord. Every one of us wonders what legacy we will leave. In other words, will our lives count for anything? Will we leave anything of lasting value? Will we finish the race well? Will anyone remember us when we're gone?

There is nothing wrong with striving for success. But if our sense of worth is wrapped up in what we do and not who we are in Christ, we can miss the opportunity we have to model the character of Christ in our work setting, community, and family.

A devotion to one's chosen profession or dedication to becoming successful is commendable. However, when such devotion and dedication become an excuse for neglecting our responsibilities or our obligation to be light to a lost world, we sacrifice our God-given purposes, talents, and potential on the altar of expediency.

Each of us has something of value to pass on to someone of value. Each of us has been given something of value by God to give to someone He values. Are you investing the treasure God has given you in the lives of your loved ones, your friends, and in the lives God has given you an opportunity to influence on His behalf? When you meet the Lord face-to-face, will He honor you for wisely investing your talents in the lives of others, or will He chastise you, as He did the servant who buried his talent in the ground? [420]

Maybe you think you have nothing of value to offer others or that no one cares what you have to offer. That is a lie from the pit of hell, and it certainly doesn't correspond to God's plans for our lives.

Begin with the End in Mind

Have you read Stephen Covey's book, *The 7 Habits of Highly Effective People*? In that book, he suggests an exercise that helps us to picture the *legacy* we want to leave.

Close your eyes. Clear your mind of everything except what I invite you to do. Don't worry about your schedule, your business, your family, your friends,

---

420 Matthew 25:14–30

what's in the oven, or what you're going to do this afternoon. Just focus on what I'm saying.

In your mind's eye, see yourself going to a funeral of a loved one. Picture yourself driving to the funeral parlor or chapel, parking the car, and getting out. As you walk inside the building, you notice the flowers, the soft organ music. You see the faces of friends and family you pass along the way. You feel the shared sorrow of losing, the joy of having known, that radiates from the hearts of the people there.

As you walk down to the front of the room and look inside the casket, you suddenly come face-to-face with yourself. This is your funeral. All these people have come to honor you, to express feelings of love and appreciation for your life.

As you take a seat and wait for the services to begin, you look at the program in your hand. There are to be four speakers. The first is from your family, immediate and also extended—possibly children, brothers, sisters, nephews, nieces, aunts, uncles, cousins, and grandparents who have come from all over the country to attend. The second speaker is one of your friends, someone who can give a sense of what you were as a person. The third speaker is from your work or profession. And the fourth speaker is from your church, where you have been involved in service.

Now think deeply. What would you like each of these speakers to say about you and your life? What kind of husband, wife, father, or mother would you like their words to reflect? What kind of son or daughter or cousin? What kind of friend? What kind of working associate?

What character would you like them to have seen in you? What contributions, what achievements would you want them to remember? Look carefully at the people around you. What difference would you like to have made in their lives?

Open your eyes. Take a few minutes to jot down your impressions. What did you jot down?

4. *We are to live by the compass and not the clock!*

The *clock* represents our commitments, appointments, schedules, goals, and activities—they drive our behavior and condition our responses. The *compass* represents our vision, values, principles, mission, direction, and destiny—what we feel is important, what we believe should lead our lives.

How many of us have climbed the ladder of success to find that it is leaning against the wrong wall. Our "success" didn't bring us the satisfaction we thought it would. Absorbed in the ascent, we left a trail of shattered relationships or missed moments of deep, rich living in the wake of the intense, over-focused effort. We simply did not take the time to do what mattered most. We promised we would be there, only to submit to the *tyranny of the urgent*, but always for what we say is the sake of the family.

As I mentioned earlier, during my daughter's senior year in high school, she repeatedly asked if I could attend one of her school's basketball games. She was a varsity cheerleader. At the time, I was a general manager of a business. I remember giving perfectly legitimate and rational reasons why it was impossible to be there. To this day, I cannot remember any of those reasons. What I remember is I wasn't there for my daughter. My primary focus was on my business sphere of influence.

One nagging question caused me to change my life dramatically and continues to influence my life daily: when I get to the end of my life and look back, how will I be remembered by my family, and what will I have accomplished of significance for the Lord?

5. *We can finish strong!*

It's not too late or too early to leave a legacy worth leaving. So how do we finish strong?

- Allow the Bible to chisel you into Christ's image.[421]
- Live a value-centered life.[422]
- Guard your heart.[423]
- Discipline your life.[424]
- Submit to being held accountable.[425]

---

421 Hebrews 4:12; Romans 12:2; 2 Timothy 3:16–17
422 1 Timothy 4:7–8; Psalm 15:1–5; 119:93
423 Proverbs 4:23; 1 Peter 5:8; Philippians 4:8
424 1 Corinthians 9:24–27; 2 Timothy 4:7–8
425 Ecclesiastes 4:9–10, 12; Colossians 3:16

Situational Lifestyles Revisited

In chapter 2 we discussed five situational lifestyles that people adopt to navigate through life: pinball wizard, electric current, Super Glue, logjam, and loose cannon. Before we explore the possible central beliefs, core values, worldview, and motives for each of these lifestyles, let's review the descriptions.

1. Pinball Wizard: Reactionary

These people react to circumstances. They live life ricocheting from one emergency to the next. If there isn't a crisis to embrace, they tend to create one to fill the void. They are often people who need to be needed and tend to see more in a given situation than is actually there. They live on the edge.

2. Electric Current: Avoidance

These people avoid problems in life by choosing the path of least resistance. Choices are embraced that cause the least amount of pain and discomfort. As character is forged over the anvil of difficulty, these folks' lives are usually shallow and undefined. They lack depth.

3. Super Glue: Transference

These people live vicariously through others who represent who they want to be, not being satisfied with who they perceive they are themselves. They attach themselves to others, losing their identity in the process. Because all humans let us down over time, extraction is painful, and latching on to someone else is predictable.

4. Logjam: Indecision

These people hate to make decisions because they are fearful of the outcome. These people decide not to decide when crisis or important issues demand a response. A "log" of indecision gets wedged in the stream of life, causing a logjam over time. The logjam is abandoned and begun again in some other place.

5. Loose Cannon: Driven

These people have one goal in life—to achieve or succeed at all costs. They "blow" through everybody and everything to attain their objectives. At the end of their lives, they have little else but their accomplishments to keep them company, with no one to share them with. They leave nothing but memories of broken lives in their wake.

As you may recall, our central beliefs *establish* our values. Our core values *inform* our perceptual attitudes or worldview. Our perceptual attitudes or worldview *condition* our motives. Our primary motives *energize* our behavior. And our behavior *reflects* the condition of our heart. Given the five situational lifestyles noted above, what possible beliefs, values, attitudes, and motives could produce such behavior?

Lifestyle	Belief	Value	Attitude	Motive	Behavior
Pinball Wizard	There is always a need	Only I can fix the problem	Life is full of crises	Rescue	Reactionary
Electrical Current	Pain is a bad thing	Comfort is desirable	Escape is preferred	Relief	Avoidance
Super Glue	I'm not good enough	Somebody else is better	An "ideal" is out there	Dissatisfaction	Transference
Logjam	A decision leads to action	Decisions lead to problems	Put it off until later	Fear	Indecision
Loose Canon	Significance is important	Achievement brings success	Success leads to recognition	Acceptance	Driven

Relationship between Beliefs, Values, Attitudes, and Motives

Let us assume that the following verses comprise a belief system to which we are committed. It may be a subset of a larger system of beliefs:

1. **Citizens of Heaven**: But our citizenship is in heaven. And we eagerly await a Savior from there, the Lord Jesus Christ, who, by the power that enables him to bring everything under his control, will transform our lowly bodies so that they will be like his glorious body.[426]

2. **Aliens and Strangers**: Dear friends, I urge you, as aliens and strangers in the world, to abstain from sinful desires, which war against your soul. Live such good lives among the pagans that, though they accuse you of doing wrong, they may see your good deeds and glorify God on the day he visits us.[427]

3. **Nonconformity with the World**: Do not conform any longer to the pattern of this world, but be transformed by the renewing of

---

426 Philippians 3:20–21
427 1 Peter 2:11–12

your mind. Then you will be able to test and approve what God's will is—his good, pleasing, and perfect will.[428]

4. **Lovers of the World**: Do not love the world or anything in the world. If anyone loves the world, the love of the Father is not in him. For everything in the world—the cravings of sinful man, the lust of his eyes, and the boasting of what he has and does—comes not from the Father but from the world. The world and its desires pass away, but the man who does the will of God lives forever.[429]

5. **Friendship with the World**: You adulterous people, don't you know that friendship with the world is hatred toward God? Anyone who chooses to be a friend of the world becomes an Enemy of God.[430]

6. **Our Mandate**: For the grace of God that brings salvation has appeared to all men. It teaches us to say no to ungodliness and worldly passions, and to live self-controlled, upright, and Godly lives in this present age, while we wait for the blessed hope—the glorious appearing of our great God and Savior, Jesus Christ, who gave himself for us to redeem us from all wickedness and to purify for himself a people that are his very own, eager to do what is good.[431]

Given this belief system the interplay between the components may be depicted graphically. Beliefs 2, 3, and 5 are related and may be summarized as our relationship with the world. Beliefs 1 and 4 are related and show our true citizenship. Belief 6 indirectly relates to both doctrines of our relationship to the world and our true citizenship.

Jesus Christ stands as the authority over these beliefs. He is the organizing center for these beliefs. Being the living word, He informs and conditions those beliefs and all that follows from them. These beliefs, in turn, establish two values, both stated as phrases. The first value comes from our relationship with the world—in the world but not of the world. The second value comes from our true citizenship—governed by the kingdom of God.

---

428 Romans 12:2
429 1 John 2:15–17
430 James 4:4
431 Titus 2:11–14

These values inform our Christian worldview; in fact, our worldview is formed by our beliefs and our values. Our values condition the motive that will compel us to act. That motive is described as missional. In other words, we act in our world because it is our mission to do so. The behavior that is produced is engagement in our world with a purpose—God's redemptive purposes.

This illustration of the relationship between beliefs, values, attitudes, motives, and behavior is ideal, but the reader should realize that such a belief system might produce other values that condition a different motive and produce different behaviors as a result. The example given is just that—an example of how the various components of the heart interact with one another to produce particular behavior.

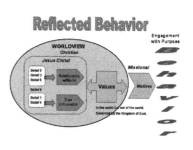

Other Examples

Lifestyle	Belief	Value	Attitude	Motive	Behavior
Resists Absolutes	There are no absolutes	Truth is relative	To each his own	Choice	Ridicule
Intimidator	Might makes right	Offense is best defense	There is only one winner	Control	Provoking
Low Self-esteem	I'm not attractive	Thin is beautiful	Beauty brings happiness	Acclaim	Insecurity
Victim Mentality	The world is against me	Others are to blame	I'm not responsible	Shift Blame	Irresponsible
Health	Body temple of the Spirit	Responsible behavior	We are stewards	Well-being	Healthy
	Health brings long life	Smoking is unhealthy	Smoking is a dirty habit	Vitality	Abstinence
Protective	Animals are to be protected	Animals have rights	Animals are as valuable	Protection	Activism
	Man is the image of God	Life is sacred	Abortion is murder	Intervention	Lobbyist
Neighborliness	Love one another	Care for strangers	Strangers are my brothers	Love	Helpful

Conclusion

Again, you can substitute your choices. I hope that you see how beliefs, values, attitudes, and motives work together to produce behavior. Behavior is a by-product of the interrelationship between these components of the heart. The goal of a life of godliness is to understand what is in our hearts; what behaviors bring dishonor to God and to us; removal of the corruption within; replacement with truth; and acting upon that truth until our lives are indeed godly.

The point, once again, is to be so controlled and influenced by the Spirit of God as to have the mind of Christ in our beliefs, values, attitudes, and motives so that our character is Christ-like and our behavior brings glory to God. To change behavior, we must have a change of heart. The final two chapters will help you with a change of heart.

BATTLE PLAN

1. What are some distractions, corruptions, or competing influences or activities you should put out of your life in order to help you focus on God's purposes for your life?
2. As you simplify your life, what are some healthy, constructive, and impacting things you should add to your life?
3. What activity are you currently involved in that you can sacrificially give up as an act of worship to God so that you can serve your church or your community?
4. If you are homebound, what could you do to serve others from your home? If you can't provide time regularly, what service project could you get involved in that could be done over time?
5. Identify personal, corrupted behaviors that you want to change. Trace the behavior back to a corrupted belief or beliefs.
6. What operational beliefs drive your behavior? Are they biblical? If so, what verses inform those beliefs?
7. Besides the family values of spiritual fruit, what other values do you employ to make your decisions? What are your values? Are they actual or preferred?
8. What is your worldview? What foundational beliefs support your worldview? Review the difference between foundational and operational beliefs (chapter 6).

9. What motivates your life? What are your primary motives that compel you to act? What circumstances, events, or people act to catalyze your motives?

CHAPTER 11
CORRECTION

What good is it, my brothers, if a man claims to have faith but has no deeds? Can such faith save him? In the same way, faith by itself, if it is not accompanied by action, is dead. But someone will say, "You have faith; I have deeds." Show me your faith without deeds, and I will show you my faith by what I do. You foolish man, do you want evidence that faith without deeds is useless? Was not our ancestor Abraham considered righteous for what he did when he offered his son Isaac on the altar? You see that his faith and his actions were working together, and his faith was made complete by what he did. You see that a person is justified by what he does and not by faith alone. As the body without the spirit is dead, so faith without deeds is dead.

James 2:14–26

What do we do about the corruption in our heart? How do we remove it and replace it with what pleases God and produces God-honoring behavior? Two suggestions are in order. The first has to do with corrective action when corruption exists. The second has to do with preventive action so that we can live a more proactive, productive life in alignment with God's redemptive purposes. I will focus on the corrective strategy in this chapter.

Although our skill in determining our central beliefs, core values, worldview, and motives is important, it is far more critical to replace corrupted, worldly, sinful beliefs, values, attitudes, and motives with biblically informed alternatives. The following process is recommended:

1. Identify corrupted, dysfunctional, sinful behaviors in your life.

2. Pray to the Father and ask Him to sensitize you to those behaviors that bring dishonor to both His and your name. The Holy Spirit

within you convicts the world of sin, righteousness, and judgment.[432] By His power He restrains sin in the world.[433] During the life of the Christian, He gives assurance, security, leads, teaches, and enables the believer.[434] By yielding to His control, the Christian becomes filled with the Spirit[435] who produces His fruit in their life.[436] The Holy Spirit will help you see your behavior as God sees your behavior. But without intentionally asking for God's help, we are incapable of accurately discerning the deeper issues of our lives.

3. Determine the primary motive that is producing the unacceptable behavior. Use the list below and check off the ones that might apply to the unacceptable behavior.

Anger	Blind Ambition	Conditional Love	Conquest	Control
Envy	Destruction	Domination	Gluttony	Greed
Hatred	Immorality	Jealousy	Lust	Materialism
Meanness	Possessiveness	Pride	Racism	Selfishness
Self-protection	Sense of Entitlement	Sexual Gratification	Superiority	Vengeance
Cruelty	Domination	Control		

All a man's ways seem innocent to him, but motives are weighed by the LORD.[437] My conscience is clear, but that does not make me innocent. It is the Lord who judges me. Therefore, judge nothing before the appointed time; wait until the Lord comes. He will bring to light what is hidden in darkness and will expose the motives of men's hearts. At that time, each will receive his praise from God.[438] What causes fights and quarrels among you? Don't they come from your desires that battle within you? You want something but don't get it. You kill and covet, but you cannot have what you want. You quarrel and fight. You do not have, because you do not ask God. When you ask, you do not receive, because you ask with wrong motives, that you

432 John 16:8–11
433 2 Thessalonians 2:6–8
434 John 14:15–27
435 Ephesians 5:18
436 Galatians 5:22–25
437 Proverbs 16:2
438 1 Corinthians 4:4–5

may spend what you get on your pleasures.[439] For the word of God is living and active. Sharper than any double-edged sword, it penetrates even to dividing soul and spirit, joints and marrow; it judges the thoughts and attitudes of the heart.[440]

4. Confess the motive if it is found to be corrupted and sinful.

5. It's possible to have a good motive but sinful belief system or corrupted value. For instance, a leader acts to protect his followers by articulating a code of conduct designed to protect them. This seems innocent enough until we learn that the leader is a white supremacist whose belief and value systems are full of venom and hate. In most cases, however, sinful behavior is the overt result of an unbridled sinful motive. Unless it is acknowledged and confessed and its underlying beliefs and values changed, the behavior will persist.

6. Try to trace the motive back to a specific core value or central belief that might be the source.

7. This may prove difficult at first. It may be helpful to speak to a close friend who understands the relationship of each heart component to behavior. It may also be helpful to write the sinful behavior and suspected motive on a sheet of paper, and speculate as to a central belief and core value that could produce such a motive and behavior. Again, ask for God's help in the process. Once you have uncovered the suspected central belief and the values that follow, confess them before the Lord and ask God to help you replace the corrupted beliefs and values with biblical beliefs and values.

8. Commit to acting on your new beliefs and values at every opportunity. Your worldview and motives will change as a direct result.

9. Remember, a belief doesn't become an ingrained belief until it's acted upon.[441] Act on the biblically based belief in obedience repeatedly.[442] As the saying goes, "Sow a thought, reap an attitude. Sow an attitude, reap an action. Sow an action, reap a habit. Sow a habit, reap a lifestyle." Beliefs can become an ingrained lifestyle. It's a matter of choice!

---

439 James 4:1–3
440 Hebrews 4:12
441 James 2:14–16
442 1 John 2:3–6; 3:18; 5:2–12

Obedience requires action on the part of the believer empowered by the Holy Spirit.

Transformational Change Steps

When an evil spirit comes out of a man, it goes through arid places seeking rest and does not find it. Then it says, 'I will return to the house I left.' When it arrives, it finds the house unoccupied, swept clean and put in order. Then it goes and takes with it seven other spirits more wicked than itself, and they go in and live there. And the final condition of that man is worse than the first. That is how it will be with this wicked generation ... The thief comes only to steal and kill and destroy; I have come that they may have life, and have it to the full.[443]

Maybe this has been your experience—confessing the same sins over and over again. Victory over the sin is elusive at best and downright annoying. The Bible says the abundant life is ours this side of heaven. Yet few of us seem to be enjoying the abundant life. Sin plagues us at every turn—some of us sin repeatedly. We confess our sin, and ask for the Holy Spirit's empowerment not to sin again in that area, only to have it repeat again and again. Some of us just give up—it is the thorn in our side that we must bear—or so we think.

I believe the problem lies with an incomplete picture of transformational change—it happens in two phases: **removal** and **replacement**. We are very familiar with the first but somewhat unfamiliar with the second. As the Scripture above implies, if you clean out sin through confession but do not replace it with something else, it may be many times worse than before the cleaning.

For instance, assume you have a decayed tooth that must be extracted by a dentist. Once it is removed, what happens if a substitute tooth or bridge is not installed? Over time, your remaining teeth will reposition and your bite will change. Your teeth might chip, your gums may become diseased, or other diseases may follow. Removal must be followed with replacement.

The following process represents a more expanded and complete journey to wholeness and holiness. The first four steps involve removal; the last

---

443 Matthew 12:43–45; John 10:10

four replacement. These eight steps of transformation easily fall under the process outlined above.

Removal

Removal begins with awareness that something is wrong. This realization is followed by prayerful reflection to clarify the cause. For change to take place, we must recognize that the sinful behavior does not measure up to God's standards for His family. It is crucial at this point that we comprehend the relationship between beliefs, values, attitudes, and motives that led to our behavior. Finally, we complete the removal process by confessing our sin, whether it was a corrupted belief, value, attitude, or motive that led to corrupted behavior.

1. *Realization (Awareness)*

First, there must be an awareness of sin, if we are to remove it. Generally, the first indication is conviction by the Holy Spirit who resides in us. He convicts the world of sin, righteousness, and judgment. He guides us into all truth—truth about ourselves. Perhaps a corrupted belief, value, attitude, or motive led to corrupted behavior. Knowing what underlies our corruption will help us recover from such corruption.[444]

2. Reflection (Prayer)

Sometimes it is not all that clear how the problem began. It may be a pattern in our lives established long ago—the cause of which has been forgotten or suppressed over time. Its effects are still felt and played out in our behavior. We may focus on the symptoms rather than the actual cause that resulted in repeated sinful behavior. Prayer can clear the fog. Again, the Holy Spirit will provide counsel and will teach us. The Bible can shed light on the cause, too.[445]

3. Recognition (Understanding)

Comprehension of the relationship between beliefs, values, attitudes, and motives as they relate to behavior is helpful at this stage. We are to guard our heart because it is out of the heart that evil springs.[446] It gushes forth in overt behavior that brings either glory and honor to the Lord or

444 John 16:8–11, 13–15
445 John 14:16–17, 26; Hebrews 4:12
446 Proverbs 4:23

dishonor and shame. Examination of our life is necessary. Identification of the root cause or causes will ensure that the problem is dealt with properly, efficiently, and effectively by God's grace and the Holy Spirit's empowerment.[447]

4. Removal (Confession)

Confession for the believer includes acknowledgment before God that our behavior is wrong; thankfulness and gratitude that God paid the penalty through His Son; appreciation that we are already forgiven and that we simply must receive that forgiveness; and finally, appropriation of the strength that is in Christ to live a more godly life. True confession recognizes that Jesus is Lord—our Master, Mediator, and Messiah. It was His sacrifice that provides atonement for our sins.[448]

Replacement

Replacement is critical to the transformational change process. Replacement begins with true repentance that leads to fruitful evidence that it has truly happened. There must be a turning away from our sinful behavior and a turning to a life of godliness. Repentance is followed by replacing the lie that gave rise to the sin with the truth that will set us free. Substitution begins with a willingness to be taught, rebuked, corrected, and trained in righteousness—to experience daily renewal in Christ. Renewal requires action. A belief or value is not real unless we act on it. Mental affirmation alone does not cut it. Finally, recalibration and realignment with our primary objective—godliness—will produce a godly life; the gift that keeps giving.

5. Repentance (Turning)

Repentance is not talked about much in many churches today. We like to keep our options open and keep control of our destiny. We forget we were bought with a price; that we are under new management; that we are to turn from what is defeating us and turn to what will give us life. Our lives should bear fruit befitting repentance. Repentance is not an option; it is a mandate from the Lord. In God's economy, there is no such thing as conditional surrender.[449]

---

447 2 Corinthians 13:5; Philippians 1:9–11
448 1 John 1:8–9; Romans 10:9–10
449 Matthew 3:8; Luke 13:3; Acts 2:38; 3:19; 26:20; 2 Peter 3:9

6. Replacement (Substitution)

Replacement with and obedience to Christ's teachings proves we are His disciples. Truth replaces the lie and brings life to the believer. The process begins with submission to biblical authority; acceptance of its critique of our lives; embracing its corrective measures; and subjecting ourselves to His training with devotion, discipline, and diligence so that we will be equipped for every good work. Once the corruption has been removed, it must be replaced with a healthy and godly alternative.[450]

7. Renewal/Restoration (Action)

The truth replacing the lie must be acted upon at every turn if transformation is to take place. If truth is not substituted for the lie and brought to vibrant life by a vibrant relationship with our life-giver—God through Christ—it will get much worse before it ever gets better. Informed faith submits to obedience before freedom, commitment before understanding, and acceptance before realization. As James said, faith without action is dead.[451]

8. Recalibration (Alignment)

Finally, recalibration to our primary objective of God's preferred lifestyle will ensure advancement and not retreat. God's grace in Christ teaches us to say no to ungodliness and worldly passions. It instructs us on how to live self-controlled, upright, and godly lives in the here and now. We are not to live with our bags packed, waiting to be ushered into glory. We have a godly life to live and a godly purpose to fulfill.[452]

Titus 2:11–14. For the grace of God that brings salvation has appeared to all men. It teaches us to say no to ungodliness and worldly passions, and to live self-controlled, upright, and godly lives in this present age, while we wait for the blessed hope—the glorious appearing of our great God and Savior, Jesus Christ, who gave himself for us to redeem us from all wickedness and to purify for himself a people that are his very own, eager to do what is good.

---

450 John 8:31–32; 2 Timothy 3:16–17; Ephesians 4:22–24
451 James 2:17, 20–22, 26; Romans 12:1–3
452 Titus 2:11–14

Guiding Transformational Prayers

The following prayers have been adapted from Neil T. Anderson's work, *Resolving Spiritual Conflicts* (1992*)* and are suggested for removing corrupted beliefs and values and sinful attitudes and motives, so that we will be engaged in God-honoring, godly behavior.

1. Ask God to reveal the corrupted motives, attitudes, values, and beliefs that are producing ungodly behavior in your life.[453] Spend time in reflection and prayer.

2. Pray this prayer or a similar one out loud, not because its utterance is magical or a supernatural formula but because it presents God's truth, boldly, unashamedly, and powerfully:

Dear heavenly Father, You have told us to put on the Lord Jesus Christ and make no provision for the flesh in regards to its lusts.[454] I acknowledge that I have given in to fleshly lusts that wage war against my soul.[455] I thank you that in Christ Jesus my sins are forgiven, but I have transgressed your holy law and given the Enemy an opportunity to wage war in my members.[456] I come before your presence to acknowledge these sins and false beliefs and to seek your cleansing[457] that I may be freed from the bondage of sin and falsehood. I now ask you to reveal to my mind the ways that I have transgressed your moral law and grieved the Holy Spirit. In Jesus' precious name, I pray. Amen.

3. Name them before the Lord and renounce them in the power of His Holy Spirit.[458]

4. Recite this prayer out loud:

Dear heavenly Father, I know that you desire truth in the inner self and that facing this truth is the way of liberation.[459] I acknowledge that

---

453 John 16:13, 24; Psalm 139:23, 24
454 Romans 13:14
455 1 Peter 2:11
456 Romans 6:12–13; James 4:1; 1 Peter 5:8
457 1 John 1:9
458 Ephesians 4:15, 25
459 John 8:32

I have been deceived by the father of lies[460] and that I have deceived myself.[461] I pray in the name of the Lord Jesus Christ that you, heavenly Father, will rebuke all deceiving spirits by virtue of the shed blood and resurrection of the Lord Jesus Christ. By faith I have received you into my life, and I am now seated with Christ in the heavenliest.[462] I acknowledge that I have the responsibility and authority to resist the devil, and when I do, he will flee from me. I now ask the Holy Spirit to guide me into all truth.[463] I ask you to "Search me, O God, and know my heart; try me and know my anxious thoughts; and see if there be any hurtful way in me, and lead me in the everlasting way."[464] In Jesus' name, I pray. Amen.

5. If it is repeated sin in a specific area, confess it before God.[465]

6. Recite this prayer out loud:

    Dear heavenly Father, You have said that rebellion is as the sin of witchcraft, and insubordination is as iniquity and idolatry.[466] I know that in action and attitude I have sinned against you with a rebellious heart. I ask your forgiveness for my rebellion and pray that by the shed blood of the Lord Jesus Christ, all ground gained by the evil one and his spirits, because of my rebelliousness, would be canceled. I pray that you will shed light on all my ways that I may know the full extent of my rebelliousness, and I now choose to adopt a submissive attitude and a servant's heart. I now confess these sins to you, and claim through the blood of the Lord Jesus Christ, my forgiveness and cleansing. I ask this in the wonderful name of my Lord and Savior, Jesus Christ. Remind me of this commitment and give me the courage to follow through with obedience. Amen.

7. Replace the corrupted belief(s) with a biblically based belief (system).[467]

---

460 John 8:44
461 1 John 1:8
462 Ephesians 2:6
463 John 16:13
464 Psalm 139:23–24
465 1 John 1:8–9
466 1 Samuel 15:23
467 John 8:31–32

Read aloud the following affirmation of faith, and do so again, as often as necessary, to remind yourself of God's truth:

I recognize there is only one true and living God (Exodus 20:2–3) *who exists as the Father, Son, and Holy Spirit and that He is worthy of all honor, praise, and glory as the Creator, Sustainer, and beginning and end of all things* (Revelation 4:11; 5:9–10; Isaiah 43:1, 7, 21).

I recognize Jesus Christ as the Messiah, the Word who became flesh and dwelt among us (John 1:1, 14). *I believe that He came to destroy the works of Satan* (1 John 3:8), *that He disarmed the rulers and authorities and made a public display of them, having triumphed over them* (Colossians 2:15).

I believe that God has proven His love for me because when I was still a sinner, Christ died for me (Romans 5:8). *I believe that He delivered me from the domain of darkness and transferred me to His kingdom, and in Him I have redemption, the forgiveness of sins* (Colossians 1:13-14).

I believe that I am now a child of God (1 John 3:1–3) *and that I am seated with Christ in the heavenlies* (Ephesians 2:6). *I believe that I was saved by the grace of God through faith, that it was a gift and not the results of any works on my part* (Ephesians 2:8).

I choose to be strong in the Lord and in the strength of His might (Ephesians 6:10). *I put no confidence in the flesh* (Philippians 3:3) *for the weapons of warfare are not of the flesh* (2 Corinthians 10:4). *I put on the whole armor of God* (Ephesians 6:10–20), *and I resolve to stand firm in my faith and resist the evil one.*

I believe that apart from Christ I can do nothing (John 15:5), *so I declare myself dependent upon Him. I choose to abide in Christ in order to bear much fruit and glorify the Lord* (John 15:8). *I announce to Satan that Jesus is my Lord* (1 Corinthians 12:3), *and I reject any counterfeit gifts or works of Satan in my life.*

I believe that the truth will set me free (John 8:32) *and that walking in the light is the only path of fellowship* (1 John 1:7). *Therefore, I stand against Satan's deception by taking every thought captive in obedience to Christ* (2 Corinthians 10:5). *I declare that the Bible is the only authoritative standard* (2 Timothy 3:15-16). *I choose to speak the truth in love* (Ephesians 4:15).

I choose to present my body as an instrument of righteousness, a living and holy sacrifice, and I renew my mind and heart by the living word of God in order that I may prove that the will of God is good, acceptable and perfect (Romans 6:13; 12:1–2). *I put off the old self with its evil practices and put on the new self* (Colossians 3:9–10), *and I declare myself to be a new creature in Christ* (2 Corinthians 5:17).

I ask my heavenly Father to fill me with the Holy Spirit (Ephesians 5:18), *lead me into all truth* (John 16:13), *and empower my life that I may live above sin and not carry out the desires of the flesh* (Galatians 5:16). *I crucify the flesh* (Galatians 5:24) *and choose to walk by the Spirit. I renounce all selfish goals and choose the ultimate goal of love* (1 Timothy 1:5). *I choose to obey the two greatest commandments, to love the Lord my God with all my heart, soul, and mind, and to love my neighbor as myself* (Matthew 22:37–39).

I believe that Jesus has all authority in heaven and earth (Matthew 28:18) *and that He is the head over all rule and authority* (Colossians 2:10). *I believe that Satan and his demons are subject to me in Christ since I am a member of Christ's body* (Ephesians 1:19–23). *Therefore, I obey the command to resist the devil* (James 4:17) *and command him in the name of Christ to leave my presence.*

Conclusion

Removal must be followed by **replacement**. Remove through confession and replace with God's truth. Then act on that truth. "If you hold to my [Jesus'] teaching, you are really my disciples. Then you will know the truth, and the truth will set you free."[468]

BATTLE PLAN

1. Identify corrupted, dysfunctional, sinful behaviors in your life. (Realize, Reflect)

2. Determine what primary motive is producing the unacceptable behavior. Use the list below, and check off the ones that might apply to the unacceptable behavior. (Recognize)

---

468 John 8:31–32

217

Anger	Blind Ambition	Conditional Love	Conquest	Control
Envy	Destruction	Domination	Gluttony	Greed
Hatred	Immorality	Jealousy	Lust	Materialism
Meanness	Possessiveness	Pride	Racism	Self-centeredness
Self-protection	Sense of Entitlement	Sexual Gratification	Superiority	Vengeance
Cruelty		Domination	Control	

3. Confess the motive if found to be corrupt and sinful. (Remove, Repent)

4. Try to trace the motive back to a specific core value or central belief that might be the source. (Recognize)

5. Commit to acting on your new beliefs and values at every opportunity. Your worldview and motives will change as a direct result. (Recalibrate, Replace, Renew/Restore)

CHAPTER 12
PREVENTION

Create in me a pure heart, O God, and
renew a steadfast spirit within me.

Psalms 51:10

This final chapter will help you develop a workable plan to ensure that you become a man after God's own heart. This plan will provide recommended actions to transform your heart so that people will know you bear in your person the imprint of Christ in what you think, say, and do. The goal is to examine what or who is feeding your heart, develop a personal battle plan to align your heart to God's word, and commit to living a life of courage, integrity, and authenticity.

In the many years I have worked with men, all too frequently a plan is developed but follow-through is lacking. Once the plan is complete, it lies dormant. I trust that will not be the case with you. There is too much at stake.

Intentionality

One reason to develop a plan is so that we reach God's designed potential for our life. God has a specific purpose for our life.[469] As mentioned earlier, we have a destiny to fulfill, a purpose to engage, a contribution to make, a ministry to complete, and a legacy to leave. We are here on this earth for a reason; we are not a product of fate, a mistake, or a coincidence. We are here by design. Aligning ourselves with God's purposes for this is extremely important. Too many of us bumble our way through life, with little thought given to what will remain of our journey after we are gone. I encourage you to live in such a way that there will be no regrets.

As I write this, I am sitting at a desk in Major Warren Lewis' bedroom. He is the brother of C. S. Lewis, in whose home in Headington, England,

469 Ephesians 2:10

I am staying as I finish this book. I find living here, steeped in the rich heritage of C. S. Lewis, particularly meaningful and inspiring. Lewis has left a godly legacy that is still enjoyed today through his books and the movies that have been made from them. His book *Mere Christianity* has a special place in my life, as I am sure it does in the lives of many who have read it. The pleasant aroma that still lingers from his life has lifted many from the misty lowlands of mediocrity. Likewise, may the aroma of your life be pleasing to God and linger long after you are gone in the lives of those God has brought within your sphere of influence.

Accountability

We will be held accountable for what we have accomplished with our life. As believers, we will appear before the judgment seat of Christ to give account for what we have done with what we have been given.

> *For we must all appear before the judgment seat of Christ, that each one may receive what is due him for the things done while in the body, whether good or bad.*[470]

For example, receiving the seed of the fruit of the Spirit at conversion requires focused attention, in tandem with the work of the Holy Spirit, to produce the fruit of God's character abundantly in our life. There must be an increase from what we have been given—but of a certain quality.

> *By the grace God has given me, I laid a foundation as an expert builder, and someone else is building on it. But each one should be careful how he builds. For no one can lay any foundation other than the one already laid, which is Jesus Christ. If any man builds on this foundation using **gold, silver, costly stones, wood, hay or straw**, his work will be shown for what it is, because the day will bring it to light. It will be revealed with fire, and the fire will test the quality of each man's work. If what he has built survives, he will receive his reward. If it is burned up, he will suffer loss; he himself will be saved, but only as one escaping through the flames.*[471]

---

470 2 Corinthians 5:10
471 1 Corinthians 3:10-15

More dramatically, if we return to God only what we have been given, with no increase, we will be treated like the unfaithful servant who did the same:

> "Again, it will be like a man going on a journey, who called his servants and entrusted his property to them. To one he gave five talents of money, to another two talents, and to another one talent, each according to his ability. Then he went on his journey. The man who had received the five talents went at once and put his money to work and gained five more. So also, the one with the two talents gained two more. But the man who had received the one talent went off, dug a hole in the ground and hid his master's money. After a long time, the master of those servants returned and settled accounts with them. The man who had received the five talents brought the other five. 'Master,' he said, 'you entrusted me with five talents. See, I have gained five more.' His master replied, 'Well done, good and faithful servant! You have been faithful with a few things; I will put you in charge of many things. Come and share your master's happiness!' The man with the two talents also came. 'Master,' he said, 'you entrusted me with two talents; see, I have gained two more.' His master replied, 'Well done, good and faithful servant! You have been faithful with a few things; I will put you in charge of many things. Come and share your master's happiness!' Then the man who had received the one talent came. 'Master,' he said, 'I knew that you are a hard man, harvesting where you have not sown and gathering where you have not scattered seed. So I was afraid and went out and hid your talent in the ground. See, here is what belongs to you.' His master replied, 'You wicked, lazy servant! So you knew that I harvest where I have not sown and gather where I have not scattered seed? Well then, you should have put my money on deposit with the bankers, so that when I returned I would have received it back with interest. Take the talent from him and give it to the one who has the ten talents. For everyone who has will be given more, and he will have an abundance. Whoever does not have, even what he has will be taken from him.

*And throw that worthless servant outside, into the darkness,
where there will be weeping and gnashing of teeth."*[472]

I hope the message is clear. As stated earlier, the only time you are
guaranteed 100 percent accuracy is when you aim at nothing—you are
bound to hit it. If you have made it through this book to this point, you
are now ready to develop your distinct, unique, and personal battle plan.
This plan will define the objectives you hope to obtain, the strategies you
intend to employ, and the tactics you will engage in becoming a man after
God's heart.

Eight Essential Facts

Certain basic and fundamental presuppositions are assumed.

1. Lasting behavioral change is not accomplished by focusing primarily
   on behavior.

   Too often, our behavior is simply a manifestation of underlying
   motives, attitudes, values, and beliefs that give rise to the behavior
   observed. When we attempt to address behavior alone, without
   attention to its underlying influences, we are simply focusing on
   symptoms rather than the cause. We place a Band-Aid on a festering
   sore, not realizing a hidden malady is producing that sore. Until one
   deals with the malady, the sore will continue to fester, even though it
   may seem to be healed for a time.

2. Behavior is fundamentally a by-product of what is stored in our
   hearts.

   Our behavior reflects the condition of our heart—the core of our
   being. Whatever is there will gush forth in demonstrable behavior
   that will honor our Savior or bring discredit upon ourselves.[473] Two
   toxic chemicals, when kept apart in separate containers, will lay inert
   until their potential is unleashed when they are combined. What lies
   dormant in our hearts can become lethal and active when stimulated
   by outside circumstances. The potential for trouble is there but not
   currently active, until a circumstance, event, or persons bring it alive,
   resulting in sinful behaviors.

---

472 Matthew 25:14–30
473 Proverbs 4:23

3. Man focuses on appearances; God focuses on the heart.

God reminded Samuel, the judge and prophet, of what He looks at in the lives of His creatures. While man is often swayed by appearances and stature, God looks at the heart.[474] Elections bring out the worst with regard to this phenomenon. How many times have you listened to commentators or read editorials about a candidate that focus almost entirely on how the candidate carries himself, dresses, looks, talks, or gestures, as if these characteristics convey unequivocally his suitability for high office? The nature of a man or woman is determined by the condition of his or her heart. Appearance might hint at his substance, but all too often, we are wrong in our judgment of appearances.

4. God is looking for men after His own heart.

After removing Saul, God made David king. In the book of Acts, the inspired writer Luke reported God's evaluation of David's life.[475] In Psalms we are told that David shepherded his people with "integrity of heart," and with skillful hands, he led them.[476] You might ask how this could be so, in light of his glaring sins. Before we are too quick to judge, God said he had one endearing quality: "he will do everything I want him to do." More subjectively, reading the Psalms he has written gives us a clue as to his heart. We can soar like an eagle or grovel in the pigpen. Aren't you glad God has not given up on us? In many ways, we are more like David than we care to admit.

5. Central beliefs, core values, worldview, and motives comprise the heart.

My research of more than eight hundred verses in the Bible regarding *heart* or one of its derivatives reveals that the heart comprises four components: beliefs, values, attitudes (worldview), and motives. Please refer to Appendix A for a more complete rendering of the evidence.

6. Our central beliefs establish our values. Our core values inform our worldview. Our world view conditions our motives. Our motives energize our behavior. Our behavior reflects what's in our hearts.

---

474 1 Samuel 16:7
475 Acts 13:22
476 Psalm 78:72

There is indeed a symbiotic connection—a relationship of mutual benefit or dependence—between the components of the heart. Although my description may appear rather linear, a kind of cause-and-effect portrayal, it is more like an ecosystem.[477] Spiritual matters are described in organic ways throughout the Bible. The concept of "heart" is no different. We can say that the heart is an ecosystem composed of a community of organisms, with a system of interacting and independent relationships, yet connected with each other. Energy flows back and forth between these organisms—between beliefs, values, attitudes, and motives. Like a real ecosystem, other factors can affect its health and well-being, such as the world, the flesh, the devil or God, the Bible, Christ, and the Holy Spirit.

7. Our objective is to be so controlled and influenced by the Spirit of God as to have the mind of Christ in our beliefs, values, attitudes, and motives, so that our character is Christ-like, and our behavior brings glory to God.

The purpose of the church universal is not to edify the body and build it up—that is the means to a greater end—but the development of Christ-likeness in its followers.[478] We are called to be holy,[479] to say no to ungodliness, and to live upright and godly lives in this present age.[480] When a follower of Christ becomes a person after God's heart, he will believe what God believes, value what God values, see the world as God sees it, and will be motivated by God's motives. His behavior, then, will reflect God's character and give ample evidence that he is a member of good standing in God's family.

8. To change behavior, we must have a change of heart.

Once again, I am reminded of Netanyahu's quote: *"Real peace,"* he says, *"does not come from the hand that signs the treaties; it comes from the head and the heart that formulates them and then forms the attitude*

---

477 A community of organisms together with their physical environment, viewed as a system of interacting and interdependent relationships, and including such processes as the flow of energy through trophic levels and the cycling of chemical elements and compounds through living and nonliving components of the system.
478 Ephesians 4:11–16
479 Ephesians 1:4; Hebrews 12:14; 1 Peter 1:15–16
480 Titus 2:11–14

toward these treaties, because true peace comes from the heart, or more precisely, it comes from a change of heart."[481] When such a change in our heart takes place, our behavior follows. The world takes notice of a man after God's heart. People may not always agree with the man, but they admire his authenticity and integrity.

Developing a Personal Battle Plan

The last chapter dealt with cleaning the heart of corruption, dysfunction, and sin. In this chapter, you will develop a **personal battle plan**, consisting of central beliefs, core values, worldview, and primary motives. This will be your battle cry, your war strategy, and your tactics for becoming a man after God's heart.

Developing a personal battle plan begins with your central beliefs, followed by core values, worldview, and primary motives.

A form to record your responses is found at the end of this chapter.

It may be easier to select your core values first. If you do this, be sure to tie each value to one or more central beliefs. Beliefs establish our values.

In any case, spend time in prayer and ask God, through Christ and the Holy Spirit, for guidance, counsel, and clarity.

Central Beliefs

Our central beliefs are the foundation for all behavior. They are more than verbal affirmations of beliefs. In other words, at our deepest core, they are what we really believe—so much so that they are a part of our being. They determine our values, affect our attitudes, and influence our motives. They ultimately determine how we behave in a given situation.

A biblical belief system might include the Ten Commandments; loving others as yourself; we are created in the image of God; man is sinful; human nature is corrupt; God loves us; apart from God, life is meaningless; salvation is the only means to wholeness; God has plans for our lives; man's chief purpose is to demonstrate God's excellence in all that we do; human life is to be cherished; widows and orphans are to be taken care of; Christ is the only means of salvation.

---

481 Rachel Ingber. "Israel's Vision of Security and Peace," in *Peacewatch*, no. 121 (February 1997).

Select a minimum of five central beliefs from the list below. This list is by no means exhaustive, and additional beliefs can be selected, but a Scripture reference supporting that belief must be identified. It's also important to select operational beliefs, as opposed to foundational beliefs. You may recall the distinction:

> **Foundational beliefs** provide the stable platform of our existence. They are absolute truths that establish our relationship with our Creator and His created world. They are foundational in nature and give us confidence, hope, and orientation for our journey. They establish the fact that we are connected to our Creator and answer the fundamental questions of our existence, identity, purpose, and destiny. They inform our journey. They have to do with our **beingness**. For instance, a Christian worldview, such as has been described earlier, is composed essentially of *foundational beliefs*.

> **Operational beliefs** are also absolute truths. The difference, however, is that they are actionable—they compel us to do something. They require a response and provide a general guideline for our behavior and actions. They provide the basis for our values—the filter through which we process our decisions, the hills on which we are prepared to die, and the principles we intend to live out in our daily lives. They have to do with our **doingness**. For instance, the Ten Commandments are essentially *operational beliefs*. They compel us to act.

Examples of Central Beliefs

You will note there is a mixture of foundational and operational beliefs in the list. Ask yourself the following questions: "How do I anticipate my life changing as a result of these beliefs?" "What kind of behavior can the members of my sphere of influence (e.g., family, friends, and associates) expect to see in me?"

- The Bible is my sole authority in faith and practice (2 Timothy 3:16–17; Hebrews 4:12).
- God loves me unconditionally (1 John 4:13–19; Galatians 2:20).
- I am a permanent member of His family (Ephesians 1:5).
- My salvation is secured forever (Ephesians 1:13–14).

- God's love knows no limits (John 3:16).
- I am forgiven (Ephesians 1:7).
- The truth sets us free when we obey it (John 8:31–32).
- The heart is to be guarded (Proverbs 4:23).
- I am to live a sober, upright, and godly life (Titus 2:11–12).
- I am to live a life worthy of His calling (Ephesians 4:1–2; Colossians 1:10).
- Christ-likeness is my objective (Ephesians 4:13, 15; Romans 8:29; 2 Corinthians 3:18).
- I have a destiny to fulfill (Jeremiah 29:11).
- I have a contribution to make (1 Corinthians 12:4–7).
- I have a ministry to complete (Ephesians 4:11–16).
- I have a legacy to leave (2 Timothy 2:2; 1 Chronicles 28:8).
- I am to love the Lord with all my heart, soul, and mind (Matthew 22:37).
- I am to love my neighbors as myself (Matthew 22:39).
- My highest purpose is to bring glory to God (1 Peter 2:9; Ephesians 1:12, 1 Corinthians 10:31).
- I am to keep God's commandments (Ecclesiastes 12:13; Matthew 5:17–19; 1 John 5:2–3).
- I am to aim my life at righteousness and godliness (1 Timothy 6:11).
- I am to abstain from immorality (1 Thessalonians 4:3–8).
- My life should be an act of worship to God (Romans 12:1–2; Colossians 3:17).
- I am to put to death what is earthly in me (Colossians 3:5–10).
- My thoughts should be honorable and pure (Philippians 4:8).
- I am to put on the whole armor of God (Ephesians 6:10–18).
- I am to love my wife as God loves the church (Ephesians 5:25).
- I am to make wise use of my time (Ephesians 5:15–16).
- I am to expose the works of darkness (Ephesians 5:11).
- I am to remember that God has raised me to a higher life (Ephesians 2:1–7).
- I am to walk by the Spirit and not my flesh (Galatians 5:16–26).

- I am to be God's love letter to the world (2 Corinthians 3:2–3).
- God is not a God of confusion but a God of peace (1 Corinthians 14:33).
- All things are to be done decently and in order (1 Corinthians 14:40).
- Love is unconditional and others-oriented (1 Corinthians 13:4–8).
- I am to seek the good of my neighbor first (1 Corinthians 10:24).
- My body is the temple of the Holy Spirit (1 Corinthians 6:19–20).
- I am to live in harmony with others (Romans 12:14–21).
- I am to never flag in zeal (Romans 12:11).
- In everything, God works for good (Romans 8:28).
- All of creation suffers as a consequence of sin (Romans 8:18–25).
- I am not to yield to wickedness (Romans 6:12–13).
- I will not be free of suffering here on earth (1 Peter 1:6; 4:13; Romans 5:3; 2 Timothy 1:8; Philippians 3:10).

Core Values

Values are the hills on which we will die; the principles we live by. They comprise our moral system. They are the filter through which life is processed and decisions are made. Values are what we esteem, and we find it hard to understand why others may not hold them in the same esteem. Terms related to values include morality, virtues, ethics, principles, rules, standards, and norms. A value becomes a virtue when it is an ingrained habit that we apply without thinking much about it.

Examples of biblically informed values might include centered living; devotion to God; family first; loyalty; justice; mercy; honesty; fairness; hard work; punctuality; self-discipline; courage; submission to the authority of God's word; being a man of integrity.

In addition to our God-given set of values—the fruit of the Spirit—select a minimum of five additional core values from the list below. Other values not on the list can be selected. The values should arise from your belief system—they should relate to the beliefs you have selected and not violate or contradict those beliefs.

To help in the selection process, ask yourself the following questions:

"What is it that I treasure so highly that I am irritated when other people don't react in the same way?"
"What are the things I respect so deeply that I tend to be resentful of those who treat them with disrespect?"
"What core value(s) do I hope my children will adopt?"
"How do I anticipate my life changing as a result of these values? What kind of behavior can the members of my group expect to see in my life?"

Personal	Spiritual	Relational
Decency	Devotion	Compassion
Courage	Diligence	Forgiveness
Perseverance	Dedication	Friendliness
Self-discipline	Faithfulness	Honesty
Centeredness	Holiness	Loyalty
Wisdom	Joyfulness	Justice
Hard Work	Obedience	Fairness
Purity	Prayerfulness	Unselfishness
Gratefulness	Godliness	Helpfulness
Truthfulness	Servanthood	Support

Once you have selected a value, draft a sentence or two that describes the value in your own terms, something you and others who read it will understand.

Then, select one or two verses from Scripture that bring the selected value into focus. This step will ensure that the value is informed by the Bible and will lead to godly behavior.

Next, select an appropriate context in which you hope to act on that value. The context will change over time, as God shows you where He wants you to exercise the value.

Finally, select a time frame in which you will proactively act on the value. When the time frame is complete, spend reflective time evaluating your progress and determining what you will do next.

Two examples follow:

Value:	**Decency**
Description:	Decency will characterize all my interactions with others, the decisions I make, and the language I use.
Focus:	1 Corinthians 13:4–8; Ephesians 4:2
Context:	My workplace
Timeframe:	Three months

Value:	**Courage**
Description:	I will be courageous in my witness for the Lord and seek to share the Gospel with any who will listen to me.
Focus:	Deuteronomy 31:6; Joshua 1:6–9
Context:	My friendships
Timeframe:	Three months

Worldview (Perceptual Attitudes)

Each of us has a set of perceptual attitudes that help shape our outlook on life. If beliefs are the foundations for our behavior, and values are the filters through which we process life's decisions, then attitudes are the lens through which we observe life around us. Our system of attitudes is also called our worldview. The term worldview refers to any "ideology, philosophy, theology, movement, or religion that provides an overarching approach to understanding God, the world, and man's relations to God and the world."

Our set of perceptual attitudes, or our worldview, determines how we perceive and interpret our observations of the world around us. The worldview we hold at any given time determines how we interpret events, draw conclusions about what we read, evaluate what we observe, assess what we hear, or process arguments.

Examples of biblically informed worldviews might include the Beatitudes (Matthew 5:3–12); God's involvement in history; humans bearing God's imprint; something good can be found in every human being; all things work together for good; theism; all creation is divinely inspired; the world is corrupted by sin; pro-life (to name just a few).

In your own words, what is your worldview, given Dr. David Clark's five essential issues that must be considered to form a worldview, as described in chapter 6? You might want to refer to the *foundational beliefs* found in chapter 6 and the key beliefs located below. Feel free to expand on the Christian worldview, described briefly below. Ask yourself the following questions: "How does my worldview relate to my central beliefs and core values? Do I see any correlation between them?"

- The nature of ultimate reality—God exists and is active in our lives.
- The nature of human personhood—humans bear the image of God.
- The basic human dilemma—the image of God is marred by sin.
- The solution to the human dilemma—the person and work of Christ.
- Our human destiny—eternal life or eternal damnation.

Some Key Beliefs of the Christian Worldview

(Adapted from chapter 2 of *Worldviews in Conflict* by Ronald Nash, 1992.)

- All human beings carry the image of God in their person. This image, marred by sin, makes us creatures capable of reasoning, love, and God-consciousness. It also explains why we are moral creatures.
- Universal moral laws exist and are ordained by God.
- The chief purpose of man is to glorify God and enjoy Him forever.
- Sin alienates us from God and enslaves us.
- All human beings long for purpose, progress, and permanence.
- Human beings have a need for forgiveness and redemption.
- Christ's redemptive work is the basis of human salvation.
- Receiving Christ as Savior and Lord brings a new birth (John 3:3–21), new heart (Galatians 2:20), new relationship with God (Hebrews 8:10–12), and a new power to live (1 John 3:1–2).

- The Christian has God's nature and Spirit within and is called to live a particular kind of life in obedience to God.
- The Bible is the Christian's ultimate authority for faith and practice.
- Physical death is not the end of our existence.
- What we do in life echoes in eternity.

Primary Motives

Motives are what stimulate our activity, mobilize us to act, and stimulate our behavior! Webster defines motive as something, such as a need or desire, that causes a person to act. It might take the form of an impulse, inducement, a prod, something that "spurs" us on. It can be seen as a driving force arising from our predispositions, biases, or habitual inclinations.

Motives compel us to take action and may arise from an external stimulus, such as an opportunity, circumstance, or event. Motives provide the bridge from thoughts (temptation) to action (behavior). Some people, for instance, are motivated by greed or jealousy. Others are motivated by love or desire. Still others might be motivated by idealism or self-interest.

Examples of biblically informed motives might be unconditional love, commitment to God, a vow, Christ-centered desires, commitment to a certain value, devotion, diligence, love of others, or self-preservation in the face of danger.

Several things cause people to act: to meet a need, solve problems, achieve, learn, grow, serve, compete, produce, win, or to be noticed—these are internal motivations. External motivations also compel us to act, such as when dealing with a challenge, crisis, emergency, or an opportunity.

From the list below, select one primary motive and one or two secondary motives for your life and behavior. Your selection should reflect your beliefs, values, and worldview but certainly your central beliefs. Ask yourself the following questions: "How can I biblically justify my primary motives?"

"How do they relate to my central beliefs, core values, and worldview?"

"How will my life give evidence of such motivation?"

Achievement	Meaning	Satisfaction
Acquisition	Newness	Service
Advancement	Obedience	Significance
Christ-likeness	Perfection	Spirituality
Discovery	Perseverance	Sponsorship
Duty	Personal Development	Status
Excellence	Pleasure	Success
Experiences	Possession/Increase	Survival
Growth	Power	Unconditional Love
Happiness	Proficiency	Uniqueness
Honor	Purpose	Valor
Improvement	Recognition	Wealth
Influence	Reconciliation	Worship
Kingdom Purposes	Redemption	Other: _____
Knowledge	Responsibility	

Some of these motives have a dark side. For instance, selecting wealth or the pursuit thereof can be good or bad. If the pursuit of wealth is to fund Christian organizations, that would be a good thing. However, if the pursuit of wealth is to secure status in society or obtain possessions for our own self-aggrandizement, that would be a bad thing. This list is not exhaustive and is meant only to suggest ideas.

Final Step of the Battle Plan

Once you have recorded your selections for beliefs, values, attitudes, and motives on the form at the end of this chapter, explain what you intend to do with the plan over the next six months. How do you intend to engage the plan to make it an observed reality in your life? Who will hold you accountable for its implementation? What steps do you intend to take? Most important, what behaviors might someone see in your life as a result of your plan? You might want to prioritize what you intend to do, so that you can focus on what is most needed at this stage of your life.

When it comes to values, you may feel the need to work on the fruit of the Spirit first, before moving on to your additional core values. I would suggest, however, that you do a bit of both at the same time. For instance, you may want to work on love, joy, and peace, while at the same time working on one or more of your core values.

Once the entire battle plan is complete, have someone you trust review it for the purpose of clarity, completeness, and congruence. In other words, does the plan make sense? Does the plan include all components (beliefs, values, attitudes, motives)? Does the plan represent your personal journey to date and what you hope to see in the future? Does it hang together, or is it a gathering of loose unassociated elements? Is there a harmony to it?

I have purposely resisted the temptation to give you an example of a completed plan for the following reasons: 1) I want your plan to be *your* plan and not a variation of another person's plan. 2) I don't want you to be intimidated by or disappointed in someone else's plan. 3) I want you to be directed by the Spirit of God in this process and not by the structure or scope of someone else's plan. This will be your battle plan, inspired by your journey and God's influence in it, through it, and over it. May God bless you as you engage the journey!

Conclusion

Now that you know what a healthy life looks like, begin to live in accordance with God's preferred lifestyle. Once you begin to implement your battle plan, it will be one step at a time. If you fall, pick yourself up and continue the journey. If you fail, begin again. If you stumble, regain your centeredness. The journey might be two steps forward and one back. At other times, it will be two steps back and one forward. Choose to live in accordance with your biblically centered beliefs, values, worldview, and motives. Lean into your fear. Commit to becoming a man after God's heart. Rely on God's empowerment. Never give up—never, never, *never!*

My primary objective throughout the journey we have just completed was to help you become a man after God's heart. You have received what I have been given from the Lord. It's up to you now to live out your personal battle plan so that your life will bring glory and honor to the Father and provide an example for your loved ones, and so you will live a legacy worth leaving in the lives of those you love and those who come under your influence. May God richly bless your quest. May His love and light shine upon you. May His Spirit renew you in the trials that lie ahead. May you finish the race well. May the following be said of you as your race concludes and you go to meet the Father: "Here is a man after God's heart—honor him!"

Prayer of Commitment

Heavenly Father, You have called me to the life of a warrior after Your heart. My shield and my sword are Yours to command. My desire is to live my life intentionally, with focused intensity, single-mindedness, and a commitment to my personal battle plan. I ask for Your blessing, the strength of Christ, and the empowerment of Your Holy Spirit. Help me to never flag in zeal; to be ever vigilant at the post You have assigned me and alert and dedicated to living all out for You; to be a trustworthy guard, a courageous warrior, a man who will stand in bold relief against the Enemy, a soldier ready to defend the helpless, a man who bears in my person the imprint of Your Son. And when all is said and done, when my journey comes to an end, may I be carried on my shield into Your presence before Your throne of grace to give praise to Your holy name. May all who remember me pay You honor for what You have done in and through my life. Amen!

In His strength and to His honor!

Greg Bourgond—comrade in arms and fellow warrior

BATTLE PLAN

Summarize your personal battle plan below.

Central Operational Beliefs

1.

2.

3.

4.

5.

Core Values

1. Value:
   Description:
   Focus (Scripture):
   Context:
   Time Frame:

2. Value:
   Description:
   Focus (Scripture):
   Context:
   Time Frame:

3. Value:
   Description:
   Focus (Scripture):
   Context:
   Time Frame:

4. Value:
   Description:
   Focus (Scripture):
   Context:
   Time Frame:

5. Value:
   Description:
   Focus (Scripture):
   Context:
   Time Frame:

Worldview (Perceptual Attitudes)

- The nature of ultimate reality

- The nature of human personhood

- The basic human dilemma

- The solution to the human dilemma

- Our human destiny

Primary/Secondary Motives

1.

2.

3.

Implementation Plan:

APPENDIX A: CATEGORIZATION OF HEART SCRIPTURES

Scriptures associated with the biblical term **heart** can be essentially assigned to four primary categories: *beliefs, values, attitudes,* and *motives.* Many verses, however, are not so easily categorized. Some can be classified in more than one category. Each verse below has been assigned one or more categories. It can certainly be argued that some of the classifications may stretch the conventional meaning of the category to which it is assigned. Nevertheless, I accept the responsibility for the assignment, arbitrary or otherwise.

Beliefs

Beliefs are what we trust in, rely on, and cling to. Commands, tenets, laws, dictates, injunctions, mandates, precepts, instructions, and the like would fall under this category. For instance, in Deuteronomy 6:5–9 and 26:16, we read: *"Love the Lord your God with all your **heart** and with all your soul and with all your strength. These **commandments** that I give you today are to be upon your **hearts**. Impress **them** on your children. Talk about **them** when you sit at home and when you walk along the road, when you lie down and when you get up. Tie **them** as symbols on your hands and bind **them** on your foreheads. Write **them** on the doorframes of your houses and on your gates … The Lord your God commands you this day to follow these decrees and laws; carefully observe them with all your heart and with all your soul."*

Also, in Mark 11:23, we read: *"I tell you the truth, if anyone says to this mountain, 'Go, throw yourself into the sea,' and does not doubt in his **heart** but **believes** that what he says will happen, it will be done for him."* In

Romans 2:14–15, we read: *"Indeed, when Gentiles, who do not have the* **law**, *do by nature things required by the* **law**, *they are a* **law** *for themselves, even though they do not have the* **law**, *since they show that the requirements of the law are* **written on their hearts**, *their consciences also bearing witness, and their thoughts now accusing, now even defending them."* And finally, in Romans 10:8–10, we read: *"But what does it say? 'The word is near you; it is in your mouth and in your heart,' that is, the word of faith we are proclaiming: That if you confess with your mouth, 'Jesus is Lord,' and* **believe** *in your* **heart** *that God raised him from the dead, you will be saved. For it is with your* **heart** *that you* **believe** *and are justified, and it is with your mouth that you confess and are saved."*

God's intention is clear. Beliefs are to be consciously meditated upon so that God's heart might be our heart. These commands are to ultimately dictate behavior. They are our foundation.

Values

Values are the hills on which we are prepared to die, the principles we intend to live by. Our values are the filter through which we process our decisions. Norms, rules, axioms, virtues, ethics, and morality reflect the nature of values. The book of Proverbs is essentially God's book of values.

In condemnation of another king, the perpetrator is reminded of why David was a man after God's heart. *"I tore the kingdom away from the house of David and gave it to you, but you have not been like my servant David, who kept my commands and* **followed me with all his heart,** *doing only what was right in my eyes."*[482] In Job 33:3, we read, *"My words come from an* **upright heart**; *my lips sincerely speak what I know."* In Psalms 94:15, we read: *"Judgment will again be founded on righteousness, and all the* **upright** *in* **heart** *will follow it."* In Proverbs 16:23, we read: *"A* **wise** *man's* **heart** *guides his mouth, and his lips promote instruction."* In Proverbs 23:26, we read: *"My son, give me your* **heart** *and let your eyes keep to my ways ..."* A warning concludes the Old Testament. In Malachi 2:2, we read: *"If you do not listen, and if you do not set your* **heart** *to* **honor** *my name,"* says the Lord Almighty, *"I will send a curse upon you, and I will curse your blessings. Yes, I have already cursed them, because you have not set your* **heart** *to* **honor** *me."*

---

482 1 Kings 14:8

In the New Testament the supreme value is to first love God and secondly to love others.[483] We also read in Luke 8:15: *"But the seed on good soil stands for those with a **noble** and good **heart**, who hear the word, retain it, and by persevering produce a crop."* In 2 Corinthians 3:2–3, we read: *"You yourselves are our letter, written on our **hearts**, known and read by everybody. You show that you are a letter from Christ, the result of our ministry, written not with ink but with the Spirit of the living God, not on tablets of stone but on tablets of human **hearts**."* And in Hebrews 10:15–16, we read: *"The Holy Spirit also testifies to us about this. First he says: 'This is the covenant I will make with them after that time,' says the Lord. **I will put my laws in their hearts, and I will write them on their minds.'"***

We were given a new heart with God's values written on it. Acting on these values produces Godly behavior.

Attitudes

Another name for the attitudes we have about life is *worldview.* Our worldview comprises the perceptual attitudes we have and by which we make judgments about what we see, hear, think, and feel. Our worldview is the lens through which we make sense of the world around us. The Ten Commandments, the Beatitudes, and other similar passages could comprise a worldview.

Many admired Solomon's worldview. In 2 Chronicles 9:23' we read: *"All the kings of the earth sought audience with Solomon to **hear the wisdom God had put in his heart**."* A biblical worldview understands that discernment comes to those who are wise in heart. We read in Psalms 90:12: *"Teach us to number our days aright, that we may **gain a heart of wisdom**."* In Proverbs 16:21, we learn: *"The wise in **heart** are called **discerning**, and pleasant words promote instruction."* In Proverbs 18:15, we are told: *"The **heart** of the discerning acquires knowledge; the ears of the wise seek it out."* In Hebrews 4:12, we read that the Bible evaluates and judges our worldview. We read: *"For the word of God is living and active. Sharper than any double-edged sword, it penetrates even to dividing soul and spirit, joints and marrow; it judges the **thoughts and attitudes of the heart**."*

Attitudes and perceptions determine how we see the world; how we connect the dots of seemingly random events and make sense of them.

---

483 Matthew 22:37–40

Motives

Motives are activated by circumstances, events, and interactions. They stimulate us to act out. They convert our thoughts to actions.

In Genesis 6:5 and 8:21, we read: *"The Lord saw how great man's wickedness on the earth had become, and that every inclination of the **thoughts** of his **heart** was only evil all the time … The Lord smelled the pleasing aroma and said in his **heart**: 'Never again will I curse the ground because of man, even though every inclination of his **heart** is evil from childhood. And never again will I destroy all living creatures, as I have done.'"* In Deuteronomy 5:29, we read: *"Oh, that their **hearts** would be inclined to **fear me and keep all my commands always**, so that it might go well with them and their children forever!"* Fear, or awesome respect for the majesty of God, is a powerful motivator. Many other passages in the Old Testament speak of motives.

In Mark 7:21–23, we have a litany of motives for behavior. We read: *"For from within, out of men's **hearts**, come evil thoughts, sexual immorality, theft, murder, adultery, greed, malice, deceit, lewdness, envy, slander, arrogance and folly. All these evils come from inside and make a man 'unclean.'"* When the Lord comes, He will judge the motives of men's **hearts**. In 1 Corinthians 4:5, we read: *"Therefore judge nothing before the appointed time; wait till the Lord comes. He will bring to light what is hidden in darkness and will expose the **motives of men's hearts**. At that time each will receive his praise from God."*

Motives compel men to act. They are laden with strong emotions and viscerally felt. They are the inner drives that push men over the threshold to full-blown action.

The following verses are identified with letters. **Beliefs** are marked with a **B**, **values** with a **V**, **attitudes** or **worldview** with a **W**, and **motives** with an **M**. All scriptural passages are in the New International Version (NIV) of the Bible. Those verses marked with an asterisk (*) are key to understanding the biblical metaphor of the heart. Only verses containing the word *heart*, as a metaphor for the center of man's being, have been included.

OLD TESTAMENT

Genesis 6:5–6 **M**
The LORD saw how great man's wickedness on the earth had become, and that every inclination of the thoughts of his **heart** was only evil all the time. The LORD was grieved that he had made man on the earth, and his **heart** was filled with pain.

Genesis 8:20–21 **M**
The LORD smelled the pleasing aroma and said in his **heart**: "Never again will I curse the ground because of man, even though every inclination of his **heart** is evil from childhood. And never again will I destroy all living creatures, as I have done.

Exodus 4:21 **M**
The LORD said to Moses, "When you return to Egypt, see that you perform before Pharaoh all the wonders I have given you the power to do. But I will harden his **heart** so that he will not let the people go.

Exodus 7:3, 13–14, 22–23 **M**
But I will harden Pharaoh's **heart**, and though I multiply my miraculous signs and wonders in Egypt. … Yet Pharaoh's **heart** became hard and he would not listen to them, just as the LORD had said. Then the LORD said to Moses, "Pharaoh's **heart** is unyielding; he refuses to let the people go. But the Egyptian magicians did the same things by their secret arts, and Pharaoh's **heart** became hard; he would not listen to Moses and Aaron, just as the LORD had said. Instead, he turned and went into his palace, and did not take even this to **heart**.

Exodus 8:15, 19, 32 **M**
But when Pharaoh saw that there was relief, he hardened his **heart** and would not listen to Moses and Aaron, just as the LORD had said. The magicians said to Pharaoh, "This is the finger of God." But Pharaoh's **heart** was hard and he would not listen, just as the LORD had said. But this time also Pharaoh hardened his **heart** and would not let the people go.

Exodus 9:7, 12, 35 **M**
Pharaoh sent men to investigate and found that not even one of the animals of the Israelites had died. Yet his **heart** was unyielding and he would not let the people go. But the LORD hardened Pharaoh's **heart** and he would not listen to Moses and Aaron, just as the LORD had said to Moses. So

Pharaoh's **heart** was hard and he would not let the Israelites go, just as the LORD had said through Moses.

Exodus 10:1, 20, 27 **M**
Then the LORD said to Moses, "Go to Pharaoh, for I have hardened his **heart** and the **hearts** of his officials so that I may perform these miraculous signs of mine among them. But the LORD hardened Pharaoh's **heart**, and he would not let the Israelites go. But the LORD hardened Pharaoh's **heart**, and he was not willing to let them go.

Exodus 11:10 **M**
Moses and Aaron performed all these wonders before Pharaoh, but the LORD hardened Pharaoh's **heart**, and he would not let the Israelites go out of his country.

Exodus 14:4, 8 **M**
And I will harden Pharaoh's **heart**, and he will pursue them. But I will gain glory for myself through Pharaoh and all his army, and the Egyptians will know that I am the LORD." So the Israelites did this. The LORD hardened the **heart** of Pharaoh, king of Egypt, so that he pursued the Israelites, who were marching out boldly.

Exodus 25:2 **M**
"Tell the Israelites to bring me an offering. You are to receive the offering for me from each man whose **heart** prompts him to give.

Exodus 35:21 **M**
And everyone who was willing and whose **heart** moved him came and brought an offering to the LORD for the work on the Tent of Meeting, for all its service, and for the sacred garments.

Leviticus 19:17 **M**
"'Do not hate your brother in your **heart**. Rebuke your neighbor frankly so you will not share in his guilt.'"

Deuteronomy 4:9 **B/W**
Only be careful, and watch yourselves closely so that you do not forget the things your eyes have seen or let them slip from your **heart** as long as you live. Teach them to your children and to their children after them.

Deuteronomy 4:29 **V**
But if from there you seek the LORD your God, you will find him if you look for him with all your **heart** and with all your soul.

Deut 5:29 **M**
Oh, that their **hearts** would be inclined to fear me and keep all my commands always, so that it might go well with them and their children forever!

Deuteronomy 6:5–9 **B**
Love the LORD your God with all your **heart** and with all your soul and with all your strength. These commandments that I give you today are to be upon your **hearts**. Impress them on your children. Talk about them when you sit at home and when you walk along the road, when you lie down and when you get up. Tie them as symbols on your hands and bind them on your foreheads. Write them on the doorframes of your houses and on your gates.

Deuteronomy 8:2 **V**
Remember how the LORD your God led you all the way in the desert these forty years, to humble you and to test you in order to know what was in your **heart**, whether or not you would keep his commands.

Deuteronomy 8:5 **B**
Know then in your **heart** that as a man disciplines his son, so the LORD your God disciplines you.

Deuteronomy 10:12 **V**
And now, O Israel, what does the LORD your God ask of you but to fear the LORD your God, to walk in all his ways, to love him, to serve the LORD your God with all your **heart** and with all your soul,

Deuteronomy 10:16 **B**
Circumcise your **hearts**, therefore, and do not be stiff-necked any longer.

Deuteronomy 11:13 **B**
So if you faithfully obey the commands I am giving you today—to love the LORD your God and to serve him with all your **heart** and with all your soul …

Deuteronomy 11:18–21 **B**
Fix these words of mine in your **hearts** and minds; tie them as symbols on your hands and bind them on your foreheads. Teach them to your children, talking about them when you sit at home and when you walk along the road, when you lie down and when you get up. Write them on the doorframes of your houses and on your gates, so that your days and the days of your children may be many in the land that the LORD swore to give your forefathers, as many as the days that the heavens are above the earth.

Deuteronomy 13:3 **V**
You must not listen to the words of that prophet or dreamer. The LORD your God is testing you to find out whether you love him with all your **heart** and with all your soul.

Deuteronomy 15:10 **M**
Give generously to him and do so without a grudging **heart**; then because of this the LORD your God will bless you in all your work and in everything you put your hand to.

Deuteronomy 26:16 **B**
The LORD your God commands you this day to follow these decrees and laws; carefully observe them with all your **heart** and with all your soul.

Deuteronomy 28:65 **M**
Among those nations you will find no repose, no resting place for the sole of your foot. There the LORD will give you an anxious mind, eyes weary with longing, and a despairing **heart**.

Deuteronomy 29:18 **W**
Make sure there is no man or woman, clan or tribe among you today whose **heart** turns away from the LORD our God to go and worship the gods of those nations; make sure there is no root among you that produces such bitter poison.

Deuteronomy 30:6–7 **B/V**
The LORD your God will circumcise your **hearts** and the **hearts** of your descendants, so that you may love him with all your **heart** and with all your soul, and live.

Deuteronomy 30:10 **B**
If you obey the LORD your God and keep his commands and decrees
that are written in this Book of the Law and turn to the LORD your God
with all your **heart** and with all your soul.

Deuteronomy 30:14 **B**
No, the Word is very near you; it is in your mouth and in your **heart** so
you may obey it.

Deuteronomy 30:17 **W**
But if your **heart** turns away and you are not obedient, and if you are
drawn away to bow down to other gods and worship them …

Deuteronomy 32:46 **B**
He said to them, "Take to **heart** all the words I have solemnly declared to
you this day, so that you may command your children to obey carefully all
the words of this law."

Joshua 22:5 **B/V**
But be very careful to keep the commandment and the law that Moses the
servant of the LORD gave you: to love the LORD your God, to walk in
all his ways, to obey his commands, to hold fast to him and to serve him
with all your **heart** and all your soul.

1 Samuel 1:13 **V**
Hannah was praying in her **heart**, and her lips were moving but her voice
was not heard. Eli thought she was drunk.

1 Samuel 2:35 **V**
I will raise up for myself a faithful priest, who will do according to what
is in my **heart** and mind. I will firmly establish his house, and he will
minister before my anointed one always.

1 Samuel 6:6 **M**
Why do you harden your **hearts** as the Egyptians and Pharaoh did? When
he treated them harshly, did they not send the Israelites out so they could
go on their way?

1 Samuel 10:9 **B**
As Saul turned to leave Samuel, God changed Saul's **heart**, and all these
signs were fulfilled that day.

1 Samuel 12:20 **V/M**
"Do not be afraid," Samuel replied. "You have done all this evil; yet do not turn away from the LORD, but serve the LORD with all your **heart**."

1 Samuel 12:24 **V/M**
But be sure to fear the LORD and serve him faithfully with all your **heart**; consider what great things he has done for you.

1 Samuel 13:14 **B/V/W**
But now your kingdom will not endure; the LORD has sought out a man after his own **heart** and appointed him leader of his people, because you have not kept the LORD's command.

1 Samuel 16:7 **B/V/W/M**
But the LORD said to Samuel, "Do not consider his appearance or his height, for I have rejected him. The LORD does not look at the things man looks at. Man looks at the outward appearance, but the LORD looks at the **heart**."

2 Samuel 17:10 **M**
Then even the bravest soldier, whose **heart** is like the **heart** of a lion, will melt with fear, for all Israel knows that your father is a fighter and that those with him are brave.

2 Samuel 24:10, 17 **B**
David was conscience-stricken after he had counted the fighting men, and he said to the LORD, "I have sinned greatly in what I have done. Now, O LORD, I beg you, take away the guilt of your servant. I have done a very foolish thing." When David saw the angel who was striking down the people, he said to the LORD, "I am the one who has sinned and done wrong. These are but sheep. What have they done? Let your hand fall upon me and my family."

1 Kings 2:4 **W**
And that the LORD may keep his promise to me: "If your descendants watch how they live, and if they walk faithfully before me with all their **heart** and soul, you will never fail to have a man on the throne of Israel."

1 Kings 2:44 **M**
The king also said to Shimei, "You know in your **heart** all the wrong you did to my father David. Now the LORD will repay you for your wrongdoing."

1 Kings 3:9 **W**
"So give your servant a discerning **heart** to govern your people and to distinguish between right and wrong. For who is able to govern this great people of yours?"

1 Kings 3:12 **W**
I will do what you have asked. I will give you a wise and discerning **heart**, so that there will never have been anyone like you, nor will there ever be.

1 Kings 8:38–40 **W/M**
And when a prayer or plea is made by any of your people Israel—each one aware of the afflictions of his own **heart**, and spreading out his hands toward this temple—then hear from heaven, your dwelling place. Forgive and act; deal with each man according to all he does, since you know his **heart** (for you alone know the **hearts** of all men).

1 Kings 8:47–48 **W**
And if they have a change of **heart** in the land where they are held captive, and repent and plead with you in the land of their conquerors and say, "We have sinned, we have done wrong, we have acted wickedly"; and if they turn back to you with all their **heart** and soul in the land of their enemies who took them captive, and pray to you toward the land you gave their fathers, toward the city you have chosen and the temple I have built for your Name …

1 Kings 8:61 **B**
"But your **hearts** must be fully committed to the LORD our God, to live by his decrees and obey his commands, as at this time."

1 Kings 9:4 **V/W**
"As for you, if you walk before me in integrity of **heart** and uprightness, as David your father did, and do all I command and observe my decrees and laws."

1 Kings 10:24 **W**
The whole world sought audience with Solomon to hear the wisdom God had put in his **heart**.

1 Kings 11:4 **W/M**
As Solomon grew old, his wives turned his **heart** after other gods, and his **heart** was not fully devoted to the LORD his God, as the **heart** of David his father had been.

1 Kings 11:9 **W**
The LORD became angry with Solomon because his **heart** had turned away from the LORD, the God of Israel, who had appeared to him twice.

1 Kings 14:8 **V**
I tore the kingdom away from the house of David and gave it to you, but you have not been like my servant David, who kept my commands and followed me with all his **heart**, doing only what was right in my eyes.

1 Kings 15:3 **V**
He committed all the sins his father had done before him; his **heart** was not fully devoted to the LORD his God, as the **heart** of David his forefather had been.

1 Kings 15:14 **V/M**
Although he did not remove the high places, Asa's **heart** was fully committed to the LORD all his life.

2 Kings 10:31 **B**
Yet Jehu was not careful to keep the law of the LORD, the God of Israel, with all his **heart**. He did not turn away from the sins of Jeroboam, which he had caused Israel to commit.

2 Kings 22:19 **M**
Because your **heart** was responsive and you humbled yourself before the LORD when you heard what I have spoken against this place and its people, that they would become accursed and laid waste, and because you tore your robes and wept in my presence, I have heard you, declares the LORD.

2 Kings 23:3 **B/V**
The king stood by the pillar and renewed the covenant in the presence of
the LORD—to follow the LORD and keep his commands, regulations
and decrees with all his **heart** and all his soul, thus confirming the words of
the covenant written in this book. Then all the people pledged themselves
to the covenant.

2 Kings 23:25 **B/V**
Neither before nor after Josiah was there a king like him who turned to the
LORD as he did—with all his **heart** and with all his soul and with all his
strength, in accordance with all the Law of Moses.

1 Chronicles 28:9 **M**
"And you, my son Solomon, acknowledge the God of your father, and
serve him with whole**heart**ed devotion and with a willing mind, for the
LORD searches every **heart** and understands every motive behind the
thoughts. If you seek him, he will be found by you; but if you forsake him,
he will reject you forever."

1 Chronicles 29:17–18 **V**
I know, my God, that you test the **heart** and are pleased with integrity. All
these things have I given willingly and with honest intent. And now I have
seen with joy how willingly your people who are here have given to you. O
LORD, God of our fathers Abraham, Isaac and Israel, keep this desire in
the **hearts** of your people forever, and keep their **hearts** loyal to you.

2 Chronicles 6:30 **B/V/W/M**
Then hear from heaven, your dwelling place. Forgive, and deal with each
man according to all he does, since you know his **heart** (for you alone
know the **hearts** of men).

2 Chronicles 6:37–38 **V/M**
And if they have a change of **heart** in the land where they are held captive,
and repent and plead with you in the land of their captivity and say, "We
have sinned, we have done wrong and acted wickedly"; and if they turn
back to you with all their **heart** and soul in the land of their captivity
where they were taken, and pray toward the land you gave their fathers,
toward the city you have chosen and toward the temple I have built for
your Name.

2 Chronicles 9:23 **W**
All the kings of the earth sought audience with Solomon to hear the wisdom God had put in his **heart**.

2 Chronicles 12:14 **V**
He did evil because he had not set his **heart** on seeking the LORD.

2 Chronicles 15:12 **V**
They entered into a covenant to seek the LORD, the God of their fathers, with all their **heart** and soul.

2 Chronicles 15:17 **V**
Although he did not remove the high places from Israel, Asa's **heart** was fully committed [to the LORD] all his life.

2 Chronicles 16:9 **B/V/W/M**
For the eyes of the LORD range throughout the earth to strengthen those whose **hearts** are fully committed to him.

2 Chronicles 17:6 **B/V**
His **heart** was devoted to the ways of the LORD; furthermore, he removed the high places and the Asherah poles from Judah.

2 Chronicles 19:3 **V**
There is, however, some good in you, for you have rid the land of the Asherah poles and have set your **heart** on seeking God.

2 Chronicles 22:9 **V/M**
He then went in search of Ahaziah, and his men captured him while he was hiding in Samaria. He was brought to Jehu and put to death. They buried him, for they said, "He was a son of Jehoshaphat, who sought the LORD with all his **heart**." So there was no one in the house of Ahaziah powerful enough to retain the kingdom.

2 Chronicles 30:19 **W**
Who sets his **heart** on seeking God—the LORD, the God of his fathers—even if he is not clean according to the rules of the sanctuary.

2 Chronicles 32:25–26 **M**
But Hezekiah's **heart** was proud and he did not respond to the kindness shown him; therefore the LORD's wrath was on him and on Judah and Jerusalem. Then Hezekiah repented of the pride of his **heart**, as did the

people of Jerusalem; therefore the LORD's wrath did not come upon them during the days of Hezekiah.

2 Chronicles 32:31 **B/V/W/M**
But when envoys were sent by the rulers of Babylon to ask him about the miraculous sign that had occurred in the land, God left him to test him and to know everything that was in his **heart**.

2 Chronicles 34:27 **M**
Because your **heart** was responsive and you humbled yourself before God when you heard what he spoke against this place and its people, and because you humbled yourself before me and tore your robes and wept in my presence, I have heard you, declares the LORD.

2 Chronicles 34:31 **B**
The king stood by his pillar and renewed the covenant in the presence of the LORD—to follow the LORD and keep his commands, regulations and decrees with all his **heart** and all his soul, and to obey the words of the covenant written in this book.

2 Chronicles 36:13 **M**
He also rebelled against King Nebuchadnezzar, who had made him take an oath in God's name. He became stiff-necked and hardened his **heart** and would not turn to the LORD, the God of Israel.

Ezra 1:5 **M**
Then the family heads of Judah and Benjamin, and the priests and Levites—everyone whose **heart** God had moved—prepared to go up and build the house of the LORD in Jerusalem.

Ezra 7:27 **V**
Praise be to the LORD, the God of our fathers, who has put it into the king's **heart** to bring honor to the house of the LORD in Jerusalem in this way

Nehemiah 2:12 **M**
I set out during the night with a few men. I had not told anyone what my God had put in my **heart** to do for Jerusalem. There were no mounts with me except the one I was riding on.

Nehemiah 7:5 **M**
So my God put it into my **heart** to assemble the nobles, the officials and the common people for registration by families. I found the genealogical record of those who had been the first to return.

Nehemiah 9:8 **B/V**
You found his **heart** faithful to you, and you made a covenant with him to give to his descendants the land of the Canaanites, Hittites, Amorites, Perizzites, Jebusites and Girgashites. You have kept your promise because you are righteous.

Job 10:13 **M**
"But this is what you concealed in your **heart**, and I know that this was in your mind."

Job 11:13 **V/M**
"Yet if you devote your **heart** to him and stretch out your hands to him ..."

Job 15:12 **M**
Why has your **heart** carried you away, and why do your eyes flash ...

Job 22:22 **B**
Accept instruction from his mouth and lay up his words in your **heart**.

Job 23:16 **M**
God has made my **heart** faint; the Almighty has terrified me.

Job 31:33 **M**
If I have concealed my sin as men do, by hiding my guilt in my **heart** ...

Job 33:3 **V**
My words come from an upright **heart**; my lips sincerely speak what I know.

Job 36:13 **M**
"The godless in **heart** harbor resentment; even when he fetters them, they do not cry for help."

Job 38:36 **W**
Who endowed the **heart** with wisdom or gave understanding to the mind?

Psalms 5:9 **M**
Not a word from their mouth can be trusted; their **heart** is filled with destruction. Their throat is an open grave; with their tongue they speak deceit.

Psalms 7:10 **V**
My shield is God Most High, who saves the upright in **heart**.

Psalms 10:3 **M**
He boasts of the cravings of his **heart**; he blesses the greedy and reviles the LORD.

Psalms 11:2 **V**
For look, the wicked bend their bows; they set their arrows against the strings to shoot from the shadows at the upright in **heart**.

Psalms 14:1 **B**
The fool says in his **heart**, "There is no God." They are corrupt, their deeds are vile; there is no one who does good.

Psalms 15:2 **V**
He whose walk is blameless and who does what is righteous, who speaks the truth from his **heart** …

Psalms 16:7 **B**
I will praise the LORD, who counsels me; even at night my **heart** instructs me.

Psalms 17:3 **B/V/W/M**
Though you probe my **heart** and examine me at night, though you test me, you will find nothing; I have resolved that my mouth will not sin.

Psalms 17:10 **B/M**
They close up their callous **hearts**, and their mouths speak with arrogance.

Proverbs 12:20 **M**
There is deceit in the **hearts** of those who plot evil, but joy for those who promote peace.

Psalms 19:8 **B/M**
The precepts of the LORD are right, giving joy to the **heart**. The commands of the LORD are radiant, giving light to the eyes.

Psalms 19:14 **B/W**
May the words of my mouth and the meditation of my **heart** be pleasing in your sight, O LORD, my Rock and my Redeemer.

Psalms 20:4 **M**
May he give you the desire of your **heart** and make all your plans succeed.

Psalms 28:3 **M**
Do not drag me away with the wicked, with those who do evil, who speak cordially with their neighbors but harbor malice in their **hearts**.

Psalms 24:3–4 **B/V/W/M**
Who may ascend the hill of the LORD? Who may stand in his holy place? He who has clean hands and a pure **heart**, who does not lift up his soul to an idol or swear by what is false.

Psalms 26:2 **B/V/W/M**
Test me, O LORD, and try me, examine my **heart** and my mind;

Psalms 27:14 **M**
Wait for the LORD; be strong and take **heart** and wait for the LORD.

Psalms 28:7 **V/W**
The LORD is my strength and my shield; my **heart** trusts in him, and I am helped.

My **heart** leaps for joy and I will give thanks to him in song.

Psalms 31:24 **M**
Be strong and take **heart**, all you who hope in the LORD.

Psalms 33:11 **B/W**
But the plans of the LORD stand firm forever, the purposes of his **heart** through all generations.

Psalms 33:13–15 **W**
From heaven the LORD looks down and sees all mankind; from his dwelling place he watches all who live on earth—he who forms the **hearts** of all, who considers everything they do.

Psalms 36:10 **V**
Continue your love to those who know you, your righteousness to the upright in **heart**.

Psalms 37:4 **M**
Delight yourself in the LORD and he will give you the desires of your **heart**.

Psalms 37:31 **B**
The law of his God is in his **heart**; his feet do not slip.

Psalms 40:8 **B**
"I desire to do your will, O my God; your law is within my **heart**."

Psalms 41:6 **M**
Whenever one comes to see me, he speaks falsely, while his **heart** gathers slander; then he goes out and spreads it abroad.

Psalms 44:21 **M**
Would not God have discovered it, since he knows the secrets of the **heart**?

Psalms 49:3 **B/W**
My mouth will speak words of wisdom; the utterance from my **heart** will give understanding.

Psalms 51:10 **B/V/W/M**
Create in me a pure **heart**, O God, and renew a steadfast spirit within me.

Psalms 51:17 **M**
The sacrifices of God are a broken spirit; a broken and contrite **heart**, O God, you will not despise.

Psalms 53:1 **B**
The fool says in his **heart**, "There is no God." They are corrupt, and their ways are vile; there is no one who does good.

Psalms 55:21 **M**
His speech is smooth as butter, yet war is in his **heart**; his words are more soothing than oil, yet they are drawn swords.

Psalms 58:2 **M**
No, in your **heart** you devise injustice, and your hands mete out violence on the earth.

Psalms 62:4 **M**
They fully intend to topple him from his lofty place; they take delight in lies. With their mouths they bless, but in their **hearts** they curse.

Psalms 62:10 **V/W/M**
Do not trust in extortion or take pride in stolen goods; though your riches increase, do not set your **heart** on them.

Psalms 64:6 **V**
They plot injustice and say, "We have devised a perfect plan!" Surely the mind and **heart** of man are cunning.

Psalms 66:18 **M**
If I had cherished sin in my **heart**, the Lord would not have listened …

Psalms 73:7 **M**
From their callous **hearts** comes iniquity; the evil conceits of their minds know no limits.

Psalms 73:26 **B**
My flesh and my **heart** may fail, but God is the strength of my **heart** and my portion forever.

Psalms 78:8 **V**
They would not be like their forefathers—a stubborn and rebellious generation, whose **hearts** were not loyal to God, whose spirits were not faithful to him.

Psalms 78:72 **V/W**
And David shepherded them with integrity of **heart**; with skillful hands he led them.

Psalms 81:12 **M**
So I gave them over to their stubborn **hearts** to follow their own devices.

Psalms 86:11 **V/W**
Teach me your way, O LORD, and I will walk in your truth; give me an undivided **heart**, that I may fear your name.

Psalms 90:12 **W**
Teach us to number our days aright, that we may gain a **heart** of wisdom.

Psalms 94:15 **V**
Judgment will again be founded on righteousness, and all the upright in **heart** will follow it.

Psalms 95:10–11 **V/W**
For forty years I was angry with that generation; I said, "They are a people whose **hearts** go astray, and they have not known my ways." So I declared on oath in my anger, "They shall never enter my rest."

Psalms 101:2 **B**
I will be careful to lead a blameless life—when will you come to me? I will walk in my house with blameless **heart**.

Psalms 101:4 **M**
Men of perverse **heart** shall be far from me; I will have nothing to do with evil.

Psalms 101:5 **M**
Whoever slanders his neighbor in secret, him will I put to silence; whoever has haughty eyes and a proud **heart**, him will I not endure.

Psalms 109:22 **V**
For I am poor and needy, and my **heart** is wounded within me.

Psalms 112:7 **B**
He will have no fear of bad news; his **heart** is steadfast, trusting in the LORD.

Psalms 112:8 **B**
His **heart** is secure, he will have no fear; in the end he will look in triumph on his foes.

Psalms 119:2 **B/V**
Blessed are they who keep his statutes and seek him with all their **heart**.

Psalms 119:7 **V**
I will praise you with an upright **heart** as I learn your righteous laws.

Psalms 119:10–11 **B/V**
I seek you with all my **heart**; do not let me stray from your commands. I have hidden your word in my **heart** that I might not sin against you.

Psalms 119:30 **B**
I have chosen the way of truth; I have set my **heart** on your laws.

Psalms 119:32 **B**
I run in the path of your commands, for you have set my **heart** free.

Psalms 119:34 **B**
Give me understanding, and I will keep your law and obey it with all my **heart**.

Psalms 119:36 **B**
Turn my **heart** toward your statutes and not toward selfish gain.

Psalms 119:58 **V**
I have sought your face with all my **heart**; be gracious to me according to your promise.

Psalms 119:69 **B**
Though the arrogant have smeared me with lies, I keep your precepts with all my **heart**.

Psalms 119:80 **B**
May my **heart** be blameless toward your decrees, that I may not be put to shame.

Psalms 119:111–112 **B**
Your statutes are my heritage forever; they are the joy of my **heart**. My **heart** is set on keeping your decrees to the very end.

Psalms 119:145 **B**
I call with all my **heart**; answer me, O LORD, and I will obey your decrees.

Psalms 125:4 **V**
Do good, O LORD, to those who are good, to those who are upright in **heart**.

Psalms 139:23 **M**
Search me, O God, and know my **heart**; test me and know my anxious thoughts.

Psalms 140:1–3 **M**
Rescue me, O LORD, from evil men; protect me from men of violence, who devise evil plans in their **hearts** and stir up war every day. They make their tongues as sharp as a serpent's; the poison of vipers is on their lips.

Psalms 141:4 **V/W**
Let not my **heart** be drawn to what is evil, to take part in wicked deeds with men who are evildoers; let me not eat of their delicacies.

Proverbs 1:23 **B**
If you had responded to my rebuke, I would have poured out my **heart** to you and made my thoughts known to you.

Proverbs 2:2 **B/W**
Turning your ear to wisdom and applying your **heart** to understanding …

Proverbs 2:10 **B/W**
For wisdom will enter your **heart**, and knowledge will be pleasant to your soul.

Proverbs 3:3 **B**
Let love and faithfulness never leave you; bind them around your neck, write them on the tablet of your **heart**.

Proverbs 3:5 **V/W**
Trust in the LORD with all your **heart** and lean not on your own understanding …

Proverbs 4:4 **B**
He taught me and said, "Lay hold of my words with all your **heart**; keep my commands and you will live."

Proverbs 4:21 **B**
Do not let them out of your sight, keep them within your **heart** …

Proverbs 4:23 **B/V/W/M**
Above all else, guard your **heart**, for it is the wellspring of life.

Proverbs 5:12 **V/M**
You will say, "How I hated discipline! How my **heart** spurned correction!"

Proverbs 6:14 **M**
Who plots evil with deceit in his **heart**—he always stirs up dissension.

Proverbs 6:18 **W/M**
A **heart** that devises wicked schemes, feet that are quick to rush into evil …

Proverbs 6:21 **B**
Bind them upon your **heart** forever; fasten them around your neck.

Proverbs 6:25 **M**
Do not lust in your **heart** after her beauty or let her captivate you with her eyes.

Proverbs 7:3 **B**
Bind them on your fingers; write them on the tablet of your **heart**.

Proverbs 7:25 **W**
Do not let your **heart** turn to her ways or stray into her paths.

Proverbs 10:8 **B**
The wise in **heart** accept commands, but a chattering fool comes to ruin.

Proverbs 11:20 **M**
The LORD detests men of perverse **heart**, but he delights in those whose ways are blameless.

Proverbs 12:23 **V**
A prudent man keeps his knowledge to himself, but the **heart** of fools blurts out folly.

Proverbs 12:25 **V**
An anxious **heart** weighs a man down, but a kind word cheers him up.

Proverbs 13:12 **V**
Hope deferred makes the **heart** sick, but a longing fulfilled is a tree of life.

Proverbs 14:10 **M**
Each **heart** knows its own bitterness, and no one else can share its joy.

Proverbs 14:30 **V**
A **heart** at peace gives life to the body, but envy rots the bones.

Proverbs 14:33 **W**
Wisdom reposes in the **heart** of the discerning and even among fools she lets herself be known.

Proverbs 15:7 **W**
The lips of the wise spread knowledge; not so the **hearts** of fools.

Proverbs 15:14–15 **W**
The discerning **heart** seeks knowledge, but the mouth of a fool feeds on folly. All the days of the oppressed are wretched, but the cheerful **heart** has a continual feast.

Proverbs 15:28 **V**
The **heart** of the righteous weighs its answers, but the mouth of the wicked gushes evil.

Proverbs 16:5 **M**
The LORD detests all the proud of **heart**. Be sure of this: They will not go unpunished.

Proverbs 16:9 **W**
In his **heart** a man plans his course, but the LORD determines his steps.

Proverbs 16:21 **W**
The wise in **heart** are called discerning, and pleasant words promote instruction.

Proverbs 16:23 **V**
A wise man's **heart** guides his mouth, and his lips promote instruction.

Proverbs 17:3 **M**
The crucible for silver and the furnace for gold, but the LORD tests the **heart**.

Proverbs 17:20 **M**
A man of perverse **heart** does not prosper; he whose tongue is deceitful falls into trouble.

Proverbs 17:22 **M**
A cheerful **heart** is good medicine, but a crushed spirit dries up the bones.

Proverbs 18:12 **M**
Before his downfall a man's **heart** is proud, but humility comes before honor.

Proverbs 18:15 **W**
The **heart** of the discerning acquires knowledge; the ears of the wise seek it out.

Proverbs 19:3 **M**
A man's own folly ruins his life, yet his **heart** rages against the LORD.

Proverbs 19:21 **B/W**
Many are the plans in a man's **heart**, but it is the LORD's purpose that prevails.

Proverbs 20:5 **B**
The purposes of a man's **heart** are deep waters, but a man of understanding draws them out.

Proverbs 21:2 **M**
All a man's ways seem right to him, but the LORD weighs the **heart**.

Proverbs 21:4 **M**
Haughty eyes and a proud **heart**, the lamp of the wicked, are sin!

Proverbs 22:11 **B/V/W/M**
He who loves a pure **heart** and whose speech is gracious will have the king for his friend.

Proverbs 22:15 **V/M**
Folly is bound up in the **heart** of a child, but the rod of discipline will drive it far from him.

Proverbs 22:17–18 **B**
Pay attention and listen to the sayings of the wise; apply your **heart** to what I teach, for it is pleasing when you keep them in your **heart** and have all of them ready on your lips.

Proverbs 23:7 **M**
For he is the kind of man who is always thinking about the cost. "Eat and drink," he says to you, but his **heart** is not with you.

Proverbs 23:12 **B**
Apply your **heart** to instruction and your ears to words of knowledge.

Proverbs 23:17 **V/M**
Do not let your **heart** envy sinners, but always be zealous for the fear of the LORD.

Proverbs 23:19 **B/W**
Listen, my son, and be wise, and keep your **heart** on the right path.

Proverbs 23:26 **V**
My son, give me your **heart** and let your eyes keep to my ways ...

Proverbs 24:1–2 **W/M**
Do not envy wicked men, do not desire their company; for their **hearts** plot violence, and their lips talk about making trouble.

Proverbs 24:12 **B/V/W/M**
If you say, "But we knew nothing about this," does not he who weighs the **heart** perceive it? Does not he who guards your life know it? Will he not repay each person according to what he has done?

Proverbs 24:32 **B/W**
I applied my **heart** to what I observed and learned a lesson from what I saw.

Proverbs 26:23 **M**
Like a coating of glaze over earthenware are fervent lips with an evil **heart**.

Proverbs 26:24 **M**
A malicious man disguises himself with his lips, but in his **heart** he harbors deceit.

Proverbs 26:25 **M**
Though his speech is charming, do not believe him, for seven abominations fill his **heart**.

Proverbs 27:19 **B/V/W/M**
As water reflects a face, so a man's **heart** reflects the man.

Proverbs 28:14 **M**
Blessed is the man who always fears the LORD, but he who hardens his **heart** falls into trouble.

Ecclesiastes 2:1 **W**
I thought in my **heart**, "Come now, I will test you with pleasure to find out what is good." But that also proved to be meaningless.

Ecclesiastes 2:10 **M**
I denied myself nothing my eyes desired; I refused my **heart** no pleasure. My **heart** took delight in all my work, and this was the reward for all my labor.

Eccl 3:11–12 **B**
He has made everything beautiful in its time. He has also set eternity in the **hearts** of men; yet they cannot fathom what God has done from beginning to end.

Ecclesiastes 7:4 **M**
The **heart** of the wise is in the house of mourning, but the **heart** of fools is in the house of pleasure.

Ecclesiastes 7:7 **M**
Extortion turns a wise man into a fool, and a bribe corrupts the **heart**.

Ecclesiastes 7:22 **V**
For you know in your **heart** that many times you yourself have cursed others.

Ecclesiastes 8:5 **V/W**
Whoever obeys his command will come to no harm, and the wise **heart** will know the proper time and procedure.

Ecclesiastes 8:11 **M**
When the sentence for a crime is not quickly carried out, the **hearts** of the people are filled with schemes to do wrong.

Ecclesiastes 9:3–4 **V/M**
This is the evil in everything that happens under the sun: The same destiny overtakes all. The **hearts** of men, moreover, are full of evil and there is

madness in their **hearts** while they live, and afterward they join the dead. Anyone who is among the living has hope—even a live dog is better off than a dead lion!

Ecclesiastes 10:2 **V/W**
The **heart** of the wise inclines to the right, but the **heart** of the fool to the left.

Isaiah 6:10 **B**
"Make the **heart** of this people calloused; make their ears dull and close their eyes. Otherwise they might see with their eyes, hear with their ears, understand with their **hearts**, and turn and be healed."

Isaiah 9:9 **M**
All the people will know it—Ephraim and the inhabitants of Samaria—who say with pride and arrogance of **heart**.

Isaiah 29:13 **W/M**
The Lord says: "These people come near to me with their mouth and honor me with their lips, but their **hearts** are far from me. Their worship of me is made up only of rules taught by men."

Isaiah 51:7 **B**
"Hear me, you who know what is right, you people who have my law in your **hearts**: Do not fear the reproach of men or be terrified by their insults."

Isaiah 59:12–13 **B**
For our offenses are many in your sight, and our sins testify against us. Our offenses are ever with us, and we acknowledge our iniquities: rebellion and treachery against the LORD, turning our backs on our God, fomenting oppression and revolt, uttering lies our **hearts** have conceived.

Isaiah 63:4 **M**
For the day of vengeance was in my **heart**, and the year of my redemption has come.

Jeremiah 3:15 **B**
Then I will give you shepherds after my own **heart**, who will lead you with knowledge and understanding.

Jeremiah 4:14 **B/M**
O Jerusalem, wash the evil from your **heart** and be saved. How long will you harbor wicked thoughts?

Jeremiah 5:23 **M**
But these people have stubborn and rebellious **hearts**; they have turned aside and gone away.

Jeremiah 7:24 **V/M**
But they did not listen or pay attention; instead, they followed the stubborn inclinations of their evil **hearts**. They went backward and not forward.

Jeremiah 9:8 **M**
Their tongue is a deadly arrow; it speaks with deceit. With his mouth each speaks cordially to his neighbor, but in his **heart** he sets a trap for him.

Jeremiah 9:26 **B**
Egypt, Judah, Edom, Ammon, Moab and all who live in the desert in distant places. For all these nations are really uncircumcised, and even the whole house of Israel is uncircumcised in **heart**.

Jeremiah 11:20 **B/V/W/M**
But, O LORD Almighty, you who judge righteously and test the **heart** and mind, let me see your vengeance upon them, for to you I have committed my cause.

Jeremiah 13:10 **M**
These wicked people, who refuse to listen to my words, who follow the stubbornness of their **hearts** and go after other gods to serve and worship them, will be like this belt—completely useless!

Jeremiah 16:12 **B/M**
But you have behaved more wickedly than your fathers. See how each of you is following the stubbornness of his evil **heart** instead of obeying me.

Jeremiah 17:5 **B/V/W/M**
This is what the LORD says: "Cursed is the one who trusts in man, who depends on flesh for his strength and whose **heart** turns away from the LORD."

Jeremiah 17:9 **M**
The **heart** is deceitful above all things and beyond cure. Who can understand it?

Jeremiah 17:10 **B/V/W/M**
"I the LORD search the **heart** and examine the mind, to reward a man according to his conduct, according to what his deeds deserve."

Jeremiah 18:12 **M**
But they will reply, "It's no use. We will continue with our own plans; each of us will follow the stubbornness of his evil **heart**."

Jeremiah 20:12 **B/V/W/M**
O LORD Almighty, you who examine the righteous and probe the **heart** and mind, let me see your vengeance upon them, for to you I have committed my cause.

Jeremiah 23:17 **M**
They keep saying to those who despise me, "The LORD says: You will have peace." And to all who follow the stubbornness of their **hearts** they say, "No harm will come to you."

Jeremiah 23:20 **B/V/W/M**
The anger of the LORD will not turn back until he fully accomplishes the purposes of his **heart**. In days to come you will understand it clearly.

Jeremiah 24:7 **B**
I will give them a **heart** to know me, that I am the LORD. They will be my people, and I will be their God, for they will return to me with all their **heart**.

Jeremiah 29:13 **B/V/W/M**
You will seek me and find me when you seek me with all your **heart**.

Jeremiah 30:24 **B/V/W/M**
The fierce anger of the LORD will not turn back until he fully accomplishes the purposes of his **heart**. In days to come you will understand this.

Jeremiah 31:33 **B**
"This is the covenant I will make with the house of Israel after that time," declares the LORD. "I will put my law in their minds and write it on their **hearts**. I will be their God, and they will be my people."

Jeremiah 32:39 **B/V/W/M**
I will give them singleness of **heart** and action, so that they will always fear me for their own good and the good of their children after them.

Jeremiah 49:16 **M**
"The terror you inspire and the pride of your **heart** have deceived you, you who live in the clefts of the rocks, who occupy the heights of the hill. Though you build your nest as high as the eagle's, from there I will bring you down," declares the LORD.

Ezekiel 11:19 **B/V/W/M**
I will give them an undivided **heart** and put a new spirit in them; I will remove from them their **heart** of stone and give them a **heart** of flesh.

Ezekiel 11:21 **B**
But as for those whose **hearts** are devoted to their vile images and detestable idols, I will bring down on their own heads what they have done, declares the Sovereign LORD.

Ezekiel 14:4 **B**
Therefore speak to them and tell them, "This is what the Sovereign LORD says: When any Israelite sets up idols in his **heart** and puts a wicked stumbling block before his face and then goes to a prophet, I the LORD will answer him myself in keeping with his great idolatry."

Ezekiel 14:7 **B**
"When any Israelite or any alien living in Israel separates himself from me and sets up idols in his **heart** and puts a wicked stumbling block before his face and then goes to a prophet to inquire of me, I the LORD will answer him myself."

Ezekiel 18:31 **B/V/W/M**
Rid yourselves of all the offenses you have committed, and get a new **heart** and a new spirit. Why will you die, O house of Israel?

Ezekiel 25:6 **M**
For this is what the Sovereign LORD says: Because you have clapped your hands and stamped your feet, rejoicing with all the malice of your **heart** against the land of Israel.

Ezekiel 28:2 **M**
Son of man, say to the ruler of Tyre, "This is what the Sovereign LORD says: 'In the pride of your **heart** you say, "I am a god; I sit on the throne of a god in the **heart** of the seas." But you are a man and not a god, though you think you are as wise as a god.'"

Ezekiel 33:31–32 **M**
My people come to you, as they usually do, and sit before you to listen to your words, but they do not put them into practice. With their mouths they express devotion, but their **hearts** are greedy for unjust gain.

Ezekiel 36:25–28 **B/V/W/M**
I will sprinkle clean water on you, and you will be clean; I will cleanse you from all your impurities and from all your idols. I will give you a new **heart** and put a new spirit in you; I will remove from you your **heart** of stone and give you a **heart** of flesh. And I will put my Spirit in you and move you to follow my decrees and be careful to keep my laws.

Daniel 5:20 **M**
But when his **heart** became arrogant and hardened with pride, he was deposed from his royal throne and stripped of his glory.

Hosea 5:4 **B/V**
"Their deeds do not permit them to return to their God. A spirit of prostitution is in their **heart**; they do not acknowledge the LORD."

Hosea 10:2 **M**
Their **heart** is deceitful, and now they must bear their guilt. The LORD will demolish their altars and destroy their sacred stones.

Joel 2:12 **B/V/W/M**
"Even now," declares the LORD, "return to me with all your **heart**, with fasting and weeping and mourning."

Joel 2:13 **B/V/W/M**
Rend your **heart** and not your garments. Return to the LORD your God, for he is gracious and compassionate, slow to anger and abounding in love, and he relents from sending calamity.

Obadiah 3 **M**
The pride of your **heart** has deceived you, you who live in the clefts of the rocks and make your home on the heights, you who say to yourself, "Who can bring me down to the ground?"

Zechariah 7:12 **B**
They made their **hearts** as hard as flint and would not listen to the law or to the words that the LORD Almighty had sent by his Spirit through the earlier prophets. So the LORD Almighty was very angry.

Malachi 2:2 **V**
"If you do not listen, and if you do not set your **heart** to honor my name," says the LORD Almighty, "I will send a curse upon you, and I will curse your blessings. Yes, I have already cursed them, because you have not set your **heart** to honor me."

Malachi 4:5–6 **V**
"See, I will send you the prophet Elijah before that great and dreadful day of the LORD comes. He will turn the **hearts** of the fathers to their children, and the **hearts** of the children to their fathers; or else I will come and strike the land with a curse."

NEW TESTAMENT

Matthew 5:8 **V**
Blessed are the pure in **heart**, for they will see God.

Matthew 5:28 **M**
But I tell you that anyone who looks at a woman lustfully has already committed adultery with her in his **heart**.

Matthew 6:21 **V**
For where your treasure is, there your **heart** will be also.

Matthew 9:4 **B/V**
Knowing their thoughts, Jesus said, "Why do you entertain evil thoughts in your **hearts**?"

Matthew 11:29 **M**
Take my yoke upon you and learn from me, for I am gentle and humble in **heart**, and you will find rest for your souls.

Matthew 12:34–35 **B/V/W/M**
You brood of vipers, how can you who are evil say anything good? For out of the overflow of the **heart** the mouth speaks. The good man brings good things out of the good stored up in him, and the evil man brings evil things out of the evil stored up in him.

Matthew 13:15 **B/V/W/M**
For this people's **heart** has become calloused; they hardly hear with their ears, and they have closed their eyes. Otherwise they might see with their eyes, hear with their ears, understand with their **hearts** and turn, and I would heal them.

Matthew 13:19 **B**
When anyone hears the message about the kingdom and does not understand it, the evil one comes and snatches away what was sown in his **heart**. This is the seed sown along the path.

Matthew 15:8–9 **B/V/W/M**
"These people honor me with their lips, but their **hearts** are far from me. They worship me in vain; their teachings are but rules taught by men."

Matthew 15:18–19 **B/V/W/M**
But the things that come out of the mouth come from the **heart**, and these make a man "unclean." For out of the **heart** come evil thoughts, murder, adultery, sexual immorality, theft, false testimony, slander.

Matthew 18:35 **M**
"This is how my heavenly Father will treat each of you unless you forgive your brother from your **heart**."

Matthew 22:37 **B/V/W/M**
Jesus replied: "Love the Lord your God with all your **heart** and with all your soul and with all your mind."

Mark 2:8 **B**
Immediately Jesus knew in his spirit that this was what they were thinking in their **hearts**, and he said to them, "Why are you thinking these things?"

Mark 7:6–7 **B**
He replied, "Isaiah was right when he prophesied about you hypocrites; as it is written: 'These people honor me with their lips, but their **hearts** are

far from me. They worship me in vain; their teachings are but rules taught by men.'"

Mark 7:20–23 **B/V/W/M**
He went on: "What comes out of a man is what makes him 'unclean.' For from within, out of men's **hearts**, come evil thoughts, sexual immorality, theft, murder, adultery, greed, malice, deceit, lewdness, envy, slander, arrogance and folly. All these evils come from inside and make a man 'unclean.'"

Mark 11:23 **B**
"I tell you the truth, if anyone says to this mountain, 'Go, throw yourself into the sea,' and does not doubt in his **heart** but believes that what he says will happen, it will be done for him."

Mark 12:30 **B/V/W/M**
Love the Lord your God with all your **heart** and with all your soul and with all your mind and with all your strength.

Mark 12:33 **B/V/W/M**
"To love him with all your **heart**, with all your understanding and with all your strength, and to love your neighbor as yourself is more important than all burnt offerings and sacrifices."

Luke 5:22 **B**
Jesus knew what they were thinking and asked, "Why are you thinking these things in your **hearts**?"

Luke 6:45 **B/V/W/M**
The good man brings good things out of the good stored up in his **heart**, and the evil man brings evil things out of the evil stored up in his **heart**. For out of the overflow of his **heart** his mouth speaks.

Luke 8:12–13 **B**
Those along the path are the ones who hear, and then the devil comes and takes away the word from their **hearts**, so that they may not believe and be saved.

Luke 8:15 **V**
But the seed on good soil stands for those with a noble and good **heart**, who hear the word, retain it, and by persevering produce a crop.

Luke 10:27 **B/V/W/M**
He answered: "Love the Lord your God with all your **heart** and with all your soul and with all your strength and with all your mind"; and "Love your neighbor as yourself."

Luke 12:29 **V**
And do not set your **heart** on what you will eat or drink; do not worry about it.

Luke 12:34 **B/V/W/M**
For where your treasure is, there your **heart** will be also.

Luke 16:15 **V**
He said to them, "You are the ones who justify yourselves in the eyes of men, but God knows your **hearts**. What is highly valued among men is detestable in God's sight."

Luke 24:25 **B**
He said to them, "How foolish you are, and how slow of **heart** to believe all that the prophets have spoken!

Luke 24:32 **B/V/W/M**
They asked each other, "Were not our **hearts** burning within us while he talked with us on the road and opened the Scriptures to us?"

Acts 1:24 **B/V/W/M**
Then they prayed, "Lord, you know everyone's **heart**. Show us which of these two you have chosen."

Acts 4:32 **B/V/W/M**
All the believers were one in **heart** and mind. No one claimed that any of his possessions was his own, but they shared everything they had.

Acts 5:3 **M**
Then Peter said, "Ananias, how is it that Satan has so filled your **heart** that you have lied to the Holy Spirit and have kept for yourself some of the money you received for the land?"

Acts 7:39 **B/V**
"But our fathers refused to obey him. Instead, they rejected him and in their **hearts** turned back to Egypt."

Acts 8:21–22 **B**
You have no part or share in this ministry, because your **heart** is not right before God. Repent of this wickedness and pray to the Lord. Perhaps he will forgive you for having such a thought in your **heart**.

Acts 13:22 **B/V/W/M**
After removing Saul, he made David their king. He testified concerning him: "I have found David son of Jesse a man after my own **heart**; he will do everything I want him to do."

Acts 15:8 **B/V/W/M**
God, who knows the **heart**, showed that he accepted them by giving the Holy Spirit to them, just as he did to us.

Acts 16:14 **B**
One of those listening was a woman named Lydia, a dealer in purple cloth from the city of Thyatira, who was a worshiper of God. The Lord opened her **heart** to respond to Paul's message.

Acts 28:27 **B/V**
For this people's **heart** has become calloused; they hardly hear with their ears, and they have closed their eyes. Otherwise they might see with their eyes, hear with their ears, understand with their **heart**s and turn, and I would heal them.

Romans 1:9 **B/V/W/M**
God, whom I serve with my whole **heart** in preaching the Gospel of his Son, is my witness how constantly I remember you.

Romans 1:21–25 **B/V/W/M**
For although they knew God, they neither glorified him as God nor gave thanks to him, but their thinking became futile and their foolish **hearts** were darkened. Although they claimed to be wise, they became fools and exchanged the glory of the immortal God for images made to look like mortal man and birds and animals and reptiles. Therefore God gave them over in the sinful desires of their **hearts** to sexual impurity for the degrading of their bodies with one another. They exchanged the truth of God for a lie, and worshiped and served created things rather than the Creator—who is forever praised. Amen.

Romans 2:5 **B/M**
But because of your stubbornness and your unrepentant **heart**, you are
storing up wrath against yourself for the day of God's wrath, when his
righteous judgment will be revealed.

Romans 2:14–16 **B**
(Indeed, when Gentiles, who do not have the law, do by nature things
required by the law, they are a law for themselves, even though they do
not have the law, since they show that the requirements of the law are
written on their **hearts**, their consciences also bearing witness, and their
thoughts now accusing, now even defending them.) This will take place
on the day when God will judge men's secrets through Jesus Christ, as my
Gospel declares.

Romans 2:29 **B**
No, a man is a Jew if he is one inwardly; and circumcision is circumcision
of the **heart**, by the Spirit, not by the written code. Such a man's praise is
not from men, but from God.

Romans 5:1–5 **V**
Therefore, since we have been justified through faith, we have peace with
God through our Lord Jesus Christ, through whom we have gained access
by faith into this grace in which we now stand. And we rejoice in the hope
of the glory of God. Not only so, but we also rejoice in our sufferings,
because we know that suffering produces perseverance; perseverance,
character; and character, hope. And hope does not disappoint us, because
God has poured out his love into our **hearts** by the Holy Spirit, whom he
has given us.

Romans 6:17–18 **B/V/M**
But thanks be to God that, though you used to be slaves to sin, you
wholeheartedly obeyed the form of teaching to which you were entrusted.
You have been set free from sin and have become slaves to righteousness.

Romans 8:26–27 **B/V**
In the same way, the Spirit helps us in our weakness. We do not know
what we ought to pray for, but the Spirit himself intercedes for us with
groans that words cannot express. And he who searches our **hearts** knows
the mind of the Spirit, because the Spirit intercedes for the saints in
accordance with God's will.

Romans 10:8–10 **B**
But what does it say? "The word is near you; it is in your mouth and in your **heart**," that is, the word of faith we are proclaiming: That if you confess with your mouth, "Jesus is Lord," and believe in your **heart** that God raised him from the dead, you will be saved. For it is with your **heart** that you believe and are justified, and it is with your mouth that you confess and are saved.

Romans 15:6 **B/V/W/M**
So that with one **heart** and mouth you may glorify the God and Father of our Lord Jesus Christ.

1 Corinthians 4:4–5 **M**
Therefore judge nothing before the appointed time; wait till the Lord comes. He will bring to light what is hidden in darkness and will expose the motives of men's **hearts**. At that time each will receive his praise from God.

1 Corinthians 10:6 **V/M**
Now these things occurred as examples to keep us from setting our **hearts** on evil things as they did.

1 Corinthians 14:25 **B/V/W/M**
And the secrets of his **heart** will be laid bare. So he will fall down and worship God, exclaiming, "God is really among you!"

2 Corinthians 1:21–22 **B/V/W/M**
Now it is God who makes both us and you stand firm in Christ. He anointed us, set his seal of ownership on us, and put his Spirit in our **hearts** as a deposit, guaranteeing what is to come.

2 Corinthians 3:2–3 **V**
You yourselves are our letter, written on our **hearts**, known and read by everybody. You show that you are a letter from Christ, the result of our ministry, written not with ink but with the Spirit of the living God, not on tablets of stone but on tablets of human **hearts**.

2 Corinthians 4:6 **B**
For God, who said, "Let light shine out of darkness," made his light shine in our **hearts** to give us the light of the knowledge of the glory of God in the face of Christ.

2 Corinthians 5:12 **M**
We are not trying to commend ourselves to you again, but are giving you an opportunity to take pride in us, so that you can answer those who take pride in what is seen rather than in what is in the **heart.**

2 Corinthians 8:16 **V**
I thank God, who put into the **heart** of Titus the same concern I have for you.

2 Corinthians 9:7 **M**
Each man should give what he has decided in his **heart** to give, not reluctantly or under compulsion, for God loves a cheerful giver.

Galatians 4:4–7 **B/V/W/M**
But when the time had fully come, God sent his Son, born of a woman, born under law, to redeem those under law, that we might receive the full rights of sons. Because you are sons, God sent the Spirit of his Son into our **hearts**, the Spirit who calls out, "Abba, Father." So you are no longer a slave, but a son; and since you are a son, God has made you also an heir.

Ephesians 1:13–14 **B/V/W/M**
And you also were included in Christ when you heard the word of truth, the Gospel of your salvation. Having believed, you were marked in him with a seal, the promised Holy Spirit, who is a deposit guaranteeing our inheritance until the redemption of those who are God's possession—to the praise of his glory.

Ephesians 1:18 **B**
I pray also that the eyes of your **heart** may be enlightened in order that you may know the hope to which he has called you, the riches of his glorious inheritance in the saints,

Ephesians 3:16–19 **B/V/W/M**
I pray that out of his glorious riches he may strengthen you with power through his Spirit in your inner being, so that Christ may dwell in your **hearts** through faith. And I pray that you, being rooted and established in love, may have power, together with all the saints, to grasp how wide and long and high and deep is the love of Christ, and to know this love that surpasses knowledge—that you may be filled to the measure of all the fullness of God.

Ephesians 4:17–19 **M**
So I tell you this, and insist on it in the Lord, that you must no longer live as the Gentiles do, in the futility of their thinking. They are darkened in their understanding and separated from the life of God because of the ignorance that is in them due to the hardening of their **hearts**. Having lost all sensitivity, they have given themselves over to sensuality so as to indulge in every kind of impurity, with a continual lust for more.

Ephesians 6:5–6 **M/B**
Slaves, obey your earthly masters with respect and fear, and with sincerity of **heart**, just as you would obey Christ. Obey them not only to win their favor when their eye is on you, but like slaves of Christ, doing the will of God from your **heart**.

Phil 4:6–7 **B**
Do not be anxious about anything, but in everything, by prayer and petition, with thanksgiving, present your requests to God. And the peace of God, which transcends all understanding, will guard your **hearts** and your minds in Christ Jesus.

Colossians 3:1–4 **B/V**
Since, then, you have been raised with Christ, set your **hearts** on things above, where Christ is seated at the right hand of God. Set your minds on things above, not on earthly things. For you died, and your life is now hidden with Christ in God. When Christ, who is your life, appears, then you also will appear with him in glory.

Colossians 3:15–17 **M**
Let the peace of Christ rule in your **hearts**, since as members of one body you were called to peace. And be thankful. Let the word of Christ dwell in you richly as you teach and admonish one another with all wisdom, and as you sing psalms, hymns and spiritual songs with gratitude in your **hearts** to God. And whatever you do, whether in word or deed, do it all in the name of the Lord Jesus, giving thanks to God the Father through him.

Colossians 3:22 **M**
Slaves, obey your earthly masters in everything; and do it, not only when their eye is on you and to win their favor, but with sincerity of **heart** and reverence for the Lord.

Colossians 3:23 **B/V/W/M**
Whatever you do, work at it with all your **heart**, as working for the Lord, not for men.

1 Timothy 1:5 **V**
The goal of this command is love, which comes from a pure **heart** and a good conscience and a sincere faith.

1 Timothy 3:1 **M**
Here is a trustworthy saying: If anyone sets his **heart** on being an overseer, he desires a noble task.

2 Timothy 2:22 **V**
Flee the evil desires of youth, and pursue righteousness, faith, love and peace, along with those who call on the Lord out of a pure **heart**.

1 Thessalonians 2:4–5 **B/V/W/M**
On the contrary, we speak as men approved by God to be entrusted with the Gospel. We are not trying to please men but God, who tests our **hearts**.

1 Thessalonians 3:12–13 **B/V**
May the Lord make your love increase and overflow for each other and for everyone else, just as ours does for you. May he strengthen your **hearts** so that you will be blameless and holy in the presence of our God and Father when our Lord Jesus comes with all his holy ones.

Philemon 20 **B/V/W/M**
I do wish, brother, that I may have some benefit from you in the Lord; refresh my **heart** in Christ.

Hebrews 3:7-19 **B/V/W/M**
So, as the Holy Spirit says: "Today, if you hear his voice, do not harden your **hearts** as you did in the rebellion, during the time of testing in the desert, where your fathers tested and tried me and for forty years saw what I did. That is why I was angry with that generation, and I said, 'Their **hearts** are always going astray, and they have not known my ways.' So I declared on oath in my anger, 'They shall never enter my rest.'" See to it, brothers, that none of you has a sinful, unbelieving **heart** that turns away from the living God. But encourage one another daily, as long as it is called today, so that none of you may be hardened by sin's deceitfulness. We have come

to share in Christ if we hold firmly till the end the confidence we had at first. As has just been said: "Today, if you hear his voice, do not harden your **hearts** as you did in the rebellion." Who were they who heard and rebelled? Were they not all those Moses led out of Egypt? And with whom was he angry for forty years? Was it not with those who sinned, whose bodies fell in the desert? And to whom did God swear that they would never enter his rest if not to those who disobeyed? So we see that they were not able to enter, because of their unbelief.

Hebrews 4:1–13 **B/V/W/M**
Therefore, since the promise of entering his rest still stands, let us be careful that none of you be found to have fallen short of it. For we also have had the Gospel preached to us, just as they did; but the message they heard was of no value to them, because those who heard did not combine it with faith. Now we who have believed enter that rest, just as God has said, "So I declared on oath in my anger, 'They shall never enter my rest.'" And yet his work has been finished since the creation of the world. For somewhere he has spoken about the seventh day in these words: "And on the seventh day God rested from all his work." And again in the passage above he says, "They shall never enter my rest." It still remains that some will enter that rest, and those who formerly had the Gospel preached to them did not go in, because of their disobedience. Therefore God again set a certain day, calling it today, when a long time later he spoke through David, as was said before: "Today, if you hear his voice, do not harden your **hearts**." For if Joshua had given them rest, God would not have spoken later about another day. There remains, then, a Sabbath—rest for the people of God; for anyone who enters God's rest also rests from his own work, just as God did from his. Let us, therefore, make every effort to enter that rest, so that no one will fall by following their example of disobedience. For the word of God is living and active. Sharper than any double-edged sword, it penetrates even to dividing soul and spirit, joints and marrow; it judges the thoughts and attitudes of the **heart**. Nothing in all creation is hidden from God's sight. Everything is uncovered and laid bare before the eyes of him to whom we must give account.

Hebrews 8:10 **B/V**
This is the covenant I will make with the house of Israel after that time, declares the Lord. I will put my laws in their minds and write them on their **hearts**. I will be their God, and they will be my people.

Hebrews 10:15–17 **B**
The Holy Spirit also testifies to us about this. First he says: "This is the covenant I will make with them after that time, says the Lord. I will put my laws in their **hearts**, and I will write them on their minds." Then he adds: "Their sins and lawless acts I will remember no more."

Hebrews 10:22 **M**
Let us draw near to God with a sincere **heart** in full assurance of faith, having our **hearts** sprinkled to cleanse us from a guilty conscience and having our bodies washed with pure water.

Hebrews 12:1–3 **V/M**
Therefore, since we are surrounded by such a great cloud of witnesses, let us throw off everything that hinders and the sin that so easily entangles, and let us run with perseverance the race marked out for us. Let us fix our eyes on Jesus, the author and perfecter of our faith, who for the joy set before him endured the cross, scorning its shame, and sat down at the right hand of the throne of God. Consider him who endured such opposition from sinful men, so that you will not grow weary and lose **heart**.

Hebrews 12:5 **V/M**
And you have forgotten that word of encouragement that addresses you as sons: "My son, do not make light of the Lord's discipline, and do not lose **heart** when he rebukes you."

James 2:14–26 **B/V/W/M**
What good is it, my brothers, if a man claims to have faith but has no deeds? Can such faith save him? Suppose a brother or sister is without clothes and daily food. If one of you says to him, "Go, I wish you well; keep warm and well fed," but does nothing about his physical needs, what good is it? In the same way, faith by itself, if it is not accompanied by action, is dead. But someone will say, "You have faith; I have deeds." Show me your faith without deeds, and I will show you my faith by what I do. You believe that there is one God. Good! Even the demons believe that—and shudder. You foolish man, do you want evidence that faith without deeds is useless? Was not our ancestor Abraham considered righteous for what he did when he offered his son Isaac on the altar? You see that his faith and his actions were working together, and his faith was made complete by what he did. And the Scripture was fulfilled that says, "Abraham believed God, and it was credited to him as righteousness," and he was called God's

friend. You see that a person is justified by what he does and not by faith alone. In the same way, was not even Rahab the prostitute considered righteous for what she did when she gave lodging to the spies and sent them off in a different direction? As the body without the spirit is dead, so faith without deeds is dead.

James 3:13–16 **M**
Who is wise and understanding among you? Let him show it by his good life, by deeds done in the humility that comes from wisdom. But if you harbor bitter envy and selfish ambition in your **hearts**, do not boast about it or deny the truth. Such "wisdom" does not come down from heaven but is earthly, unspiritual, of the devil. For where you have envy and selfish ambition, there you find disorder and every evil practice.

James 4:7–10 **V**
Submit yourselves, then, to God. Resist the devil, and he will flee from you. Come near to God and he will come near to you. Wash your hands, you sinners, and purify your **hearts**, you double-minded. Grieve, mourn, and wail. Change your laughter to mourning and your joy to gloom. Humble yourselves before the Lord, and he will lift you up.

1 Peter 1:22 **B/V**
Now that you have purified yourselves by obeying the truth so that you have sincere love for your brothers, love one another deeply, from the **heart**.

1 Peter 3:15–16 **B**
But in your **hearts** set apart Christ as Lord. Always be prepared to give an answer to everyone who asks you to give the reason for the hope that you have. But do this with gentleness and respect, keeping a clear conscience, so that those who speak maliciously against your good behavior in Christ may be ashamed of their slander.

1 John 3:19–20 **V**
This then is how we know that we belong to the truth, and how we set our **hearts** at rest in his presence whenever our **hearts** condemn us. For God is greater than our **hearts**, and he knows everything.

1 John 5:10 **B**
Anyone who believes in the Son of God has this testimony in his **heart**. Anyone who does not believe God has made him out to be a liar, because he has not believed the testimony God has given about his Son.

Revelation 1:3 **B**
Blessed is the one who reads the words of this prophecy, and blessed are those who hear it and take to **heart** what is written in it, because the time is near.

APPENDIX B: PERSONAL BIO

GREGORY W. BOURGOND, Dmin, Edd
Shoreview, Minnesota 55126
Office: (651) 308-1530
Fax: (651) 486-7193
Email: GWBourgond@aol.com

Dr. Greg Bourgond earned a bachelor's degree in psychology from Chapman University (1979), a master of divinity degree from Bethel Seminary in San Diego (1983), a doctor of ministry degree in church leadership from Bethel (1997), and a doctor of education degree in instructional technology and distance education (2001) from Nova Southeastern University. He completed post-graduate studies at Harvard Graduate School of Education (2003).

His previous experience includes ten years in the defense industry and commercial business and over fourteen years in various ministry positions. He has held positions as a principal analyst for Analysis & Technology, Inc., senior project engineer for Hughes Aircraft Company, unit manager for General Electric, and general manager for an auto dealership. He held several leadership positions at Bethel University. He is currently the executive pastor of a large church in Minnesota. In ministry he has been a deacon, elder, ministry director, associate pastor, and executive pastor. He completed twenty-nine years of active and reserve duty in enlisted and officer ranks in the U.S. Navy.

Greg serves as a consultant and teacher in the areas of leadership formation and development, spiritual and personal formation, legacy, organizational systems, strategic planning, men's ministries, and small group dynamics. He is the president and founder of Heart of a Warrior Ministries, a ministry dedicated to helping men live lives of integrity and honor under the authority of God. He has taught in many schools, churches, and organizations. Greg has been happily married for forty-three years and enjoys his six grandchildren every chance he gets.

APPENDIX C: HEART OF A WARRIOR MINISTRIES

Heart of a Warrior is a ministry born out of a desire to change the hearts of men from the inside out so that the lives they live will bring glory and honor to God. It began in 1991 with fifteen men in San Diego, California. The ministry was stimulated by a recognition that we were meant to fly like eagles and to live life in victory, not defeat. I grew weary of men living in the "misty lowlands of mediocrity," abdicating their responsibility to be godly leaders within their sphere of influence, forgetting their identity in Christ, wasting their energies  on non-significant activities, and losing their passion for what matters to God. To become men after God's heart, spiritual surgery was necessary. The journey to wholeness began. Since then, scores of men have taken the journey and are living more productive and God-centered lives.

MISSION: To help men live lives of integrity[484] and honor[485] under the authority of God.

VISION: Heart of a Warrior is committed to developing men after God's heart so that they bear, in their person, the imprint of His character reflected in all they think, say, and do. To this end we are committed to bringing reconciliation between men and God, men and their families, and men and their calling. Four ministries are provided for these purposes: **Foundations of a Warrior—Setting Firm Faith Foundations; Heart of a Warrior (Phase I)—Establishing a Compass for Your Life; Focus of a Warrior (Phase II)—Developing a Map for Your Life;** and **Purity of a Warrior—Dealing with Sexual Addictions.** These ministries are designed to grow and expand as God gives us opportunity to secure a biblical identity for men, to embrace God's preferred lifestyle for men, to help men fulfill their God-ordained obligations and responsibilities, and to bring men into alignment with God's purposes for their lives.

FOUNDATIONAL BELIEFS

- Guard your heart for it is the wellspring of life. *Proverbs 4:23*
- The Lord looks at the heart, not appearances. *1 Samuel 16:7*

---

484 **Integrity:** living with uprightness, honesty, and sincerity. Such a man lives in congruity with biblically centered beliefs so that his conduct reflects those beliefs regardless of the circumstances he faces, the trials he confronts, or the stresses he endures. He strives to live in such a way so that there will be no discrepancy between what he appears to be and who he really is. Such integrity does not allow our words to violate what is in our heart. **Psalm 15:1–6** (OT—Joshua & Caleb; Numbers 13:1, 14:38; NT—Barnabas: Acts 9:26–31; 11:22–26; 15:1–41)

485 **Honor:** living forthrightly in alignment with biblical principles. A man after God's heart seeks to live a life of honor based on God's word, the Bible. He has a desire to bring honor to the name of Christ by living for Him no matter the cost. This means he commits to living life in accordance with biblical values, to developing a keen sense of right and wrong, to adhering to action and principles considered right and true, and to bringing respect and nobility to one's life. **Titus 2:11-14** (OT—Joseph: Genesis 37:1, 50:26; NT—The Sinful Woman: Luke 7:36–50)

- God searches hearts and rewards conduct accordingly. *Jeremiah 17:10*
- The heart's secrets are betrayed by the mouth. *Matthew 12:33–34*
- The mouth reveals what is in the heart—the ear determines what goes into it. *Proverbs 2:2*
- From within, out of the heart, comes evil. *Mark 7:21–23*
- Where your treasure is, there your heart will be as well. *Matthew 6:21*
- The heart is deceitful above all things. *Jeremiah 17:9*
- At judgment God will expose the hidden counsels of the heart. *1 Corinthians 4:5*
- The heart needs to be educated. *Proverbs 22:17–18*
- The heart functions as the conscience. *Psalm 51:10*
- The Spirit of God must give humans a new heart. *Jeremiah 31:33; Ezekiel 36:26*
- Faith purifies a new heart. *Acts 15:9; Ephesians 3:17*
- First clean the inside, and then the outside will be clean. *Matthew 23:26*
- Removal and replacement of corruption is essential for lasting change. *1 John 1:9; John 8:31–32*
- Believers set the heart on things above. *Colossians 3:1; Philippians 4:8*
- Love the Lord God with all your heart—a conscious, volitional commitment. *Matthew 22:37*

KEY ASSUMPTIONS

- Lasting behavioral change is not accomplished by focusing primarily on behavior.
- Behavior is fundamentally a by-product of what is stored in our hearts.
- Man focuses on appearance; God focuses on the heart.
- God is looking for believers after His own heart.
- Central beliefs, core values, worldview, and motives comprise the heart.
- Our central beliefs establish our values. Our core values inform our worldview. Our worldview conditions our motives. Our motives energize our behavior. Our behavior reflects what's in our hearts.

- The objective is to be so controlled and influenced by the Spirit of God as to have the mind of Christ in our beliefs, values, attitudes, and motives so that our character is Christ-like and our behavior brings glory to God.
- To change behavior, we must have a change of heart.

CORE VALUES

1. Salvation through Christ is the only hope for wholeness.[486]
2. Real faith is beliefs in action.[487]
3. We are called to the high road.[488]

---

486 **Ephesians 1:3–14** *Praise be to the God and Father of our Lord Jesus Christ, who has blessed us in the heavenly realms with every spiritual blessing in Christ. For he chose us in him before the creation of the world to be holy and blameless in his sight. In love he predestined us to be adopted as his sons through Jesus Christ, in accordance with his pleasure and will—to the praise of his glorious grace, which he has freely given us in the One he loves. In him we have redemption through his blood, the forgiveness of sins, in accordance with the riches of God's grace that he lavished on us with all wisdom and understanding. And he made known to us the mystery of his will according to his good pleasure, which he purposed in Christ, to be put into effect when the times will have reached their fulfillment—to bring all things in heaven and on earth together under one head, even Christ. In him we were also chosen, having been predestined according to the plan of him who works out everything in conformity with the purpose of his will, in order that we, who were the first to hope in Christ, might be for the praise of his glory. And you also were included in Christ when you heard the word of truth, the Gospel of your salvation. Having believed, you were marked in him with a seal, the promised Holy Spirit, who is a deposit guaranteeing our inheritance until the redemption of those who are God's possession—to the praise of his glory.*

487 *Hebrew scholars attest to the fact that real faith is beliefs in action. They see no separation between one's beliefs and one's actions. More specifically, a belief doesn't become an ingrained belief until it's acted upon. Repeated application of one's beliefs indicates what one really believes. If there is a disconnect between the two, one's beliefs and one's actions, then they are not really beliefs but simply affirmations or aspirations. Our central beliefs establish our values. Our core values inform our worldview. Our worldview conditions our motives, our primary motives energize our behavior, and our behavior reflects the condition of our heart.* **James 2:17** *Faith by itself, if it is not accompanied by action, is dead.* **James 2:26**

488 The high road is one that Jesus Christ took to the cross (Phil. 2:6–11). As men after God's heart we are to *embrace "whatever is true, whatever is noble,*

4. A life of godliness is not an option, it is a necessity.[489]
5. Christ-likeness is our primary objective.[490]
6. Removal and replacement is essential for lasting change.[491]
7. We are to fulfill God's purposes for us.[492]
8. Kingdom service is mandatory.[493]

---

whatever is right, whatever is pure, whatever is lovely, whatever is admirable—if anything is excellent or praiseworthy—think about such things." **Philippians 4:8**

489 **Titus 2:11–14** *For the grace of God that brings salvation has appeared to all men. It teaches us to say no to ungodliness and worldly passions, and to live self-controlled, upright and godly lives in this present age, while we wait for the blessed hope—the glorious appearing of our great God and Savior, Jesus Christ, who gave himself for us to redeem us from all wickedness and to purify for himself a people that are his very own, eager to do what is good.*

490 **2 Corinthians 3:18** *And we, who with unveiled faces all reflect the Lord's glory, are being transformed into his likeness with ever-increasing glory, which comes from the Lord, who is the Spirit.* **Ephesians 4:13–15** *Until we all reach unity in the faith and in the knowledge of the Son of God and become mature, attaining to the whole measure of the fullness of Christ. Then we will no longer be infants, tossed back and forth by the waves, and blown here and there by every wind of teaching and by the cunning and craftiness of men in their deceitful scheming. Instead, speaking the truth in love, we will in all things grow up into him who is the Head, that is, Christ.*

491 **Removal: 1 John 1:9** *If we confess our sins, he is faithful and just and will forgive us our sins and purify us from all unrighteousness.* **Replacement: John 8:31–32** *To the Jews who had believed him, Jesus said, "If you hold to my teaching, you are really my disciples. Then you will know the truth, and the truth will set you free."*

492 **Ephesians 2:10** *For we are God's workmanship, created in Christ Jesus to do good works, which God prepared in advance for us to do.* **Colossians 1:10–14** *And we pray this in order that you may live a life worthy of the Lord and may please him in every way: bearing fruit in every good work, growing in the knowledge of God, being strengthened with all power according to his glorious might so that you may have great endurance and patience, and joyfully giving thanks to the Father, who has qualified you to share in the inheritance of the saints in the kingdom of light. For he has rescued us from the dominion of darkness and brought us into the kingdom of the Son he loves, in whom we have redemption, the forgiveness of sins.*

493 **Matthew 5:16** *In the same way, let your light shine before men, that they may see your good deeds and praise your Father in heaven.* **2 Corinthians 9:8–9** *And God is able to make all grace abound to you, so that in all things at all times, having all that you need, you will abound in every good work.* **2 Timothy 2:21**

Gregory W. Bourgond, DMin, EdD
Founder and President, Heart of a Warrior Ministries
Phone: 651-308-1530
E-mail: GWBourgond@aol.com
Website: www.heartofawarrior.org
Blog: www.heartofawarrior.typepad.com

If a man cleanses himself from the latter, he will be an instrument for noble purposes, made holy, useful to the Master and prepared to do any good work. **Titus 3:8** *This is a trustworthy saying. And I want you to stress these things, so that those who have trusted in God may be careful to devote themselves to doing what is good. These things are excellent and profitable for everyone.* **1 Peter 2:12** *Live such good lives among the pagans that, though they accuse you of doing wrong, they may see your good deeds and glorify God on the day he visits us.*